KANT ON THE FRONTIER

LIT Z

Sara Guyer and Brian McGrath, series editors

Lit Z embraces models of criticism uncontained by conventional notions of history, periodicity, and culture, and committed to the work of reading. Books in the series may seem untimely, anachronistic, or out of touch with contemporary trends because they have arrived too early or too late. Lit Z creates a space for books that exceed and challenge the tendencies of our field and in doing so reflect on the concerns of literary studies here and abroad.

At least since Friedrich Schlegel, thinking that affirms literature's own untimeliness has been named romanticism. Recalling this history, Lit Z exemplifies the survival of romanticism as a mode of contemporary criticism, as well as forms of contemporary criticism that demonstrate the unfulfilled possibilities of romanticism. Whether or not they focus on the romantic period, books in this series epitomize romanticism as a way of thinking that compels another relation to the present. Lit Z is the first book series to take seriously this capacious sense of romanticism.

In 1977, Paul de Man and Geoffrey Hartman, two scholars of romanticism, team-taught a course called Literature Z that aimed to make an intervention into the fundamentals of literary study. Hartman and de Man invited students to read a series of increasingly difficult texts and through attention to language and rhetoric compelled them to encounter "the bewildering variety of ways such texts could be read." The series' conceptual resonances with that class register the importance of recollection, reinvention, and reading to contemporary criticism. Its books explore the creative potential of reading's untimeliness and history's enigmatic force.

KANT ON THE FRONTIER

Philosophy, Politics, and the Ends of the Earth

Geoffrey Bennington

Fordham University Press

New York 2017

This book was originally published in French as Geoffrey Bennington, *Frontières kantiennes*, Copyright © Éditions Galilée, 2000.

Visit us online at www.fordhampress.com.

Library of Congress Cataloging-in-Publication Data available online at http://catalog.loc.gov.

Printed in the United States of America

19 18 17 5 4 3 2 1

First edition

Contents

Preface to the English Edition

This book is the outcome of a long and quite involved history. Its distant origins lie in a graduate seminar I conducted at the University of Sussex from 1989 to 1992, as one of the Collège international de philosophie's first group of corresponding program directors. That Sussex seminar, conducted in English under the general title "Frontiers," met once a week for three academic years, focusing on Kant (1989–90), Hegel (1990–91), and Frege and Wittgenstein (1991–92). I took the opportunity to present a "seminar" in something more like the French sense, writing out a continuous text that I read to the group every two weeks, with intervening weeks devoted to student presentations and more informal reading and discussion sessions, sometimes of other authors (Kafka's "Great Wall of China" and "The Burrow" gave us food for thought, for example).[1] I subsequently published the surviving written sessions of those seminars in *Frontiers: Kant, Hegel, Frege, Wittgenstein* (CreateSpace, 2003). At the 1992 Cerisy conference Le passage des frontières: à partir de Jacques Derrida, I presented a summary of some of the work done in the Sussex seminar.[2] The seminars bear a number of traces of their historical moment, including the fall of the Berlin Wall (I was especially struck by the fact that the first reported piece of graffiti on the East German side of the wall read "the wall is gone") and a subsequent flurry of enthusiasm in the press for Kant's political writings, taken more or less naïvely to predict the European Union eventually formed in 1993, and seen, by some at least, as representing some kind of "end of history."

1. The further elaboration of the seminar materials here owes a good deal to the students who followed this seminar and brought their own work to it. My warm thanks go to my then-doctoral students Richard Beardsworth, Scott Davidson, Jonathan Derbyshire, Suhail Malik, and Diane Morgan, to name only those for whom Kant was a major object of study.

2. See "La frontière infranchissable," in *Le passage des frontières: autour du travail de Jacques Derrida*, ed. Marie-Louise Mallet, 69–81 (Paris: Galilée, 1994). Other pieces from this period that draw on and summarize this seminar material include "The Frontier: Between Kant and Hegel," in my *Legislations: The Politics of Deconstruction*, 259–73 (London: Verso Books, 1994), and "Frontiers: Of Literature and Philosophy," delivered as a lecture in 1996 and published in my *Other Analyses: Reading Philosophy*, 239–67 (CreateSpace, 2005).

Starting again from the Kant material, I wrote in 1995 the continuous draft of what subsequently became *Frontières kantiennes* (Galilée, 2000). The book starts from the seminar material on Kant (and some of the Cerisy Frege material), elaborates it considerably in the detail and depth of the readings, and departs from it most saliently in the long treatment of the Critique of Teleological Judgment in chapter 5. The present volume is a somewhat adapted translation of that French book: it still follows the French text closely, and maintains some of the "French philosophy" features of the writing, but I have taken many liberties in the interests of readability that I would not take translating the text of another author. I have also removed a number of remarks that bore specifically on the often inaccurate published French translations of Kant and taken the opportunity to correct a few errors of my own, to clarify the argument here and there and to delete a handful of more speculative remarks (often in footnotes) that no longer seem justified to me. A few longer footnotes have been incorporated into the body of the text. I have also included as an Appendix an essay originally written in French for a conference, also in 1995, focusing directly on Kant's use of the terms *Grenze* and *Schranke* and their cognates in his many discussions of frontier questions.[3]

Many fine books and articles on Kant have of course been published in several languages since this book was first published. Given its focus, however, and its quasi-narrative (quasi-teleological) movement toward the still not widely read Critique of Teleological Judgment, I have not tried to update it with reference to recent scholarship. My current understanding of some of the issues addressed here has certainly benefitted from more recent reading of excellent and important books by, among others, Peter Fenves, Olivia Custer, Peter Szendy, and Catherine Malabou,[4] all of which deal to some extent with salient issues addressed here, and with all of whom there would also be differences to explore; but direct engagement with them here would have introduced an awkward element of anachronism into the book and interrupted the continuity of the argument. Nor have I tried to address the influential recent anti-Kantianism associated with the "new realism," which

3. This essay was originally delivered at a conference organized by Michel Lisse in Louvain-la-Neuve and subsequently published as "De la fiction transcendantale," in *Passions de la littérature: avec Jacques Derrida*, ed. Michel Lisse, 141–60 (Paris: Galilée, 1996).

4. Peter Fenves, *Late Kant: Towards Another Law of the Earth* (London: Routledge, 2003); Olivia Custer, *L'exemple de Kant* (Leuven, Belgium: Editions Peeters, 2012); Peter Szendy, *Kant chez les extraterrestres: Philosofictions cosmopolitiques* (Paris: Minuit, 2011), tr. Will Bishop as *Kant in the Land of Extraterrestrials* (New York: Fordham University Press, 2013); Catherine Malabou, *Avant demain: épigénèse et rationalité* (Paris: Presses Universitaires de France, 2014).

I believe to be largely misguided in its aims and inaccurate in much of its understanding of Kant, and to which I hope to respond elsewhere.

The stakes of the argument presented here essentially revolve around a claim about the interrupted or self-interrupting structure of teleological schemas, a claim that can be summed up in the slogan "the end is the end": the end in the sense of goal or *telos* is also the end in the sense of *finis*, or death. Kant, or so I argue, provides textual resources for thinking through the difficult consequences of this thought (which I believe is one possible way of understanding Derrida's still enigmatic slogan "la différance infinie est finie"). I try to develop this claim first on the basis of Kant's writings on history and politics, subsequently in his explicit thinking about teleology, but also, throughout, on the persistent analogies he mobilizes between these two apparently separate parts of his philosophy, and indeed on the explicit discussion of analogy itself. I do not think that the structures that emerge from these readings can adequately be thought in terms of the "Idea in the Kantian sense," at least as usually interpreted (nor *a fortiori* in terms of the Idea in the Platonic sense). The claimed interruption or disruption of teleological schemas that "the end is the end" tries to capture has immediate consequences for how we think about history and politics, but also (in another persistent analogy) how we think about *reading*, and perhaps more especially the reading of philosophical works. And thereby how we think about thinking itself (especially if it be accepted that the concept of "concept" is teleological and therefore interrupted too, as suggested here in the brief polemical reading of Frege). I believe that philosophy most often tends to repress the question of reading and that reintroducing that question has philosophical effects that exceed the reach of hermeneutics (philosophy's best—but inadequate—effort at a theory of reading) and are most clearly and productively thought through in deconstruction. The apparently analogical communication between the political implications of this interrupted structure of teleology on the one hand, and its implications for reading and doing philosophy more generally on the other, cannot satisfactorily be left in the hands of the concept of analogy, however, unless we push very hard at what Kant himself identifies as the "point of heterogeneity" that really *is* the point of analogy and that might justify the introduction of a notion of *ananalogy* to describe it. This point of heterogeneity, which is what we are interested in but cannot quite understand in an analogy, is what exposes critique in the Kantian sense to deconstructive reading and, given the continued prevalence of Kantian schemas in moral and political thinking at least, seems to promise the possibility of reformulating habitual ways of addressing such issues, including the predominantly historicist ways that currently—and I believe unfortunately—dominate academic work in the humanities.

If Kant's Critique of Teleological Judgment is no longer much read, I imagine this is because it is widely thought that Darwinism provided an answer to the at least apparent natural purposiveness that Kant is trying to understand. Kant is confident that the schemas of mechanical causality could *never* account for organisms (and by extension for nature as a whole), and Darwin, it seems, provides just such a mechanical explanation with the theory of natural selection. By the same token, the whole issue of teleological judgment and its theological extensions would seem to become otiose, and commentators who do not want simply to abandon Kant altogether in favor of more or less militant promotion of an atheistic scientism would seem to be justified in concentrating their attention on the *aesthetic judgment*, which, after all, Kant himself suggests is the essential part of the third *Critique*. My interest in the teleological judgment in spite of the completely compelling claims of Darwinism does not at all lie in any attempt to rehabilitate the Kantian account of nature's "technic" and all that seems to flow from it, and still less to afford any credence to the absurdities of "creationism." Rather, to suggest *on the one hand* that the teleological is not quite as readily abandoned as might be imagined, and that attempts to abandon it can give rise to its perverse return (in the very concept of the "selfish gene," for example, and in militant forms of neo-Darwinism that often take on a quasi-religious and even crusading character), and *on the other* that, as I read it here, teleology undoes or interrupts itself anyway because of a curious internal logic that could be shown to affect evolutionism as much as teleologism. One way of pursuing this thought would involve showing how there is a more or less secret convergence between Kant's thinking about natural ends (where the end of nature is to have given rise to a humanity able to set its own ends independently of the natural end it thereby also seems to fulfill) and the thinking of evolutionary biology or psychology (where the end of the evolutionary process is the production of an animal capable of understanding that process and thereby significantly escaping from it, i.e., an animal capable of setting its own ends independently of that process and perhaps bringing it to an end). Either way we are faced with a structure of end-setting that interrupts the process leading up to it and demands analysis of its internal interruptions and impossibilities, the more radically so now that it seems likely to many that that end-setting interruptive of natural processes (a currently fashionable name for which is the Anthropocene) really might be tending toward the End. Although this book was written long before the concept of the Anthropocene was widely used in the humanities, and despite some recent claims that deconstruction has nothing to say about issues such as human-induced climate change, I believe that working with the structures of interruption described here can indeed help in thinking about such questions, if only ananalogically.

Parts of this book have previously appeared in English. Part of Chapter 5 was published as "The End Is Here," in *Tekhnema* 6 (2001): 34–50; part of Chapter 4 appeared as "Kant's Open Secret," in *Theory, Culture and Society* 28, no. 7–8 (2011): 26–40, a small section of which also figured in "Rigor: Or, Stupid Uselessness," in *Southern Journal of Philosophy* 50, Spindel Supplement (2012): 20–38; the Appendix, "On Transcendental Fiction," appeared in *Discourse: Journal for Theoretical Studies in Media and Culture* 29, no. 1 (2007): 169–88 and is used here with the permission of Wayne State University Press. I am grateful to those publications for permission to reuse that material here.

New York City
June 2015

Pre-liminary

If the point here were to do metaphysics (again), my claim, which would then be extraordinarily immodest, would be that "frontier" is nothing less than the primary philosophical concept and the origin of all others. *F(r)ons e(s)t origo.* And indeed, we shall see that there is no concept in general that does not presuppose the concept of the frontier—as we shall verify with Frege, without a (concept of the) frontier, there would simply be no concept at all. So if I manage to construct a rigorous concept of the frontier in this book, I might want to claim I had (re-)grounded metaphysics by giving it a master-concept that could stand up to all others.

Such is not my ambition. Not that I particularly doubt the rigor of what is argued here (except to doubt the concept of rigor itself beyond a certain point, once we have crossed a certain frontier): I do think I can show that the philosophical concept of concept cannot be constructed without presupposing the concept of frontier and that, therefore, within the philosophical order, this concept has absolute priority over others. But I also think I can show that this very priority withdraws the frontier from the order of the concept that presupposes it. For as we shall see, if every concept must have a frontier if it is to be the concept that it is, it follows that there can be no concept of frontier. Whence two consequences, the first of which is quite classical and the second of which repeats but then erases the first: 1) all philosophical concepts rest on a nonconceptual (nonphilosophical) ground that philosophy is incapable of thinking (of conceptualizing); but then 2) in fact, there are no (philosophical) concepts, for if, for there to be a concept, we need a (concept of the) frontier, and if the frontier by definition escapes conceptualization—and so in all rigor we cannot know what it is and even if there is one—then all concepts turn out to be pre-concepts awaiting the *telos* of a clarification (a clear and clean frontier) that will never, even in an ideal future, come to be drawn at their limits. The very concept of "concept" would thus, because of the frontier, be both fundamentally teleological and (following a logic developed more especially in Chapter 5 of this book) constitutively cut from its *telos*, a mere promise of a concept, forever promised and never fulfilled.

From the conjunction of these two consequences (because we cannot simply abandon the first in favor of the second), a number of paradoxes seem to flow. For example, according to the first consequence, there would be an outside of philosophy (its origin, if you like) that cannot be brought into philosophy for conceptualization. So if one wanted to think this outside (this origin), one would have above all not to try to do so philosophically. But according to the second consequence, this outside would already be inside philosophy, which would mean that, from the first, philosophy is not entirely philosophical. Either philosophy remains dependent on an origin it is in no position to assimilate (and it is therefore not philosophical through and through) or else it assimilates that origin (and it is therefore not philosophical through and through). According to this second consequence, one might still hope to *think* the frontier with means that look almost indistinguishable from those of philosophy, with the slight difference that on this view there is no philosophy (and never has been), which is why there is a "history" of philosophy, and that just is philosophy.[1]

It might still seem, nevertheless, as though, while trying to refuse a metaphysics of the frontier, we are granting it (the word *frontier* as well as the "thing" it designates) a singular privilege that cannot fail to bring back a more pernicious metaphysics still. Because in spite of the arguments just sketched out, which will be developed at length in the pages that follow, one might legitimately suspect that behind this privilege there is the return of an obscurantist or even mystical metaphysics. The frontier, alpha and omega, first and last truth? Which cannot be clearly exhibited to consciousness and reason? The proper name for what supposedly underlies all philosophy?

This suspicion, dictated by a critical concern that must always be kept alert, cannot be fully answered here, before we even start, because the book lives only in the disquiet it represents. We really do run the risk, every time we say "frontier," of doing metaphysics. We can mitigate this risk (but not avoid it, on the contrary, it is a fine risk) by insisting on the fact that everything we are saying assumes that "frontier" is not *the* name of some *thing* that would be *one* thing. So there is not, as one might assume, a something = x that might be called, among other things perhaps, "frontier" (which would then be nothing other than Being, which, as Aristotle famously says, is diversely named).[2] It is true that the reader will not fail to find (or so we hope) that "frontier" is here trying to name something that looks (just) like what has elsewhere been

1. I place "history" in scare quotes so as not to suggest any adequation, even a dialectical one, between philosophy and its history: rather, philosophy "is" its history to the extent that it is never quite itself.

2. *Metaphysics*, γ, 1003a 33; δ, 1017a 8–24; ζ, 1028a 10, etc.

called "difference" (or even "différance"), "différend," "sense," and so on.[3] But it is not sufficient to point out this family resemblance (which is real, and to which I am the first to lay claim), because we would have understood nothing of this movement of thought if we do not realize that what is thus diversely named, without being nothing, is no thing and indeed escapes the order of (the thinking of) Being. So "frontier" is not a new name for a same old thing—the same thing, the thing itself, is always Being, comes down to (being nothing but) Being.

Not that one can escape (the thinking of) Being by looking somewhere else, in another world. The frontier, at least as I try to unfold its quasi-concept here, is neither simply in metaphysics nor simply outside it but precisely (on) its frontier; it is neither before nor after, neither beneath like its foundation, nor at its heart like its inner hidden truth, nor above it like its transcendental condition. Rather, like some fractal curves, the frontier tendentially fills the space of metaphysics without ever completely saturating it. I shall try to show that the frontier is literally everywhere. Imagine a space populated by different fractal curves. Each curve is singular and confused with no other. These curves intersect in many places, more or less unpredictably. But as they develop (for some fractals, perhaps all, have an irreducible temporal dimension), they all tend to fill the whole space in which they are found, to the point of being literally everywhere at the same time. Whence, sometimes, the maximalist impression made by the type of thinking I have just cited, even as that thinking constantly insists on the singularity of its objects.

So "frontier" does not name the same thing as "différance," "différend," or "sense," all the while recognizing itself in them, and all the while tending to merge with them. If I am so attached to it (when other words, all the other words, appeal to me as well), this is perhaps for a reason I will state here elliptically, hoping it will become clearer as we proceed. I like "frontier" because "frontier" *is a frontier*. Wherever there is "frontier" there is a frontier. Not in the sense that one might think that a referent can sometimes be present alongside its sign. I am not saying that wherever one reads the word *frontier* there is a frontier outside the word, designated by it, but that the word *frontier*

3. Jacques Derrida, "La différance," in *Marges—de la philosophie*, 3–29 (Paris: Minuit, 1972), tr. Alan Bass as "Differance" in *Margins of Philosophy*, 1–27 (Chicago: University of Chicago Press, 1982); Jean-François Lyotard, *Le différend* (Paris: Minuit, 1983), tr. Georges van den Abbeele as *The Differend* (Minneapolis: University of Minnesota Press, 1989); Jean-Luc Nancy, *Le sens du monde* (Paris: Galilée, 1993), tr. Jeffrey S. Librett as *The Sense of the World* (Minneapolis: University of Minnesota Press, 1997).

in the text is itself a frontier. And as we shall see that there never is, never could be, *one* frontier, this means several different things, some of which we will be trying to follow.

—|—

There are, it seems, two major traditional concepts of the frontier, or meanings of the word *frontier*. The first (which indeed comes first in both the *Oxford English Dictionary* and Merriam-Webster) refers to the line that separates two entities of the same type: France and Germany, the USA and Canada. In this sense the frontier—which here is bilateral and so already more complex than a simple line—marks separation where one might not otherwise notice it, imposes a crossing, or at least a mark of difference. According to this first concept, the frontier is artificial (even if it always might coincide with what is called, after the fact, a natural frontier—river, mountains, coastline), a nonnatural tracing in nature. The frontier thus defined is essentially traversable (it is there to control crossing, not to make it impossible) and therefore contestable (one can always cross it in an effort to erase it or declare it nonexistent). The frontier is a place of confrontation and violence, of friction, the place where, even in peacetime, the possibility of war is announced. At the frontier, where the identity of the country is permanently announced and threatened, it is reinforced by means that are symbolic (flags, inscriptions) and real (barbed wire, soldiers, customs houses).

There is another concept of the frontier or (and here there may be a translation issue, an issue of crossing linguistic borders) of The Frontier in what is more obviously the "American" sense of the word. Here we are at the limit of civilization or of known civilization, on its edge or its point that advances or believes itself to be advancing. This is the place of adventure and the adventurer, the pioneer, the frontiersman, precisely. Beyond this limit there be monsters, the jungle, the desert, places of uncertainty and terror, of the radically unknown. Crossing the frontier in the first sense (into another country) is nothing compared to what happens here, for here we can precisely not cross: We are *on* the frontier or rather *in* the frontier that we carry with us. Pushing back the frontier, we bring "civilization" with us, redefining the limit from which the infinite beyond draws us to its futural void, calls out from the emptiness where by definition we will never be. This untraversable frontier is where nature starts, where what starts is always in the position of nature with respect to our civilization, an archaic nature that we are supposed to have left behind but in which, by the same token, we have never yet been, an absolute past that calls to us from the future. There may be no natural frontiers, but the frontier in this sense is nature (and thus, contrary to all mythology, history too, for it is the same thing). Beyond the frontier, the future is the past; no surprise that science fiction, which deals with just this frontier, should so systematically link futurist technologies and prehistoric fantasies. The frontiersman, at the point of civilization advancing, gaining on nature, is also man returned to nature, become again somewhat animal, beast-like, brutish. Life on the frontier, where we are already ahead of ourselves, is essentially rough and primitive; the limits of civilization are places where, in its advance, civilization has left itself behind, forgetting—despising—its comforts and securities that will slowly follow this heroic and ambiguous advance. The point is isolated, sent back to the origins, it always has to sharpen itself in contact with raw materials, old ways, getting back to hunting and snares, wearing animal skins, eating its food raw. The thrusting, virile advance of civilization confirms its ambivalent virility by identifying at least a little with the feminine nature that delimits it.

This frontier is essentially mobile. It is usually thought of as being more or less irresistibly pushed back (but it takes infinite vigilance to prevent burgeoning nature from regaining ground behind the line). Culture is supposed to conquer nature, bringing with it light and knowledge. And that is its paradox: Push back the frontier to find what is beyond, and what was beyond is no longer beyond, because you are already there, the beyond has retreated beyond again; you will never get there.

But in fact these two concepts of the frontier, which seem to confront each other along a conceptual frontier traced within the word itself, merge into one. Bilateral frontiers squeeze into their vanishing but infinite line all the nature that the other concept imagined it could find beyond, by advancing. What remains of nature in the bilateral frontier (but that just is nature; we shall see that nature is only ever its own remains, its own double or phantom) is still there, but in imploded form: the gap between the paving stones in which we think we can sense the beach, but where monsters or bears also live in the dark; the black monolith at the end of *2001: A Space Odyssey*. And in the apparent erasure of the frontier between these two concepts of the frontier, the frontier itself, the never-established difference between its two meanings or concepts, suddenly appears everywhere, nature rediscovered in its potential violence on every little daily frontier, line scribbled across the whole surface, filling it as we watch, feeling at the same time the solid ground of "we" or "I" giving way, losing the vantage from which we were watching.

—|—

"If the point here were to do metaphysics . . . ," we were saying at the beginning. But it might be time to say that *there is no metaphysics*. The reason is both simple and ungraspably complex: "Metaphysics" is metaphysical. To claim to identify something as metaphysics is the very gesture of metaphysics. But if, as I will be trying to show here, this identificatory gesture is impossible or at least radically unfinished, it would follow not only that metaphysics is impossible, in the sense that one can no longer permit oneself to go in for it these days (as though it depended on our historical moment, on a decision we would have to take, or even a noble renunciation of a temptation that is henceforth forbidden or outmoded), but that metaphysics is impossible in the sense that there never could have been any such thing. What we more or less calmly call "metaphysics" is thus not metaphysical (without being any other determinable thing). Metaphysics would consist in the gesture of identifying metaphysics. But that gesture can never be completed.

Equally and conversely, there has never been anything other than metaphysics. We wanted to identify and delimit metaphysics in order to separate ourselves from it and hold it at arm's length; but as it is not something strictly identifiable, that separation never happens, and we find ourselves in it, like it or not. In order to escape metaphysics, it would suffice to fulfill it by saying what it is, to escape from it and finally do something else (and thus, according to a logic we shall be seeing a lot of in this book, the end of metaphysics would be the end of metaphysics). But this is quite impossible, and always has been. In this situation, we cannot fail to give the impression of having found in the frontier a new metaphysical, foundational, concept. But the frontier itself, moving always elsewhere in its nonlinear dynamic, will always bely that impression.

Here, on the frontier of the book.

Prolegomena

We are, then, going to be spending time on the frontier.[1] On the frontier, which is also to say on the border, the extremity, the limit, the marches, the confines, on the edge, the periphery, around the rim, on the boundary, the shore, the threshold, the end. And perhaps especially on the frontier one can imagine passing between these various words and concepts, or rather these terms (a term is a frontier). According to one traditional (philosophical) approach to philosophy, our task here would consist in establishing as precisely as possible the frontier between these diverse words and concepts (in order to determine, for example, whether we are really dealing with different concepts or the same concept under different names), and doing so successfully might be thought to be a condition of their conceptual status, if they are to achieve such status. For, or so one might think, a concept is only a concept if it can be precisely and completely delimited. I am borrowing the formula for this eminently philosophical demand not from, say, Descartes or Kant, but, for strategic reasons to do with the style or manner of philosophy being practiced here, from Gottlob Frege. Here, in the *Grundgesetze der Arithmetik*:

> The concept must have a sharp boundary [der Begriff muss Scharf begrenzt sein]. If we represent concepts in extension by areas [Bezirke] on a plane, this is admittedly a picture [ein Gleichnis] that may be used only with caution, but here it can do us good service. To a concept without sharp boundary there would correspond an area that had not a sharp boundary-line all round, but in places just vaguely faded away into the background [stellenweise ganz verschwimmend in die Umgebung überginge: note that here the boundary or frontier of the concept apparently separates it from an *Umgebung*, a milieu, an environment or a fringe-area that are apparently imprecise, a wasteland rather than other concepts, perhaps even a liquid medium in which the concept might be swimming]. This would not really be an area at all; and likewise a concept that is not sharply defined is wrongly termed a concept. Such quasi-conceptual constructions [solche begriffsartige Bildungen] cannot be recognized as con-

1. In the French text I was able to write "nous allons passer du temps à la frontière," which can also be read quite pertinently as meaning "we are going to move from time to the frontier," which captures one distant aspiration of the book—namely, to insist on the resistance of spatiality to its philosophical sublation into time.

> cepts by logic; it is impossible to lay down precise laws for them [note this language of legislation: the point for Frege, very Kantian here, is to delimit a territory with a view to legislation]. The law of excluded middle is really just another form of the requirement that the concept should have a sharp boundary. Any object δ that you choose to take either falls under the concept or does not fall under it; *tertium non datur*. E.g. would the sentence "any square root of 9 is odd" have a comprehensible sense at all if *square root of 9* were not a concept with a sharp boundary? Has the question "Are we still Christians?" really got a sense, if it is indeterminate whom the predicate "Christian" can truly be ascribed to, and who must be refused it?[2]

This demand of Frege's, repeated from beginning to end of his work,[3] this demand that is the demand of philosophy itself, this demand that is legitimate if ever a demand were legitimate—drawing a clear frontier is the beginning of legitimacy—has several immediate and paradoxical consequences:

1. If one is to speak clearly and be recognizable by logic, and indeed to mean anything at all, one must have concepts with sharp frontiers.
2. The need or obligation in which we find ourselves to draw or find such sharp frontiers assumes that in fact we find cases where such frontiers have not been traced, pseudo-conceptual constructions that must be got rid of.[4]

2. Gottlob Frege, *Grundgesetze der Arithmetik* (Hildesheim, Germany: Georg Ohms, 1962), vol. 2, §56; partial translation in *Translations from the Philosophical Writings of Gottlob Frege*, ed. Peter Geach and Max Black (Oxford: Blackwell, 1970), 139. I address Wittgenstein's comments on this demand of Frege's in *Frontiers: Kant, Hegel, Frege, Wittgenstein* (CreateSpace, 2003), 372–75.

3. I quote Frege's papers from *Kleine Schriften*, ed. Igancio Angelelli (Hildesheim, Germany: Georg Ohms, 1967), tr. Hans Kaal as *Collected Papers on Mathematics, Logic and Philosophy*, ed. Brian McGuinness (Oxford: Blackwell, 1984). In the text "On the Law of Inertia" (1891), for example, "If something fails to display this sharp boundary [diese scharfe Begrenzung], it cannot be recognized in logic as a concept"; in "Function and Concept" (1891), he states that "as regards concepts we have a requirement of sharp delimitation [scharfe Begrenzung]" (135/148), or "If something fails to display a sharp boundary, it cannot be recognised in logic as a concept" (122/133), and constantly warns against any "blurring" of boundaries. Thus in a polemical exchange from 1906 with a certain Korselt, "I have been at pains to draw sharp boundaries; Mr Korselt, it seems, diligently blurs them once again" (281/293), or more generally, and crucially for Frege's uncompromising realism, he is determined to "prevent the blurring of the boundary between psychology and logic" (343/352).

4. Frege goes so far as to make of this the motor of the history of science, while contesting the role of contradiction in this respect. According to Frege, a concept can perfectly well involve a contradiction without for all that ceasing to be a concept or

3. As every concept must have such a frontier to ensure its definition, every concept presupposes the frontier, and so there can be no concept of frontier that does not presuppose that its object is already known.
4. Which is why we have to speak in images (*bildlich*), metaphorically rather than conceptually.
5. Which means that not only do we not have a sharply defined concept of what a frontier is, but nor do we have a sharply defined concept of what a concept is in general (not having a concept of frontier, but rather a metaphorical illustration, although the frontier defines the concept: so the concept as such, and not just the frontier, is being defined metaphorically).
6. Which means that in the end it remains indeterminate to what the concept "concept" can be assigned in truth, given that the non- or quasi-conceptuality of the frontier means that the concept "concept" is not clearly defined and remains a quasi-concept. The definition of the concept "concept" cannot be complete, because it depends on the definition of the frontier that delimits it—and the frontier defining the concept cannot be defined, not being a concept but the preconceptual condition of any concept.

---

calling for any development or sublation. Recall that in *The Foundations of Arithmetic* it is the contradictory concept "not equal to itself" that helps Frege define the zero, from which all the rest is supposed to follow. This idea is developed in "On the Law of Inertia":

> The concept of not being identical with itself contains a contradiction and remains none the less what it is and always was, and still does not look as if it was about to develop further. It has a good claim to being recognized in logic as a concept, for its boundary is as sharp as it can possibly be; and one can make good use of it in defining the number 0, as I have shown in my book, *The Foundations of Arithmetic*. In our case too, it is not contradictions in the concept of motion that are the driving force behind its development. Contradictions have indeed appeared; but it is not as if they had been created by combining mutually contradictory characteristic marks in the definition; they have, rather, been created by treating as a concept something that was not a concept in the logical sense because it lacked a sharp boundary. In the search for a boundary line, the contradictions, as they emerged, brought to the attention of the searchers that the assumed boundary was still uncertain or blurred, or that it was not the one they had been searching for. So contradictions were indeed a driving force behind the search, but not contradictions in the concept; for these always carry with them a sharp boundary: it is known that nothing falls under a contradictory concept; it is therefore impossible to doubt whether or not a given object falls under the concept, once the contradiction in it has been recognized. The real driving force is the perception of the blurred boundary [die Wahrnehmung der verschwommenen Begrenzung]. (*Kleine Schriften*, 123/134)

Frege's philosophical difficulties repeatedly confirm this slightly brutal analysis. For example, in "On Concept and Object" (1892), written in response to a certain Kerry:

> Kerry contests what he calls my definition of "concept." I would remark, in the first place, that my explanation is not meant as a proper definition. One cannot require that everything shall be defined, any more than one can require that a chemist shall decompose every substance. What is simple cannot be decomposed, and what is logically simple cannot have a proper definition [was logisch einfacht ist, kann nicht eigentlich definiert werden]. Now something logically simple is no more given to us at the outset than most of the chemical elements are; it is reached only by means of scientific work. If something has been discovered that is simple, or at least must count as simple for the time being, we shall have to coin a term for it, since language will not contain an expression which exactly answers. On the introduction of a name for something logically simple, a definition is not possible; there is nothing for it but to lead the reader or hearer, *by means of hints* [durch Winke anzuleiten; to lead by allusions, pointers, insinuations, almost winks, the wink of a slightly secret and perhaps shameful complicity] to understand the word as is intended. (*Kleine Schriften*, 167–68/182–83; my emphasis)[5]

5. See too, a little later: "Kerry holds that no logical rules can be based on linguistic distinctions; but my own way of doing this is something that nobody can avoid who lays down such rules at all; for we cannot come to an understanding with one another apart from language, and so in the end we must always rely on other people's understanding words, inflexions, and sentence-construction in essentially the same way as ourselves. As I said before, I was not trying to give a definition, but only hints [Winke]; and to this end I appealed to the general feeling for the German language [das allgemeine deutsche Sprachgefühl]. It is here very much to my advantage that there is such good accord between the linguistic distinction and the real one" (169–70/184–85; neither the first nor the last German philosopher to find to his satisfaction that his language accords so well with reality). This problem returns constantly: "I admit that there is a quite peculiar obstacle in the way of an understanding with the reader. By a kind of necessity of language, my expressions, taken literally, sometimes miss my thought; I mention an object, when what I intend is a concept. I fully realize that in such cases I was relying upon a reader who would be ready to meet me half-way [ein wohlwollendes Entgegenkommen des Lesers]—who does not begrudge a pinch of salt [einem Körnchen Salz]" (177/193). See too the paper "What Is a Function?" (1904): Frege has just said that functions, unlike numbers, are unsaturated, and he continues: "Of course this is no definition; but likewise none is here possible. I must confine myself to hinting at what I have in mind by means of a metaphorical expression [Ich muss mich darauf beschränken, durch einbildlichen Ausdruck auf das hinzuweisen, was ich meine], and here I rely on my reader's agreeing to meet me half-way" (280/292). I have tried to

Because "concept" is the name of something logically simple, it cannot be defined, and we cannot know whether it has a clear-cut frontier. It will be objected that this is a straightforward consequence of what is sometimes called Frege's Paradox—namely, that because in Frege "concept" (or "function"; it is by an extension of the mathematical notion of function that Frege develops his concept of concept) always names a predicate (i.e., an incomplete or unsaturated expression of the type ". . . is the capital of the German Empire" [Frege's example]), one cannot *name* a concept without transforming it into what Frege calls an object (an object being what is properly named by a name, and a name what properly names an object), which object is, precisely, the other of the concept or function. There is between object and concept a clear frontier that means one cannot directly address the concept without transforming it into an object:

> It must indeed by recognized that here we are confronted by an awkwardness of language, which I admit cannot be avoided, if we say that the concept *horse* is not a concept, whereas, e.g., the city of Berlin is a city, and the volcano Vesuvius is a volcano. Language is here in a predicament [ein Zwangslage] that justifies the departure from custom. The peculiarity of our case is indicated by Kerry himself, by means of the quotation-marks around "horse"; I use italics to the same end. There was no reason to mark out the words "Berlin" and "Vesuvius" in a similar way. In logical discussions one quite often needs to say something about a concept, and to express this in the form usual for such predications—viz. to make what is said about the concept into the content of the grammatical predicate. Consequently, one would expect that what is meant by the grammatical subject would be the concept; but the concept as such cannot play this part, in view of its predicative nature; it must first be converted into an object, or, more precisely, an object must go proxy for it. (170–71/185–86)

So if one wishes to insist on the clear-cut definition of the concept, we must first find the definitional frontiers of the object. But this is no more possible on the side of the object, if we are to believe Frege, than on the side of the concept:

> When we have thus admitted objects without restriction as arguments and values of functions, the question arises what it is that we are here calling an object. I regard a regular definition [ein schulgemässe Definition] as impossible,

show elsewhere that this type of appeal to the reader condemns philosophy to what it calls "metaphor"; see my "Lecture—de Georges Bataille," in my *Géographie et autres lectures*, 5–32 (Paris: Hermann, 2011).

> since we have here something too simple to admit of logical analysis. It is only possible to indicate [hinzudeuten] what is meant. Here I can only say briefly: An object is anything that is not a function [i.e., a concept], so that an expression for it does not contain any empty place. (134/147)

So we will never have a definition of the concept or of the object. This turns out to be part of the very logic of definition: In a little text on formal theories in arithmetic (1885), Frege, seeking "a certain sharpness of delimitation, a certain logical completeness [eine gewisse Schärfe der Abgrenzung, eine gewisse logische Vollkommenheit]," intends to show that arithmetic can be entirely derived from logic, that (for once) "there is no sharp boundary [keine scharfe Grenze] between the two" (103/112). In the course of this argument, Frege devotes a development to the question of definition, precisely:

> In the case of any definition whatever we must presuppose as known something by means of which we explain what we want understood by this name or sign. We cannot very well define an angle without presupposing knowledge of what constitutes a straight line. To be sure, that on which we base our definitions may itself have been defined previously; however, when we retrace our steps further, we shall always come upon something which, being a simple, is indefinable, and must be admitted to be incapable of further analysis. And the properties belonging to these ultimate building blocks [Urbansteinen] of a discipline contain, as it were in a nutshell [im Keime, in germ, as seeds], its whole contents. [. . .] Now it is clear that the boundaries of a discipline are determined by the nature of its ultimate building blocks. (104/113–14)

The frontiers of a science are thus traced, in their necessary clarity (if we are trying to say there is no such frontier between arithmetic and logic, this is in order to assert that, precisely, they are *not* separate sciences), by the ultimate blocks that are their basis. These blocks, assumed to be simple,[6] which can only be simple, are precisely what cannot be defined, and they condemn us, even in logic, to metaphors and hints or winks, and thus to nonsimplicity.[7]

6. But this cannot be demonstrated just because of the impossibility of definition—the same impossibility that is supposed to confirm the simplicity in question. This is why the Wittgenstein of the *Tractatus* makes of this type of simplicity a logical necessity: There *must* be simples, even if we are not in a position to describe their nature. These simples in the *Tractatus* (2.02) are strictly logical and not to be confused with any empirical simple, as some positivists have thought.

7. Frege's frustration is, in fact, a frustration with language itself. In the first of the *Logical Investigations* (entitled simply "Thoughts"), we find the following: "I am not here in the happy position of a mineralogist who shows his audience a rock-crystal [or per-

The impossibility of arriving at a clear definition of the frontier, and thus of the concept of concept, means that no more can one be certain of the frontiers of a science, which inherit the lack of sharpness that thus affect its constitutive elements, the building blocks that contain the germ (note that Frege, condemned to metaphor, does not wield it with any great care or logic). As Jacques Derrida has taught us, the foundation of an institution, its very institution, the institution of the institution, including the institution of a science, and even of a science of logic, cannot be understood by that institution, can only be violent with respect to that institution.[8] What I am trying to show here is that the frontier is the enduring (uncrossable) trace of that violent institution of the institution in general, and that this violence marks all concepts with the trace of a constitutive nonconceptuality. Frege, who is a bit disgusted by all this, can only give hints, slightly shady winks, base himself on a common precomprehension of the language, or else speak metaphorically to get across the frontier and get us to logic, conceptuality, and clarity. At the root of Fregean logicism, and of all the philosophy of language that is inspired by it, there is, then, a constitutive and unthought murkiness (unthought and unthinkable in the terms of such a philosophy), a nonlogical frontier of logic, a frontier that cannot be traced clearly, a poorly defined zone that is named, for want of anything better, by "image," "metaphor," or "indication." Even a logical notation, such as the *Begriffschrift* proposed by Frege in 1879, which is at the root of all subsequent logical notations, necessarily has its roots in this zone. All of Frege's philosophy (and therefore a few others' too) tries desperately to repress this nonlogical "origin" of logic

haps a pinch of salt]: I cannot put a thought in the hands of my readers with the request that they should examine it from all sides. Something in itself not perceptible by sense, the thought, is presented to the reader—and I must be content with that—wrapped up in a perceptible linguistic form. The pictorial aspect of language [die Bildlichkeit der Sprache] presents difficulties. The sensible always breaks in and makes expressions pictorial and so improper. So one fights against language [there is "ein Kampf mit der Sprache"], and I am compelled to occupy myself with language although it is not my proper concern here. I hope I have succeeded in making clear to my readers what I mean by 'a thought'" (350n4/360n6).

8. See, for example, Jacques Derrida, *Force de loi: le "fondement mystique" de l'autorité* (Paris: Galilée, 1994), tr. Mary Quaintance as "Force of Law: The 'Mystical Foundation' of Authority" in *Acts of Religion*, ed. Gil Anidjar, 231–98 (London: Routledge, 2002), 242; and "Mochlos, ou le conflit des facultés," in *Du droit à la philosophie*, 397–438 (Paris: Galilée, 1990), 435, tr. Jan Plug as "Mochlos or the Conflict of the Faculties" in *Eyes of the University: Right to Philosophy 2*, 83–112 (Stanford, CA: Stanford University Press, 2002), 109–10.

behind dogmatic demands and stipulations—whence its deep-seated moralism. This murkiness that defines the definition itself and makes it indefinite, and is, therefore, the indefinite definition of definition, the quasi-conceptual nature of conceptuality, undermines *all* the bases of this philosophy, up to and including the famous and untenable distinction between *Sinn* and *Bedeutung*, and condemns Frege to the very fiction and metaphor he tried so hard to avoid. If, as Derrida claims in *Schibboleth*, the indecision of the frontier between the philosophical and the poetical is what most provokes philosophy to think,[9] then it must be said that the philosophy that appeals more or less directly to Frege is the philosophy that most firmly tries to block thinking. Not only do we not find a concept of frontier in Frege, but we find in him and his successors that the essential lack of that concept means there is no concept of concept either, nor indeed of anything else. We will, then, never know if we are still Christians, or even, it seems, if that question has any meaning. We will never cross the frontier into absolute clarity.

Having got stuck here, how are we going to move forward? Our book on the frontier really is on the frontier, and even on the frontier of the frontier, apparently unable to define its object, to draw a frontier that would allow us to cross over and get started. (For the more sharply a frontier is drawn, the easier it is to cross, according to a law we would need to formalize—or that is the law of formalism itself.)

As we have seen, in attempting to approach our object philosophically, we have rapidly run up against an impossibility, or even a *petitio principii*: Not being able to define the concept of frontier without presupposing the possibility of drawing nonconceptualizable frontiers around it condemns us to a mode of indirectness that shows up right here, from the start, in the form of an inevitable resort to what philosophy would call analogy, image, or metaphor. This "metaphor" of the frontier is not neutral or innocent but immediately leans toward a geometric or cartographic, and ultimately geopolitical, language. Rather than remaining stuck on the metaphor of conceptual frontiers, why not turn to the apparently literal sense of that metaphor? If we cannot make the conceptual frontier literal, and if it will remain forever metaphorical, might we not, instead, pursue the "literal," geopolitical frontier?

9. Jacques Derrida, *Schibboleth: pour Paul Celan* (Paris: Galilée, 1986), 80, tr. Thomas Dutoit as "Schibboleth: For Paul Celan" in *Sovereignties in Question*, 1–64 (New York: Fordham University Press, 2005), 44.

There are two ways of proceeding here, and we need to distinguish them at least provisionally, to draw a frontier between them. The first would consist in claiming a certain failure of philosophy: having failed to produce a concept of the frontier, philosophy sees conceptuality itself collapse. According to this first way of proceeding, if we want to pursue our inquiry, we would need to drop philosophical demands as illusory and be content with an empirico-positive study of frontiers. We cannot follow that route here, because in spite of all the interesting things that might be said within the framework of such a study (especially, perhaps, at the present moment) it would sooner or later come up against the fact that it cannot fail to presuppose that it knows what a frontier is, that therefore it has a concept of the frontier, when it claims to draw its whole supposed legitimacy from the fact that no such concept can be produced. Which means it is indulging in what Derrida might call "transcendental contraband."[10]

The second way of proceeding, the one we will follow here, consists not in forgetting philosophy but in retreating more modestly—and provi-

10. This is not only the case with the so-called human sciences, in that philosophy falls very easily into this trap. This seems to be notably the case with Foucault, who can in principle say everything except how it is possible for him to say what he says. The case of Deleuze seems more complex. In the zone of our immediate preoccupations, one can find a very interesting exploitation of a "political" language in the conceptual domain: "Thought as such is already in conformity with a model that it borrows from the State apparatus, and which defines for it goals and paths, conduits, channels, organs, an entire *organon*. There is thus an image of thought covering all of thought; it is the special object of 'noology' and is like the State-form developed in thought. This image has two heads, corresponding to the two poles of sovereignty: the *imperium* of true thinking operated by magical capture, seizure or binding, constituting the efficacy of a foundation (*mythos*); a republic of free spirits proceeding by pact or contract, constituting a legislative and juridical organization, carrying the sanction of a ground (*logos*). [. . .] But confining ourselves to the image, it appears that it is not simply a metaphor when we are told of an *imperium* of truth and a republic of spirits. It is the necessary condition for the constitution of thought as principle, or as a form of interiority, as a stratum" (Gilles Deleuze and Félix Guattari, *Capitalisme et Schizophrénie: Mille plateaux* [Paris: Minuit, 1980], 465–66, tr. Brian Massumi as *A Thousand Plateaus: Capitalism and Schizophrenia* [Minneapolis: University of Minnesota Press, 1987], 374–75; the translation makes the passage a little more assertive than the original, in which the verbs in the first two sentences quoted above are in the conditional). And more generally, everything that is described in terms of territorialization and deterritorialization, and even nomadism, goes in the direction of what we are proposing here. But Deleuze clearly gives priority to one of the terms in these descriptions. So politics (the State form) is supposed to be the key to the concept, and within this "politics," the nomad always has a privilege (a privilege one might find a little "romantic") over the sedentary.

sionally—from logic or pure or fundamental philosophy in order to move toward a philosophy that claims to deal directly with the region in which we have located the "literal" sense of the frontier (i.e., political philosophy). This retreat can only be provisional, because we shall see that the very project of delimiting something like a "region" presupposes frontiers that will constantly refer us from politics to logic, from a logic of politics to a politics of logic, in a movement that can come under neither logic nor politics, at least as they are usually understood.

What do we find in political philosophy as to the frontier? Basically, not very much. Let me put forward the hypothesis that, in general, political philosophy tries to think *the* State or *the polis* in the singular. This object must be delimited and defined, thus surrounded by a frontier, but to the extent that the object is usually presented as essentially singular, this frontier is more often presupposed than thought. In classic political philosophy, it appears that we first try to define or deduce the State (Plato and Aristotle would be the obvious *loci classici*), and if one asks questions about the relations this State can have with other States, this is done later, as though it were a secondary problem. Rousseau's *Social Contract*, for example, seems to be coherent in spite of the absence in the main text of any reflection on the frontier of the State and, therefore, its relation with other States.[11] Here, via analysis of some texts of Kant's, I will be trying to show that, in fact, the problem of the frontier is the primary problem of political philosophy, that this problem entails the thought of what I shall call an "absolute exteriority," and that it cannot be resolved dialectically. We shall never cross over this frontier.

11. The final chapter of the work, entitled simply "Conclusion," reads as follows in its entirety: "After setting down the true principles of political right and trying to found a State on its basis, it would remain to buttress the State by its external relations; which would include the right of nations, commerce, the right of war and conquests, public right, leagues, negotiations, treaties, etc. But all this forms a new object too vast for my short sight; I should always have fixed it nearer to myself" (tr. Victor Gourevitch in *The Social Contract and Other Later Political Writings*, 39–152 [Cambridge: Cambridge University Press, 1997], 152). See the commentary by Peggy Kamuf in *Signature Pieces: On the Institution of Authorship* (Ithaca, NY: Cornell University Press, 1988).

KANT ON THE FRONTIER

1. The End of Nature

> If the biblical theologian meddles with his reason in any of these tenets, then, even granting that reason strives most sincerely and earnestly for that same objective, he leaps (like Romulus's brother) over the wall [so überspringt er . . . die Mauer] of ecclesiastical faith, the only thing that assures his salvation, and strays into the free and open fields of private judgment and philosophy. And there, having run away from the Church's government, he is exposed to all the dangers of anarchy.
>
> —Immanuel Kant, *The Conflict of the Faculties*

> Natural science must not jump over its boundaries [muß sie ihre Grenze nicht überspringen] in order to bring within itself as an indigenous principle that to whose concept no experience at all can ever be adequate and upon which we are authorized to venture only after the completion of natural science.
>
> —Immanuel Kant, *Critique of the Power of Judgment*

Displacing slightly the classical form of the question, let's ask no longer "What *is* a frontier?" but "What is the *nature* of a frontier?" In a famous passage, Marx says that exchange must have begun in an external way at the frontier of natural communities.[1]

What is the relation between exchange, nature, and frontier (these are

1. Karl Marx, *Capital*, vol. 1, ch. 2: "Objects in themselves are external to man, and consequently alienable by him. In order that this alienation may be reciprocal, it is only necessary for men, by a tacit understanding, to treat each other as private owners of those alienable objects, and by implication as independent individuals. But such a state of reciprocal independence has no existence in a primitive society based on property in common, whether such a society takes the form of a patriarchal family, an ancient Indian community, or a Peruvian Inca State. The exchange of commodities, therefore, first begins on the boundaries of such communities, at their points of contact with other similar communities, or with members of the latter. So soon, however, as products once become commodities in the external relations of a community, they also, by re-action, become so in its internal intercourse" (tr. Ben Fowkes [Harmondsworth, UK: Penguin Books, 1976], 182). And, for the value of nature, *Grundrisse* (tr. Martin Nicolaus [Harmondsworth, UK: Penguin Books, 1973], 204), where barter, "the first phenomenal form of exchange-value" begins "accidentally" "at the borders of the natural communities, in their contact with strangers." Accidentally or *contingently*, where such communities touch each other (*contingere* from *con-tangere*). As we shall see, the frontier is always a place of contingency.

also the three key terms in Aristotle's derivation of economics and chrematistics)?[2] We would need to ask what a "natural community" might be and whether "natural" communities have so-called natural frontiers. We shall see that, as has become a truism, there are no natural frontiers, that what are called natural frontiers (shores, rivers, mountains) are named thus only by analogy with nonnatural frontiers, once they have been crossed.[3] Only after the fact, after nature, does a "natural" frontier become a true frontier, nonnatural, instituted, therefore traversable. And yet, we shall see that in a deeper and more persistent sense, all frontiers can be called natural, in the sense that they are frontiers *of nature*, lines where nature stops, the point of transition or transgression at which nature turns into one or other of its others (culture, law, *technē*, politics, etc.). In this sense all frontiers are (on) the frontier of nature. Where there is a frontier, there is (at least one) nature.

So let's displace our question again. How does a frontier happen to nature? Or, perhaps, how does a frontier return to nature? What is the event of a frontier? Here is a description of a frontier happening (or rather, but this is [in] its nature, precisely, its nature as returning to nature), not quite happening:

> Remus, the story goes, was the first to receive a sign—six vultures; and no sooner was this made known to the people than double the number of birds appeared to Romulus. The followers of each promptly saluted their master as king, one side basing its claim upon priority, the other upon number. Angry words ensued, followed all too soon by blows, and in the course of the affray Remus was killed. There is another story, a commoner one, according to which Remus, by way of jeering at his brother, jumped over the half-built walls of

2. Aristotle: "the members of the primitive household used to share commodities that were all their own, whereas on the contrary a group divided into several households participated also in a number of commodities belonging to their neighbors, according to their needs for which they were forced to make their interchanges by way of barter, as also many barbarian tribes do still; for such tribes do not go beyond exchanging actual commodities for actual commodities, for example giving and taking wine for corn, and so with the various other things of the sort. Exchange on these lines therefore is not contrary to nature, nor is it any branch of the art of wealth-getting, for it existed for the replenishment of natural self-sufficiency; yet out of it the art of business in due course arose. For when they had come to supply themselves more from abroad by importing things in which they were deficient and exporting those of which they had a surplus, the employment of money necessarily came to be devised" (*Politics*, tr. H. Rackham [Cambridge, MA: Harvard University Press, 1932], 1257a 20–32). Marx regularly pays tribute to Aristotle's analyses in *Capital* (see, for example, 152).

3. See G.W. F. Hegel, *Philosophy of Right*, remark to §247, and more recently Michel Foucher, *Fronts et frontières: un tour du monde géopolitique* (Paris: Fayard, 1988).

> the new settlement, whereupon Romulus killed him in a fit of rage, adding the threat, "So perish whoever else shall overleap my battlements."[4]

For now, let's take from this famous passage the idea that the frontier is drawn in the context of a prior violence or discord, or rather that tracing it involves its originary transgression—that the frontier, drawn against natural violence, arrives always too late not to be itself violent. Drawing a frontier always represents an act of violence in a context of violence (but the very concept of context presupposes that of frontier and so cannot explain it) and invites further violence: jealousy, mockery, revenge, threat, warfare.[5]

Here is another, more recent, description of a frontier happening (or rather, as always, not quite happening):

> Wherever two regions are about to form a boundary [. . .], the third region [. . .] establishes a chain of outposts. In order that these outposts do not form bilateral borders with their neighbours, they in turn are surrounded by chains of islands in a structure which is repeated down to infinitely small dimensions [. . .]
>
> What may seem almost impossible as a boundary between three "countries" can be extended without any mathematical difficulty to situations with 4, 5, 6 [. . .] competing domains. The boundary is made up entirely of points where 4, 5, 6 [. . .] countries meet.[6]

This passage comes from a popularizing book about fractals. Without addressing the specifically mathematical aspects of fractals,[7] let's note in this description the incautious mix of the language of nature and the language of politics: There is talk of "islands" but also of "countries," of "competing domains" that have "neighbors." Note also the whiff of a purposiveness (we shall see that there is no frontier and no nature without the question of teleology arising) in the phrase "in order that these outposts do not form." Where

4. Livy, *The Early History of Rome*, tr. Aubrey de Selincourt (London: Penguin Books, 1960), 37.

5. We could reread here Lyotard's strange little text *Le mur du pacifique* (Paris: Galilée, 1979) as a way of wondering whether Rome might not be taken as the paradigmatic case of the frontier in general. I attempt a preliminary reading of this text in "'Ces petits différends . . .': Lyotard and Horace," in *Legislations: The Politics of Deconstruction*, 152–71 (London: Verso Books, 1994).

6. H.-O. Peitgen and P. H. Richter, *The Beauty of Fractals: Images of Complex Dynamical Systems* (Berlin: Springer Verlag, 1987), 19.

7. See the now classic book by Benoît Mandelbrot, *Fractals: Form, Chance and Dimension* (New York: W. H. Freeman, 1977), and the popularizing work by James Gleick, *Chaos: Making a New Science* (New York: Viking, 1988).

does the competition come from, and what is the force that would prevent bilateralism in the name of a more complex plurality? No doubt we could describe the frontier between the natural and the political in fractal terms, but let's beware of the more or less hidden metaphysics in such descriptions and of our desire to appeal to a "scientific" description as the final arbiter of all our problems.[8] Nonetheless, fractal geometry will often return to give us precious analogies for thinking the structure of the frontier, up to the point when the structure of the frontier will oblige us to examine the structure of analogy itself.

It is, then, impossible not to talk about nature if we want to talk about frontiers. We proposed two apparently contradictory hypotheses about this: On the one hand, that there are no natural frontiers, and on the other, that all frontiers are natural or else *of nature* in the sense that every frontier would mark the spot where nature begins or ends. If we manage to hold these two hypotheses together (which we cannot do by simply leaving nature behind), we may be able to understand why nature turns out to be (especially in political philosophy, perhaps) such a critical concept (critical because always precritical, always awaiting decision and division, the *krinein* of the *nomos*). As we shall see, nature is what we find at, on, or in the frontier. The frontier comes down to nature, still belongs to it, because nature is what comes back at the frontier, returns to the frontier. The nature of the frontier is nature, and the nature of nature is to return at (on or in) the frontier.

So it is certainly not by chance that Kant talks a great deal about nature in the two texts we shall first be reading (and that will provide us with what those same texts would call a "guiding thread" for reading Kant more generally).[9] For these two texts, as we shall see, are devoted to thinking

8. This is no doubt the major problem of Jean-François Lyotard's *La condition postmoderne* (Paris: Minuit, 1979), tr. Geoffrey Bennington and Brian Massumi as *The Postmodern Condition* (Minneapolis: University of Minnesota Press, 1983): Lyotard argues against crossing the frontier between language games but then does exactly that in finding a model for postmodern justice in postmodern science. His slightly later treatment in *Le différend* (1983) is more cautious in this respect.

9. Immanuel Kant, "Idea for a Universal History with a Cosmopolitan Purpose," in *Kant's Political Writings*, ed. Hans Reiss, 2nd enlarged ed., 41–53 (Cambridge: Cambridge University Press, 1991) (hereinafter *KPW*), and *Perpetual Peace: A Philosophical Sketch*, *KPW*, 93–120. I will not insist on everything that separates the manner and stakes of my reading from, for example, that of Jürgen Habermas, in *La paix perpétuelle: le bicentenaire d'une idée kantienne*, tr. Rainer Rochlitz (Paris: Le Cerf, 1996). Alongside the thinkers who have most influenced my reading (who indeed taught me how to read), most notably Jacques Derrida and Jean-François Lyotard, my under-

the frontier or—this will be the whole problem—thinking frontiers in the plural. It would not be easy to extract from them a simple doctrine as to so-called natural frontiers. On the one hand, Kant recognizes that there are at the very least divisions or separations that seem to be quite natural—"The community of man is divided by uninhabitable parts of the earth's surface such as oceans and deserts" (*KPW*, 106)—but immediately points out the means of crossing such boundaries or frontier-zones: "but even then, the *ship* or the *camel* (the ship of the desert) make it possible for them to approach their fellows over these ownerless tracts, and to utilize as a means of social intercourse that *right to the earth's surface* which the human race shares in common" (*KPW*, 106).

This is part of a more general doctrine of natural providence, or at least of a quasi-natural providence, a doctrine carefully subdivided into three aspects and given the supplementary gravitas of Latin terminology.

This use of Latin is not at all insignificant in Kant and, in fact, engages with a whole politics of language in its relation to philosophy:

> In the great wealth of our languages, the thinking mind often finds itself at a loss for an expression that exactly suits its concept, and lacking this it is able to make itself rightly intelligible neither to others nor even to itself. Coining new words is a presumption to legislate in language that rarely succeeds, and before we have recourse to this dubious means it is advisable to look around in a dead and learned language to see if an expression occurs in it that is suitable to this concept; and even if the ancient use of this expression has become somewhat unsteady owing to the inattentiveness of its authors, it is better to fix on the meaning that is proper to it (even if it is doubtful whether it always had exactly this sense) than to ruin our enterprise by making ourselves unintelligible.[10]

Kant returns to this issue, annoyed, in the preface to the second *Critique*:

> I have no fear, with respect to this treatise, of the reproach that I want to introduce a *new language*, because the kind of cognition itself approaches popularity.

standing of Kant owes a great deal to some more specialized essays and commentaries. Among those that have had the greatest impact, let me mention Eric Weil, *Problèmes kantiens* (Paris: Vrin, 1963); Gilles Deleuze, *La philosophie critique de Kant* (Paris: PUF, 1963); Françoise Proust, *Kant: le ton de l'histoire* (Paris: Payot, 1991); and, in English, Howard Caygill, *Art of Judgment* (Oxford: Blackwell, 1989) and *A Kant Dictionary* (Oxford: Blackwell, 1995); Peter Fenves, *A Peculiar Fate: Metaphysics and World History in Kant* (Ithaca, NY: Cornell University Press, 1991).

10. Immanuel Kant, *The Critique of Pure Reason*, tr. Paul Guyer and Allen Wood (Cambridge: Cambridge University Press, 1999), A312/B369 (hereinafter *CPR*).

> This reproach with respect to the first *Critique* could also not have occurred to anyone who had thought it through and not merely turned over the pages. To invent new words where the language already has no lack of expressions for given concepts is a childish effort to distinguish oneself from the crowd, if not by new and true thoughts yet by new patches on an old garment.[11]

Kant's irritation continues for a while. In a note called by the last sentence of this same paragraph, he claims to fear more than obscurity the misunderstanding of popular or ordinary expressions. He takes the example of his use of "permitted" and "forbidden" and as if by chance the problem of linguistic invention returns to illustrate how this "somewhat unusual" usage (which might have looked like a new construction) is not, however, "altogether foreign" to ordinary usage: "It is *forbidden* to an orator, as such, to forge new words or constructions; this is to some extent *permitted* to a poet" (*CPrR*, 9). And this can be further related to a note to §17 of the third *Critique*: "Models of taste with regard to the arts of discourse must be composed in a dead and learned language: the former, in order not to have to suffer the alterations that unavoidably affect living languages, which make noble expressions flat, common ones outmoded, and newly created ones of only brief currency; the latter, so that it should have a grammar that is not subject to any willful change of fashion but has its own unalterable rules."[12] These passages do not appear to be taken into account in Jean-Luc Nancy's brilliant account of Kant,[13] where there is, however, the following important reminder: "The language of Kant himself abounds in archaisms, in multiple borrowings, sometimes from dialectal usages, sometimes from the old language of the law courts, and in idiosyncrasies of spelling, morphology and syntax. [. . .] Kant's problem is also that of a language and a people" (69–70n45/155n20; tr. mod.). Recall that in the passage from the first *Critique* that we just quoted, Kant refers to "our languages" in the plural, which scatters the problem beyond the uncertain frontiers of Germany. "Kant's problem" might depend in part on the fact that,

11. Immanuel Kant, *The Critique of Practical Reason*, tr. Mary Gregor, rev. ed. (Cambridge: Cambridge University Press, 2015), 8 (hereinafter *CPrR*).

12. Immanuel Kant, *Critique of the Power of Judgment*, tr. Paul Guyer (Cambridge: Cambridge University Press, 2000), 116n. On Kant's use of Latin, see also Jacques Derrida's remarks in *La vérité en peinture* (Paris: Flammarion, 1979), 104–5, tr. Geoff Bennington and Ian McLeod as *The Truth in Painting* (Chicago: University of Chicago Press, 1983), 91–92.

13. Jean-Luc Nancy, *Le discours de la syncope, I: Logodaedalus* (Paris: Aubier-Flammarion, 1976), tr. Saul Anton as *The Discourse of the Syncope: Logodaedalus* (Stanford, CA: Stanford University Press, 2007).

on the one hand, the philosopher, at least at his best, is indeed the "legislator of human reason" (itself essentially legislative), whereas on the other hand, as we saw, to present oneself as a legislator in question of language is most often doomed to failure. For this difficult position of the legislator more generally, see my *Dudding: des noms de Rousseau* (Paris: Galilée, 1991).

Providence, duly latinized, then, falls into three aspects: "original" providence (*providentia conditrix*), which has been active since the beginning of time; ruling providence (*providentia gubernatrix*), which keeps nature's course running according to universal purposive laws; and directive providence (*providentia directrix*), which brings about particular ends that man could not have foreseen (*KPW*, 108n). This distinction forms part of the demonstration that perpetual peace is guaranteed by Nature herself. Providence, in fact, is just a name for Nature seen from the point of view of its purposive form, a form that becomes intelligible to us not through an act of theoretical knowledge but to the extent that we analogically supplement our lack of such knowledge in this domain by comparing nature to the work of a human *artifex*.[14]

This view of natural purposiveness can seem amusing. Isn't it wonderful [*bewunderenswürdig*], exclaims Kant, that moss can still grow in Arctic regions, so that reindeer can eat it, so that men in their turn can eat them! Also wonderful, perhaps especially wonderful, the camel, "which seems as if it had been created for traveling over [the sandy salt deserts] in order that they might not be left unutilized" (*KPW*, 110). And Kant goes on to wonder at the fact that the inhabitants of the Arctic should also have available to them whales and walruses, and to admire still more the fact that nature brings driftwood to those shores where trees cannot grow. We might be tempted to laugh, as we might laugh at Voltaire's Pangloss admiring the fact that men have two legs so they can wear breeches or at Bernardin de Saint-Pierre and his melon naturally designed to be eaten *en famille*.

Kant's nature, and his providence, however, are more complicated than this would suggest. Like Rousseau (whose own notion of the state of nature

14. This is the argument of the *Critique of Teleological Judgment*, which will detain us at great length in Chapter 5. See especially §75. Kant is extremely cautious in his appeal to Providence here, writing that "in contexts such as this, where we are concerned purely with theory and not with religion, we should also note that it is more in keeping with the limitations of human reason to speak of *nature* and not of *providence*, for reason, in dealing with cause and effect relationships, must keep within the bounds of possible experience. *Modesty* forbids us to speak of providence as something we can recognize, for this would mean donning the wings of Icarus and presuming to approach the mystery of its inscrutable intentions" (*KPW*, 109).

is often misunderstood), Kant is very clear that such a view of nature ("Isn't nature wonderful?") is stupidity itself, as he makes very clear in the text on universal history:

> [. . .] an Arcadian, pastoral existence of perfect concord, self-sufficiency and mutual love. But all human talents would remain hidden forever in a dormant state, and men, as good-natured as the sheep they tended, would scarcely render their existence more valuable than that of their animals. The end for which they were created, their rational nature, would be an unfilled void. (*KPW*, 45)

In fact, the idea or fantasy of a simply sweet and gentle nature is not Kant's but one he imputes to man himself, insofar as man has always already lost any such nature. Because nature is precisely not what man would wish for: "Man wishes concord, but nature, knowing better what is good for his species, wishes discord" (*KPW*, 45). Let's see in this the first indication of an idea that will not cease to pursue us: namely, that man is not entirely natural or that his nature is to double or shadow nature with a second, artificial, nature. And this nature that is not really natural will recall what we were saying about frontiers, which, although not natural, are nonetheless *of nature*. Kant himself says in a note to the sixth proposition of this same text, "Man's role is thus a highly artificial one [*künstlich*]" (*KPW*, 47n). We will consistently see that this opposition between nature and artifice is insufficient to think what we are dealing with here.

We should, in any case, beware of any simple reading of nature. If we must indeed avoid the Arcadian reading that might have tempted us at first, we must not for all that switch over to a simple reading of nature's wanting discord. The text of the fourth proposition continues:

> Man wishes to live comfortably and pleasantly, but nature intends that he should abandon idleness and inactive self-sufficiency and plunge instead into labour and hardships, so that he may by his own adroitness find means of liberating himself from them in turn. The natural impulses which make this possible, the sources of the very unsociableness and continual resistance which cause so many evils, at the same time encourage man towards new exertions of his powers and thus towards further development of his natural capacities. They would thus seem to indicate the design of a wise creator—not, as it might seem, the hand of a malicious spirit who had meddled in the creator's glorious work or spoiled it out of envy. (*KPW*, 45)

A little dialectic goes a long way. Kant seems to fit neatly enough here between, say, Rousseau and Hegel, at least in the standard reading of those authors. But let's not allow this conciliatory perspective to absorb too rapidly the negativity implied in the idea that "Nature wants discord." For we might imagine that, according to Kant, man is on the point of stagnating in the deep peace of Arcadia only to have nature wake him up by a more or less catastrophic intervention. It will be remembered that that is the Rousseauist schema of the *Essay on the Origin of Languages*, where a simple movement of God's finger tilts the earth's axis and thus gives rise to climatic—and thereby linguistic and characteriological—differentiation, which sets history going.[15] In fact, Kant is not simply reproducing this traditional (Biblical) schema, according to which an essentially peaceful state of nature is subsequently interrupted or overturned by violence. But, as we shall see, there is a heavy price to pay for giving up on this schema: one cannot think an originarily violent nature (as Kant does) without more or less rapidly coming to the conclusion that nature is not entirely natural. We shall see that this is, in fact, an analytic consequence of our double hypothesis about natural frontiers.

Kant has just said that nature, in its wisdom, "wants" discord. As opposed to Rousseau, for whom nature was peaceful but nonetheless gave rise to a subsequently unavoidable violence, Kant conceives of a nature that is already violent but whose fundamental violence will be compensated for by a teleological movement toward perpetual peace. But it would be a mistake to see in Kant a disagreement with Rousseau situated on the same logical level, as it were. Rousseau thought that the natural state of man was one of dispersion and that in such a dispersion there would reign the peace of indifference; whence his violent disagreement with Hobbes's doctrine of nature as war of all against all. Kant can avoid all such anthropological speculations (even if he does not always do so). For him, the state of nature can *de facto* be either a state of peace or a state of war; but as nothing prevents it from becoming violent if it is not already violent, then it is *de jure* violent, even if a profound peace reigns in fact. (Let's note in passing this precious hint about the asymmetrical character of oppositions such as that of peace and war or peace and violence: potential violence is already violence, whence the idea that the only peace worthy of the name would be perpetual peace.)[16]

This transcendental argument is advanced, as one might expect, in the text

15. As explicated by Jacques Derrida in *De la grammatologie* (Paris: Minuit, 1967), esp. 361ff, tr. Gayatri Chakravorty Spivak as *Of Grammatology* (Baltimore, MD: Johns Hopkins University Press, 1974), 255ff.

16. The very beginning of the *Perpetual Peace* text makes a distinction between a mere truce or suspension of hostilities ("ein bloßer Waffenstillstand, Aufschub der Feindseligkeiten") and true peace, which "means an end to all hostilities, and to attach the adjective 'perpetual' to it is already suspiciously close to pleonasm" (*KPW*, 93).

on perpetual peace: "A state of peace among men living together is not the same as the state of nature (*status naturalis*), which is rather a state of war. For even if it does not involve active hostilities, it involves a constant threat of their breaking out" (*KPW*, 98; adding the Latin omitted in the translation). A footnote explains:

> Man [. . .] in a mere state of nature [im bloßen Naturstande; in a pure or naked state of nature] robs me of any such security [Kant is contrasting the state of nature with a "legal civil state," of which more anon] and injures me [lädiert mich; this is a latinate, juridical term for "injury"] by virtue of this very state in which he co-exists with me. He may not have injured me actively (*facto*) [*tätig* is Kant's word, not far from *tätlich*, violent], but he does injure me by the very lawlessness of his state (*statu iniusto*), for he is a permanent threat to me, and I can require him either to enter into a common lawful state along with me or to move away from my vicinity. (*KPW*, 98n)[17]

"I can oblige him . . . ," "ich kann ihn nötigen . . . ." A lot here hangs on Kant's *kann*. It cannot easily mean that I have the capacity to make him do something, which would presuppose that I am stronger than my neighbor and that I would simply exercise that superior force against him. For if I exercised that force against him according to the first prong of the dilemma posed by Kant, in order to oblige him to enter into a lawful state with me,

17. In *Religion within the Boundaries of Mere Reason*, Kant cites Hobbes: "Hobbes's statement, *status hominum naturalis est bellum omnium in omnes*, has no other fault apart from this: it should say, *est status belli* . . . etc. For, even though one may not concede that actual hostilities are the rule between human beings who do not stand under external and public laws, their condition (*status iuridicus*), i.e. the relationship in and through which they are capable of rights (of their acquisition and maintenance) is nonetheless one in which each of them wants to be himself the judge of what is his right vis-a-vis others, without however either having any security from others with respect to this right or offering them any: and this is a condition of war, wherein every man must be constantly armed against everybody else. Hobbes's second statement, *exeumdum esse e statu naturali*, follows from the first: for this condition is a continual violation of the rights of all others through the presumption of being the judge in one's own affairs and of not allowing any security to other human beings in theirs save one's own power of choice" (tr. Allen Wood [Cambridge: Cambridge University Press, 1998], 108n). Kant does not follow Hobbes further than this; see the whole second section of the essay on "Theory and Practice" (*KPW*, 61–92). In the *Religion* book, Kant distinguishes between a juridical state of nature and an ethical state of nature: It is possible (and, in fact, inevitable) to remain in the second even having left the first. For now, let's note that if "state of nature" can be qualified as "ethical" or "juridical," it is already not so very natural.

to carry him in spite of himself over the frontier that still separates us from legality (and therefore from the possibility of peace), the force I would use to do this would no longer really be quite natural, in that it would already be directed toward right or law. So my naturally superior force would no longer be wholly natural but already at least somewhat a force of right, if not of law, to the extent that this force would be exercised against my neighbor *justly*. I would already have left the state of nature without my neighbor, and I could no longer count on mere natural force to oblige him to leave it with me. So the *ich kann* must mean, rather, that I *have the right* to make my neighbor leave the state of nature. But this interpretation is difficult too, in that we are *ex hypothesi* supposed to be in a state of nature where there is no right but merely force, which is why my neighbor injures me and always might be stronger than I. In the lawless violence of the state of nature, there is apparently a *right to right*, which means that, in the state of nature, I am indeed in a state of always at least possible violence but already enough in a state of right to be able to leave it behind, either with my neighbor or against him. But if my neighbor hears the obligation by which he is supposedly bound and decides to leave the state of nature with me, then he must already have been in enough of a state of right to hear the call of this obligation and is to that extent not simply in the state of nature either—and in that case it would rather be me who had injured him by imagining that he was injuring me by remaining in the state of nature whereas he was on the way out of it before me. Even if, hearing the obligation to leave the state of nature, he decides to ignore it and stay in that state, simply moving away from my vicinity, he has nonetheless been receptive enough to the call to refuse to submit to the obligation it bespeaks and to that extent is already no longer in the state of nature in which he is supposedly choosing to remain. In order to understand how this confusing situation is possible, and how I can cross the frontier that separates natural violence from the state of right (assuming that there is such a frontier and that one can cross it) we shall need to take a long detour before returning to the *ich kann*.[18]

18. In §44 of the "Doctrine of Right" section of the *Metaphysics of Morals* (tr. Mary Gregor [Cambridge: Cambridge University Press, 1996], [hereinafter *MM*]), Kant, having restated the argument we have just read, implicitly recognizes the existence of a right before right in the state of nature: "If no acquisition were recognized as rightful even in a provisional way prior to entering the civil condition, the civil condition itself would be impossible. For in terms of their form, laws concerning what is mine or yours in the state of nature contain the same thing that they prescribe in the civil condition, insofar as the civil condition is thought of by pure rational concepts alone. The differ-

"Nature," then, or at least "state of nature," is the name in Kant for a situation where law is absent and therefore violence (at least potentially) holds sway. Any idea of "natural law" or "natural right" would then be clearly delimited by this transcendental argument: Any such supposed right would be merely a play of opposing forces (and nature would then be what it indeed is to a purely theoretical or scientific gaze). Natural law would in that case be mere law of nature, in the sense that the concepts of law and, therefore, of necessity are constitutive of nature in the theoretical sense. This would leave us with a nature that is on the one hand constitutively *lawful* (in the eyes of science) and on the other absolutely *illegal* (in the eyes of morality or politics). In leaving the state of nature, assuming that that is intelligible, man must leave lawfulness for legality, thus marking the becoming nonnatural of nature.

The very idea of natural right thus involves a paradox, clearly stated by Spinoza in his political writings. *In* nature, the only right is natural force, which is not a right strictly speaking; and once man has left nature, he is no longer natural enough to lay claim to nature as grounding any right. Here is what Spinoza says in the *Political Treatise*:

> And so by natural right I understand the very laws or rules of nature, in accordance with which everything takes place, in other words, the power of nature itself. And so the natural right of universal nature, and consequently of every individual thing, extends as far as its power: and accordingly, whatever any man does after the laws of his nature, he does by the highest natural right, and he has as much right over nature as he has power.[19]

And, a little later:

> But inasmuch as in the state of nature each is so long independent, as he can guard against oppression by another, and it is in vain for one man alone to try and guard against all, it follows hence that so long as the natural right of man is determined by the power of every individual, and belongs to everyone, so long it is a nonentity, existing in opinion rather than fact, as there is no assurance of making it good. And it is certain that the greater cause of fear every individual has, the less power, and consequently the less right, he possesses. To this must

ence is only that the civil condition provides the conditions under which these laws are put into effect (in keeping with distributive justice). So if external objects were not even provisionally mine or yours in the state of nature, there would also be no duties of Right with regard to them and therefore no command to leave the state of nature" (*MM*, 90).

19. Baruch Spinoza, *A Theological-Political Treatise and A Political Treatise*, tr. R. H. M. Elwes (Mineola, NY: Dover Publications, 1951), 292.

> be added, that without mutual help men can hardly support life and cultivate the mind. And so our conclusion is, that that natural right, which is special to the human race, can hardly be conceived, except where men have general rights, and combine to defend the possession of the lands they inhabit and cultivate, to protect themselves, to repel all violence, and to live according to the general judgment of all. For the more there are that combine together, the more right they collectively possess. And if this is why the schoolmen want to call man a sociable animal—I mean because men in the state of nature can hardly be independent—I have nothing to say against them. (*Political Treatise*, 296–97)

First of all, natural right must be reduced to natural force, which means it disappears *qua* right. It follows that there can be natural right only once man has left nature behind. Natural right does not belong to nature[20] but to what comes after nature. It is, therefore, no longer quite natural. Man, as agent (or patient) of nature's getting outside itself in this way, is thus essentially a social or political animal (as Spinoza recognizes), a *zoon politikon*.[21]

20. In fact, Kant says little about natural right and natural law. One finds the following, however, in the introduction to the *Metaphysics of Morals*: "Obligatory laws for which there can be an external lawgiving are called external laws (*leges externae*) in general. Those among them that can be recognized as obligatory a priori by reason even without external lawgiving are indeed external but natural laws, whereas those that do not bind without actual external lawgiving (and so without it would not be laws) are called positive laws. One can therefore conceive of external lawgiving that would contain only positive laws; but then a natural law would still have to precede it, which would establish the authority of the lawgiver (i.e., his authorization to bind others by his mere choice)" (*MM*, 17). So there is indeed a certain priority of natural law that gives law to positive law, but this natural law is anything but the law of nature as a putative state. Law always *comes out* of nature.

21. This is also, almost, the conclusion of the *Anthropology*: "The sum total of pragmatic anthropology, in respect to the vocation of the human being and the Characteristic of his formation, is the following. The human being is destined by his reason to live in a society with human beings and in it to *cultivate* himself, to *civilize* himself, and to *moralize* himself by means of the arts and sciences. No matter how great his animal tendency may be to give himself over *passively* to the impulses of comfort and good living, which he calls happiness, he is still destined to make himself worthy of humanity by *actively* struggling with the obstacles that cling to him because of the crudity of his nature" (*Anthropology from a Pragmatic Point of View*, tr. Robert B. Louden [Cambridge: Cambridge University Press, 2006], 229–30). I am not claiming that Kant is Spinozist; see, for example, *CPrR*, 85, and *Critique of the Power of Judgment*, tr. Paul Guyer and Eric Matthews (Cambridge: Cambridge University Press, 2000), §§73 and 85 (hereinafter *CJ*), which we shall be reading in Chapter 5. For Kant's reaction to an accusation of Spinozism, see "What Is Orientation in Thinking?" (*KPW*, 246n).

+

It is not enough, however, to say that man leaves nature behind (or should leave nature behind) to become truly human. Spinoza clearly shows that "nature" is the name of its own having-left-itself-behind. From which we should conclude not that nature should be denied, abandoned, or denounced in the name of all its others, and especially history and politics (this was the gesture of the so-called human sciences and everything that still takes its bearings from them), but that "nature," having not been left behind, insists now *as* that which one is supposed to have left behind. "Nature" then becomes the name not of a state supposed to have existed before social or political organization (a state before the State), but the name of the never-accomplished crossing of its own frontier.

This schema, which is classical (Aristotelian, as we shall see in a moment), gives man an exorbitant privilege with respect to what is usually thought of as an animality situated on the other side of a clear-cut frontier. The animal is on the "nature" side of the frontier that defines man as already having crossed it. Arcadia is for the sheep, to the extent that for man nature is an unsustainable state, and therefore not a state at all. *There is no state of nature*, except as a fiction in the text; in fact, nature is always already political. Which also means, paradoxically, that, even though one has always already left the state of nature behind, one cannot ever quite leave it (or, therefore, animality) behind:

> In a civil constitution, which is the highest degree of artificial improvement of the human species' good predisposition to the final end of its vocation, *animality* still manifests itself earlier and, at bottom, more powerfully than pure *humanity*. (*Anthropology*, 232)

Nature is therefore nothing other than its own frontier with humanity, a frontier that corresponds to politicization. The complex logic we have seen to be at work thus allows for all imaginable metaphors and analogies between nature and its others.[22]

22. Thus, for example, this passage from the *Anthropology* in which the frontier between nature (as animality as well as natural mechanism) and nonnature (political organization) is constantly being traversed in both directions: "The human being was not meant to belong to a herd, like cattle, but to a hive, like the bee.—Necessity to be a member of some civil society or other./ The simplest, least artificial [i.e., most natural] way to establish such a society is to have one leader in this hive (monarchy).—But many such hives next to each other will soon attack each other like robber bees (war); not, however, as human beings do, in order to strengthen their own group by uniting with others—for here the comparison ends—but only to use by cunning or force *other's* industry *for themselves*. Each people seeks to strengthen itself through the subjugation

Nature, then, is naturally and immediately unsustainable, goes outside itself in the shape of man in order to name itself nature after the fact and know itself teleologically in view of its own teleological knowing (teleological and not theoretical knowing, not demonstrable, and therefore analogical, as we shall see in detail in Chapter 5). We just said that this schema is essentially Aristotelian, which we shall now rapidly verify.

At the beginning of the *Politics*, Aristotle affirms that the State is a type of association (*koinonia*), that every association is made with a view to an end (i.e., a good, because all human actions are carried out with a view to a good [*agathon*] or at least what is assumed to be a good). It follows that the association that includes all the others, and thus aims at the highest good, is the highest association: such an association is the State (*polis*). We should not assume, however, that all associations are of the same type (at least as concerns the exercise of power). One can bring out the difference between king, magistrate, and father, says Aristotle, who has Plato in his sights here, "in accordance with our regular method of investigation" (1252a 17–18), i.e., by analytically decomposing complexes into their elements, while expositing synthetically a process of natural growth that will lead from these simple elements, which are found at the origin [*arches*], to the whole that we are investigating.

This archeo-teleological analysis (or ana-synthesis) begins with the first association, the original association, which is marked by its necessity: that of man and woman, without which association nothing could ensue. This association, with a view to the continuation of the species by procreation, is also natural: "not of deliberate purpose, but with man as with the other animals and plants there is a natural instinct to desire to leave behind one

---

of neighboring peoples, either from the desire to expand or the fear of being swallowed up by the other unless one beats him to it. Therefore civil or foreign war in our species, as great an evil as it may be, is yet at the same time the incentive to pass from the crude state of nature to the *civil* state. War is like a mechanical device of Providence, where to be sure the struggling forces injure each other through collision, but are nevertheless still regularly kept going for a long time through the push and pull of other incentives" (*Anthropology*, 235). The extreme difficulty Kant has in bringing his analogy to a close comes from a reciprocal contamination of each side of the frontier by the other: on the political side mankind organizes himself into a beehive; on the natural side bees are therefore political animals. This movement (and the bees) can also be found at the beginning of the "Universal History" text: On the one hand, Kant draws a sharp frontier between animals, who simply follow their instincts (and who, therefore, have a "law-governed history," as with bees and beavers [*KPW*, 41–42]), and men, who act willfully but not in fact always rationally; but on the other hand, it is precisely from observation of animals that we can draw the idea of a teleological system of nature pursuing an end.

another being of the same sort as oneself" (1252a 26–27). This is the first trace of what will be an erasure, in the name of nature, of sexual difference. In human procreation, the procreating individual does not know to what extent his or her offspring will be "of the same sort" as regards gender. But nature has also given to the male the gift of commanding (which no doubt separates humans from other animals and plants and thus is the first minimal mark of politics, which thus begins to separate itself from a *certain* animal or vegetable nature): "and the union of natural ruler and natural subject for the sake of security" (1252a 30–32). This first association, then, is the result of the individual's inability to maintain him or herself in the state of nature, the necessity that there be two individuals who cannot be substituted the one for the other; here, the association involves an immediate asymmetry and hierarchization. In this case sexual difference is primordial. Both natural and the principle of the first step outside nature toward politics, it will be almost immediately forgotten or erased.

Another association (having proposed to begin at the beginning and to follow a line of development, Aristotle does not here make the order clear or linear): nature, which alone provides for procreation and which also gives command,[23] also wants this command to be with the more intelligent or at least foresightful individual and wants that the less intelligent be a slave.[24]

23. The equivalence or confusion between commencement and commandment (*arkhe* and *archon*) in Aristotle is a theme strongly brought out by Sylviane Agacinski in *Volume: philosophies et politiques de l'architecture* (Paris: Galilée, 1992), 38–44.

24. The *Economics* (a text not certain to be entirely by Aristotle) is much clearer as to the order here: "nothing is more natural than the tie between female and male" (*The Complete Works of Aristotle: The Revised Oxford Translation*, 2 vols., ed. Jonathan Barnes, tr. E. S. Forster and G. C. Armstrong [Princeton, NJ: Princeton University Press, 1984], 2:1343b 7–8). As we shall see, however, the State itself can also be said to be the most natural association. This confusion at the origin is just what we are tracking under the name "nature." The same principle of confusion is visible in the supplementary remarks to be found in the *Economics* on the naturality of procreation. Here it is specified that "among the other animals, this intercourse is not based on reason" but on instinct, whereas it is based on reason for human animals who are therefore less purely natural (especially as regards children, the closest final cause of the male-female association, with regard to whom the parents have a calculative relation that aims to secure an advantage later in life) (1342b 20–24). But because man behaves rationally in this respect, it also follows that he is also more natural than the other animals because he is closer to the ends of nature. Both the *Politics* and the *Economics* quote a line from Hesiod ("First and foremost a house, a woman, and an ox for the plough"), the former to see in the ox a figure of the slave, the second to insist on a primordiality of the maternal relation to the earth: "agriculture is natural; for by nature all derive their sustenance from their mother, and so men derive it from the earth" (1343a 30–1343b 1).

We must not, however, think that these two associations (which are co-originary, or all but) can be superimposed on each other. It does not follow from the equally "natural" character of these two relations that the woman, who is subject to the command of the man, should be in the position of the slave, the nonintelligent (or else, we could say, if she is in the position of a slave, that is not natural, or follows the will of a nature other than the nature that will become political). For it is tempting to confuse woman and slave in this analysis, and Aristotle thwarts that temptation by making this confusion the mark of the non-Greek, the barbarian, the one who is outside the bounds of the city we are on our way to defining. If the woman is not the slave, this is again because of natural teleology: nature destines each being to *one* end, and so if one is a woman one cannot simply be a slave:

> Thus the female and the slave are by nature distinct (for nature makes [...] one thing for one purpose; for so each tool will be turned out in the finest perfection, if it serves not many uses but one). Yet among barbarians the female and the slave have the same rank; and the cause of this is that barbarians have no natural rulers, but with them the conjugal partnership is a partnership of female slave and male slave. (*Politics*, 1252b 1–7)

The barbarians confuse woman and slave and by that very fact are slaves, through lack of intelligence, through stupidity: Whoever confuses woman and slave must by that very fact be a slave. Barbarity is not just a matter of linguistic identification but of the confusion of naturally willed hierarchies: The barbarians are therefore both more natural than the Greeks, closer to the origin (more brutish, in a word), and much less natural because they are incapable of following nature's commands when it comes to commanding. The barbarians, all naturally slaves, are thus incapable of authority. They do not command, or rather only command their women, but with the wrong form of command: the one that would be appropriate for a master—which they cannot be, for want of intelligence—to exercise over true slaves.

The relations that Aristotle is positing between these first two associations are not entirely clear. The French translation of the *Politics* by J. Tricot (Paris: Vrin, 1995), the one used in the original writing of this book, tries to separate them out by associating the commanding-commanded relation exclusively with the master-slave couple. I prefer the interpretation that links this relation both to the man-woman couple and the master-slave couple, without for all that suggesting that the woman simply is a slave. This interpretation can find support in the *Economics*, for which woman and slave are both part of the man's *goods* (1343a 17), and, more importantly, by the famous later discussion of slavery in the *Politics*, where the example of the man-woman couple returns to shore up the thesis of the natural status of the relation of subordination in general: "As between the sexes, the male is by nature superior and the female inferior, the male ruler and the female subject" (1254b 13–14). This first book of the *Politics* can appear to posit the equiprimordiality of three relations, at least for the analysis of the family—master-slave, husband-wife, father-children—but the deduction of slavery that suggests the priority of the male-female relation is based on the analogical claim about the authority of the soul over the body ("it is in a living creature, as we say, that it is first possible to discern the rule both of master and of statesman: for the soul rules the body with the sway of a master, the intelligence rules the appetites with that of a statesman or a king" [1254b 1–5]), then passing via the relations between man and animals and men and women, before concluding that "the same must also necessarily apply in the case of mankind as a whole" (1254b 15). So it seems that the male-female relation does indeed precede the master-slave relation in the order of nature. But this whole argument is affected by a twist that is hard to ignore, to the extent that its general principle is that "to discover what is natural we must study it preferably in things that are in a natural state, and not in specimens that are degenerate" (1253a 35): Nature is, naturally enough, what we find in nature.

The *Economics* (1343b 25–1344a 8) ground the power relation between man and woman on natural qualities (strength/weakness, courage/timidity, outside/inside, activity/passivity, education/nourishment), which will be standard elements of Western culture as regards sexual difference, but (at least in Book III, probably apocryphal) explicitly give woman authority over the inner domestic space (as will also be the case in both Kant and Levinas). In any case, the authority that may devolve to the woman (or the slave-overseer) remains essentially limited and so, as with the barbarians, subject to the paradox of more or less natural—slaves and women remain closer to nature in that they cannot progress to the more properly political, and to that extent less natural, levels of authority, and so are not in fact so natural, given that it is by becoming political that man will fulfill his natural finality. But this movement that takes man out of the house and into the City might also make him flee the City itself and destroy its integrity. It will follow (notably in Hegel, with the irony of the community) that only a certain femininity can guarantee the maintenance of any political organization, precisely by maintaining it under the sign of nature, whence it definitionally emerges, but into which it risks falling back at any moment.[25] There is more than a trace of this already in Aristotle when he recognizes that the authority of man over

25. See too Jacques Derrida, *Glas* (Paris: Galilée, 1974), 210–11, tr. John P. Leavey Jr. and Richard Rand as *Glas* (Lincoln: University of Nebraska Press, 1990), 187–88.

woman—which is natural, as we have seen—is nonetheless political (which implies that women, unlike slaves, indeed possess the deliberative part of the soul [1260a 12–13]), even if in her case that part is, mysteriously enough, devoid of authority.

We are not yet at the end of the difficulties presented by the relation between these two (equi-)primordial associations. The next association in the synthetic line followed by Aristotle is the household, the *oikos*, formed by association of the two prior associations. Henceforth, subsequent associations are going to be formed by simple aggregation (beyond the household, further associations will be formed by the association of apparently similar associations), but here we have an asymmetrical association between two already asymmetrical associations: the man-woman association marked by the asymmetry of sexual difference and by a certain power relation that remains (and in the *Politics* at least will remain) ill-defined; and the master-slave association marked by the asymmetry of command, grounded in the fact of being intelligent or not.[26] The point where these two associations meet is man: not *anthropos* but *aner*, the male, because the husband of one is the master of the other. The *oikos* is, thus, natural, just like the other associations: "The partnership that comes about in the course of nature for everyday purposes is the 'house', [... made up of] 'meal-tub-fellows' [...] 'manger-fellows'" (1252b 12–15).

The *oikos* can now associate with other *oikoi* to form, still naturally, what Aristotle calls a "village" (*komē*). In fact, the village retains the traces of the asymmetries we have identified at work in its component parts, because a village is less an association of *oikoi* on the same footing than a grouping hierarchized according to a genealogical history, in that it is formed of an *oikos* and other *oikoi* that are its colonies or its offspring (*apoikiai*), populated by children and grandchildren (*homogalaktas*, those fed with the same milk). The village has, in any case, taken a step toward the *polis* itself, which authorizes a series of analogies despite Aristotle's caution when he opens his book by warning against any confusion of household and State:

> The primary partnership made up of several households for the satisfaction of not mere daily needs is the village. The village according to the most natural account seems to be a colony from a household, formed of those whom some people speak of as "fellow-sucklings," sons and sons' sons. It is owing to this

26. Here too the *Economics* gives a more differentiated picture, distinguishing between slaves, for it turns out that some slaves are less slave than others (overseers, or those who "have more liberal occupations"), who deserve greater consideration.

> that our cities were at first under royal sway and that foreign races [ta ethne] are so still, because they were made up of parts that were under royal rule. (1252b 17–21)

We then arrive at the *polis*, formed by the "natural" association of several villages, with a view to *autarkeia*, a self-sufficiency that goes beyond mere subsistence but that also aims at the good life.[27]

As we have said, this is supposed to be a natural progression, which begins from the individual incapable of sustaining him or herself in nature and ends up in self-sufficiency, *autarkeia*, supposed to be reached only at the level of the State. At each stage, one loses and gains in "nature," for at every stage mankind gets further from the origin (which is nature), but at each stage supposedly realizes a little more fully his "nature," which is, as is all too well-known, to be *zoon politikon*. The *polis* is, then, the natural fruit of a natural and quasi-genetic process. The *polis*, the association furthest removed from the natural origin, in fact capitalizes the nature of each stage of the process, just by being its end:

> The partnership finally composed of several villages is the city-state; it has at last attained the limit of virtually complete self-sufficiency, and thus, while it comes into existence for the sake of life, it exists for the good life. Hence every city-state exists by nature, inasmuch as the first partnerships so exist; for the city-state is the end of the other partnerships, and nature is an end, since that which each thing is when its growth is completed we speak of as being the nature of each thing [telos gar aute ekeinon e de physis telos estin], for instance of a man, a horse, a household. Again, the object for which a thing exists, its end, is its chief good; and self-sufficiency is an end, and a chief good. From these things therefore it is clear that the city-state is a natural growth, and that man is by nature a political animal. (1252b 30–1253a 2)

The *polis* is, then, not only natural, a natural object among others, a natural association among other natural associations, but it is also the very nature of these other natural associations from which is proceeds and from which

27. See too *Economics*, 1343a 10–11: "A city is an aggregate [plethos] made up of households and land and property self-sufficient with regard to the good life." The text of the *Politics* curiously qualifies the *autarkeia* of the *polis* as being "more or less," "just as though," "os epos eiein," "so to speak," "as it were." See also 1261b 12–13, where Aristotle argues against Plato that self-sufficiency is not the same as unification or oneness (which are, in fact, exemplified by the non-self-sufficient individual) and so a *less* unified City has a greater chance of achieving the autonomy it needs. We shall see later the importance of these slight hesitations in the definition of the City in terms of its *autarkeia*.

it is born. Precisely because it is the end of the process, it is the true nature of that process, the nature of nature. The associations of men and women, masters and slaves, households and villages, are themselves natural, but in fact attain their nature, or the nature of their nature, only in the *polis* in which they reach, or all but reach, their end (i.e., self-sufficiency), which is the end and the good of nature in general. Man as the becoming-politics of nature is thus the end of nature as *zoon politikon*: The process is one of moving to ever (no) more nature.[28]

This double status of nature explains why the argumentation can appear to reverse direction here. In a gesture that will resonate throughout the tradition at least up until Marx, Aristotle proudly follows the analytic order of decomposition, all the while telling a story that starts off synthetically from the origin thus discovered: The method moves upstream and divides things up; the exposition moves downstream, finding that each association of elements is born of the preceding one. Just as narrative in general (as we have known since Barthes and Genette at least)[29] is structured by a final causality presenting itself as a linear causality, according to the paralogisms of *post hoc*

28. See too *Metaphysics* A (tr. Hugh Tredennick [Cambridge, MA: Harvard University Press, 1933]), 982b 3–8: "that science is supreme, and superior to the subsidiary, which knows for what end each action is to be done; i.e. the Good in each particular case, and in general the highest Good in the whole of nature." This end is also an *end*, what *puts an end*, in a mortal logic that will be giving us a great deal of food for thought: "Further, the Final cause of a thing is an *end*, and is such that it does not happen for the sake of some thing else, but all other things happen for its sake. So if there is to be a last term of this kind, the series will not be infinite; and if there is no such term, there will be no Final cause. Those who introduce infinity do not realize that they are abolishing the nature of the Good (although no one would attempt to do anything if he were not likely to reach some limit); nor would there be any intelligence in the world, because the man who has intelligence always acts for the sake of something, and this is a limit, because the *end* is a limit [telos peras estin]" (994b 8–16). According to the *Nicomachean Ethics* (1094a–b), the highest science is not, in fact, metaphysics but politics. This tension between philosophy and politics will run throughout the tradition, up to and including Jacques Rancière's *La mésentente* (Paris: Galilée, 1995). Following the thread of nature, we shall be attempting to move behind this distinction between metaphysics and politics, just as later, on the basis of Kant's teleology, we shall try to move behind the distinction between theory and practice.

29. See Roland Barthes, "Introduction à l'analyse structurale du récit," *Communications* 8 (1966): 7–33, tr. Stephen Heath as "Introduction to the Structural Analysis of Narrative" in *Image, Music, Text*, 79–124 (New York: Hill and Wang, 1978); Gérard Genette, "Vraisemblance et Motivation," in *Figures II*, 71–99 (Paris: Seuil, 1969), tr. David Gorman as "*Vraisemblance* and Motivation," *Narrative* 9, no. 3 (2001): 239–58. The practical demonstration of this is already to be found in Sartre's early novel *La Nausée* (1938).

ergo propter hoc and *hysteron proteron*—themselves denounced as sophistical by Aristotle himself[30]—and can thus be said to have its end before its beginning, so we can say that the *polis*, the end of the story Aristotle tells, is, in fact, the beginning, or even precedes the beginning, and so Aristotle can say that it is "naturally prior" (*proteron de te physei*, this pretension to absolute priority being the very nature of nature) to the associations that appeared to precede it. If the *polis* comes at the end of a natural process, all of whose stages were natural, then the fact is that those states were not yet entirely natural, to the extent that the nature of nature is to tend toward the *autarkeia* that is realized (more or less realized) only at the end. The end, which is nature, arrives only at the end, which is therefore the true beginning:

> Thus also the city-state is prior in nature to the household and to each of us individually. For the whole must necessarily be prior to the part; since when the whole body is destroyed, foot or hand will not exist except in an equivocal sense, like the sense in which one speaks of a hand sculptured in stone as a hand; because a hand in those circumstances will be a hand spoiled, and all things are defined by their function and capacity, so that when they are no longer such as to perform their function they must not be said to be the same things, but to bear their names in an equivocal sense. It is clear therefore that the state is also prior by nature to the individual; for if each individual when separate is not self-sufficient, he must be related to the whole state as other parts are to their whole, while a man who is incapable of entering into partnership, or who is so self-sufficing that he has no need to do so, is no part of a state, so that he must be either a lower animal or a god. (1253a 19–29)

Man is political to the extent that he becomes natural *qua* member of a *polis*. Politics does not so much come about because man leaves nature, but because man is only fully natural to the extent that he tends, naturally, to be part of the *polis*. One might wonder why man should be pre-eminently destined for this political nature (for there are many animals for whom an isolated individual is in principle no more self-sufficient than an isolated human, and indeed there are many other political animals, as Aristotle recognizes). This is because of *logos*, for man is the most political animal only to the extent that he is an animal endowed with speech, and thereby capable of the good (i.e., the end), for discourse is teleologically caused by its practical purposiveness:

> And why man is a political animal in a greater measure than any bee or any gregarious animal is clear. For nature, as we declare, does nothing without

30. See, for example, *Poetics*, 1452a, and *Sophistical Refutations*, 167b.

> purpose; and man alone of the animals possesses speech [logos]. The mere voice [phonē], it is true, can indicate [semeion] pain and pleasure, and therefore is possessed by the other animals as well (for their nature has been developed so far as to have sensations of what is painful and pleasant and to indicate [semanein] those sensations to one another), but speech is designed to indicate [sempheron] the advantageous and the harmful [to deloun kai to blaberon], and therefore also the right and the wrong [dikaion kai to adikon; the just and the unjust]; for it is the special property of man in distinction from the other animals that he alone has perception of good and bad [agathon kai kakon] and right and wrong and the other moral qualities, and it is partnership in these things that makes a household and a city-state. (1253a 7–18)

Man is, then, the animal that he is, "rational" or at least language-using, to the extent that his nature is to realize the end of nature by defining himself from the start as a practical member of a *polis*. It follows that a man who does not do so is not truly human, like the stone hand is not truly a hand, and that by not naturally being member of a *polis*, man comes back to another, denatured nature—that of brute beasts or gods.

By suggesting an essential continuity between Aristotle's natural teleology and Kant's, I might seem to be ignoring all of Heidegger's warnings as to what gets lost in the transition and translation of Greek into Latin and beyond: *Physis* is not *natura*, nor therefore *Natur* or *nature*, and by behaving as though we were dealing with synonyms here, we are dismissing everything that separates a *physis* thought of as blossoming and perdurance and a *natura* thought as "the motions of material things."[31] However, as Heidegger is the first to admit, the word *physis* in Greek philosophy "began quite early to take on a more restrictive sense" that prefigures the Roman translation as *natura* (as would be the case in Aristotle's *Physics*, for example). This would mean that there is a pretranslation already inscribed in the Greek term, at least in some of its usages, that would have guided in advance the "de-naturing" translation. It is true that, wanting to show that the supposedly originary sense is not entirely lost in Greek philosophy, Heidegger quotes Aristotle himself, and more especially the famous opening of Book γ of the *Metaphysics*, where Aristotle defines metaphysics as the science of being *qua* being, *to on e on* (1003a 20; curiously though, Heidegger does not mention here *Metaphysics* δ, §4 [1014b 16ff], which deals much more directly with *physis*). Even within

31. Martin Heidegger, *Introduction to Metaphysics*, tr. Gregory Fried and Richard Polt (New Haven, CT: Yale University Press, 2000), 17, and, more generally, "The Origin of the Work of Art," in *Pathmarks*, tr. Julian Young and Kenneth Haynes, 1–56 (Cambridge: Cambridge University Press, 2002).

Heidegger's perspective, we might be tempted to try to justify our hypothesis of a profound continuity between Aristotle and Kant by imagining that the word *physis* in the *Politics* would correspond to the more restricted and "physical" use of the word, which could then communicate with Kant's "modern" usage—but this would not be a very plausible hypothesis, as it seems clear that *physis* in the passages we have just been reading is far from the restricted sense that Heidegger is tracking. So we might want to prefer the converse possibility, according to which there would remain in the restricted, Roman and post-Roman translation of *physis* at least a trace of the supposedly originary sense and that this trace would be operative in Kant (at least), even where he seems to come close to a modern and "scientific" sense of nature. Thus, for example, the first sentence of the Preface to the *Metaphysical Principles of Natural Science* (tr. Michael Friedman in Kant, *Theoretical Philosophy after 1781* [Cambridge: Cambridge University Press, 2010], 183) invokes a "formal" sense of nature ("the first inner principle of all that belongs to the existence of a thing"), which is distinct from the "material" sense that is close to what Heidegger attributes to the Latin translation and that seems to retain an echo, however distant, of the supposedly "originary" sense of blossoming and perdurance. (See too *Critique of Pure Reason* A419/B446n.) This hypothesis would have the advantage of explaining at least the possibility for Heidegger to claim some access to this original sense, to "hear with a Greek ear" and to retranslate it for us, but would also tend to avoid the powerful Heideggerian *pathos* about the Greek language and the supposed primary sense of words.[32]

According to Aristotle, a man who does not naturally belong in the *polis*, who does not assume his political nature, falls precisely into what Kant, after many others, will call the state of nature—warfare:

> From these things therefore it is clear that the city-state is a natural growth, and that man is by nature a political animal, and a man that is by nature and not merely by fortune citiless is either low in the scale of humanity or above it (like the "clanless, lawless, hearthless" man reviled by Homer, for one by nature unsocial is also "a lover of war") inasmuch as he is solitary, like an isolated piece at draughts. (1253a 3–5)

32. The principle of this remark could be extended to the important 1939 text devoted explicitly to the concept of *physis* in Aristotle ("On the Essence and Concept of *physis* in Aristotle's *Physics* B, I," tr. Thomas Sheehan in Martin Heidegger, *Pathmarks*, 183–230 [Cambridge: Cambridge University Press, 1998]), and especially its slightly brutal discussion of Kant (200ff). I discuss this at greater length in the full version of "Emergencies," *Oxford Literary Review* 18 (1997): 175–216, 210n21.

This counter-natural tendency, the possibility of which at least is here admitted into nature by Aristotle (it is possible that a man regress naturally from his nature toward that of the brutes, and, in fact, below that of the brutes, because that a brute be a brute is in the nature of a brute, but that a man be a brute is clearly enough counter-purposive, and thus in opposition to the nature of nature, which counter-purposiveness, in the human political context, leads to war), will be explicitly and dialectically integrated by Kant, as we have seen, into the very concept of "nature" itself:

> [. . .] the *unsocial sociability* of men, that is, their tendency to come together in society, coupled, however, with a continual resistance which constantly threatens to break this society up. This propensity is obviously rooted in human nature. Man has an inclination to *live in society*, since he feels in this state more like a man, that is, he feels able to develop his natural capacities. But he also has a great tendency to *live as an individual*, to isolate himself, since he also encounters in himself the unsocial characteristic of wanting to direct everything in accordance with his own ideas. (*KPW*, 44)[33]

We left Kant at the moment when the *ich kann* of the transition from state of nature to state of right was causing us a problem. The "I can" seemed to resolve into an intractable dilemma, given the ambiguity of the verb: capacity or right? Are we any further along after our detour via Aristotle? Yes and no. Because we have seen that it is quite possible to think a nature such that it is naturally possible to leave it while yet remaining in it. In the *Politics*, man leaves pure natural necessity by entering into the *polis*, but the *polis* is not only natural but the most natural because it is the natural end of nature. Kant gives us exactly this process in which nature turns into its other while remaining itself in, for example, the fifth proposition of the "Idea for a Universal History:"

> The highest purpose of nature—i.e. the development of all natural capacities—can be fulfilled for mankind only in society, and nature intends that man should

33. This is still an Aristotelian point. See an important passage at the beginning of the *History of Animals*, in which Aristotle fleshes out considerably the specificity of the human in the context of other animals, especially other political animals such as ants, wasps, bees, and cranes, and recognizes that man is "mixed" with respect to his gregarity and solitariness (487b 33–488a 14). "Mixed" here is a way of translating the verb *epamphoterikein*, which is used by Aristotle in his works on animals in situations where the phenomenon in question does not fall unambiguously on one side of a classificatory frontier: So the sea anemone is both animal and plant (*Parts of Animals* 681b 1), monkeys are both biped and quadruped (689b 32), seals are both sea animals and land animals (566b 27).

> accomplish this, and indeed all his appointed ends, by his own efforts. This purpose can be fulfilled only in a society which has not only the greatest freedom, and therefore a continual antagonism among its members, but also the most precise specification and preservation of the limits of this freedom in order that it can co-exist with the freedom of others. The highest task which nature has set for mankind must therefore be that of establishing a society in which *freedom under external laws* would be combined to the greatest possible extent with irresistible force, in other words of establishing a perfectly just civil constitution. For only through the solution and fulfilment of this task can nature accomplish its other intentions with our species. (*KPW*, 45–46)

Nature, then, pushes us to leave nature and enter into the law. However, this departure is said still to be natural so as not to choose between necessity and obligation. We were trying to find out if the departure were made by force (natural necessity) or right (moral obligation), or whether the relation between force and right had to be thought otherwise in view of the paradoxes we encountered when we tried to choose between them. It is perhaps no surprise, given the natural character of everything that is happening here (nature is natural; leaving nature is natural; the *polis* is natural) that Kant will reply: both force and right. Men leave the state of nature by necessity, and they ought to leave it. Here first is necessity, more marked in the text on universal history:

> Man, who is otherwise so enamoured with unrestrained freedom, is forced to enter this state of restriction by sheer necessity. And this is indeed the most stringent of all forms of necessity, for it is imposed by men upon themselves, in that their inclinations make it impossible for them to exist side by side for long in a state of wild freedom. (*KPW*, 46)

And then obligation, especially marked in later texts, such as the *Perpetual Peace* essay ("can and ought to demand of the others that they should enter with it into a constitution" [*KPW*, 102]) or the "*Doctrine of Right*" ("a state of nature [. . .] a state one *ought* to leave in order to enter a lawful condition" [§61, *MM*, 119, emphasis added]). Is it necessary to enter into right (in which case one remains, as it were, still subject to the state of nature, to natural necessity) or is it an obligation (by natural right: in which case the state of nature is already a state of right)? A law of nature or a natural law? Kant does indeed say that in a perfect civil constitution, right annexes to itself an irresistible force, which would make it turn back into something just like nature (in the supposedly "restricted" sense of the term), a simulacrum of nature.[34] For the problem that is tormenting these texts of Aristotle as much as those of Kant depends on the very structure (or the nature) of the frontier itself: If we cross the frontier between nature and right by nature, by necessity and natural force, we remain short of the frontier, on the side of nature, while claiming to cross it. If, however, we cross the frontier out of duty, we do not really cross it, because we were already on the other side, in right, just when we were supposed not to be there yet. The frontier between nature and right, then, does not really exist, even if there is this frontier. The nonlinear dynamics of these relations between nature and its others—*physis* and *nomos*, necessity and obligation, violence and peace, the always-already but yet never accomplished crossing of the frontier that separates these opposing terms—is precisely what we are here calling "nature," some paradoxical consequences of which we are just beginning to see.

34. Perhaps this is the place to refer to Derrida's fundamental text *Force de loi*, which explores this paradox on the basis of Pascal's famous *pensée* that begins "*Justice, force*. It is just that what is just be followed, it is necessary that what is stronger be followed" (Blaise Pascal, *Pensées*, ed. Louis Lafuma [Paris: Seuil, 1962], no. 103). Curiously, in this text Derrida does not mention Paul de Man's reading of the same *pensée* in "Pascal's Allegory of Persuasion," in *Allegory and Representation*, ed. S. Greenblatt, 1–25 (Baltimore, MD: Johns Hopkins University Press, 1981). I sketched a critical reading of de Man's reading in "Aberrations: De Man (and) the Machine," in *Reading de Man Reading*, ed. Wlad Godzich and Lindsay Waters, 209–22 (Minneapolis: University of Minnesota Press, 1989), reprinted in *Legislations: The Politics of Deconstruction* (London: Verso Books, 1995), 137–51.

2. The Return of Nature

> Since I have always censured and warned against the mistake of straying beyond the limits of the science at hand or mixing one science with another, this is the last fault I could be reproached with.
>
> —Immanuel Kant, *The Conflict of the Faculties*

> As soon as we allow two different callings to combine and run together, we can form no clear notion of the characteristic that distinguishes each by itself.
>
> —Immanuel Kant, *The Conflict of the Faculties*

Let us suppose that Kant has succeeded in thinking through the crossing of the frontier between state of nature and state of law, in spite of all the aporias we have pointed out in passing. Let us even suppose that he has succeeded in thinking through everything to do with the internal organization of the State and that the problems that occupy the greater part of treatises on political philosophy have been resolved. Let us jump over everything that concerns sovereignty, legislation, the forms of government, suffrage, private property, everything that is the bread and butter of political philosophy. Once these problems have been solved (but we shall see that they can never be solved, and that is politics), the question arises of the relation between the State in question (which up to now will have been called simply THE State, with a curious generic singular) and the other States we suddenly realize surround it. The Greek *polis*, which remains the fundamental model for the State in political philosophy, is essentially circular, the circle of citizens around the empty ("de-real") space in the middle.[1] It is as though the members (the men) of the city, finding themselves at the end of their immediate (i.e., internal) political preoccupations, turned away from the empty space that defines the circle in which they are standing and saw, to their great surprise, that the space around them is full of other groups, other circles. In fact, the existence of several States (and we shall see that there must be several) should

1. See Jean-François Lyotard, *Des dispositifs pulsionnels* (Paris: Union générale d'édition, 1973), 268. In fact, this empty space at the heart of the City can only be thought as resulting from an invagination of the outside—indeed, a radical exteriority—that we are, precisely, calling "the frontier."

prevent us from thinking—with the whole tradition—the analogical form of the State as being that of a circle: Circles can touch each other, but only tangentially, and cannot have frontiers in common. We shall need a more complex geometry to think politics.

The problem, simply put, is that the state of nature, left behind by the foundation (or at least the description) of the *polis*, keeps coming back as soon as that *polis* has to enter into contact with other *poleis*. One of the passages we quoted from the *Metaphysics of Morals* (§61), in fact, concerns not individuals in a state of nature but States in their relations among themselves. Here is the passage again, this time without omissions:

> Since a state of nature among nations, like a state of nature among individual men, is a condition that one ought to leave in order to enter a lawful condition, before this happens any rights of nations, and anything external that is mine or yours that states can acquire or retain by war, are merely provisional. Only in a universal association of states (analogous to that by which a people becomes a state) can rights come to hold conclusively and a true condition of peace come about. (*MM*, §61, 119)

We thought we had crossed the (analogical) frontier separating state of nature from state of law, but this frontier returns as soon as we pose the question of the (real) frontier of the State. The frontier that surrounds the *polis* and marks it off from nature (even if that separation is inspired by nature, even if it is in a sense natural) also immediately marks the return of nature or the return to nature in the relations between States, as soon as we take its outer limit into account.

This situation brings formidable difficulties with it, and if I have chosen to follow them in Kant, this is because he seems to confront these difficulties more directly than others. Let me say immediately that it seems to me that this problem of the frontier is intractable and that it has been the object of a foreclosure in traditional political philosophy.[2]

2. I use the word "foreclosure" here to name a problem, because it seems necessary to have understood the frontier to understand foreclosure (in the psychoanalytical sense). See Lyotard, *Le différend*, §218. What Lyotard calls "differend" is, moreover, not so different from what Kant calls "state of nature," as suggested by Kant's further analysis in the "Doctrine of Right" (§42): "It is true that the state of nature need not, just because it is natural, be a state of injustice (*iniustus*), of dealing with one another only in terms of the degree of force each has. But it would still be a state devoid of justice (*status iustitia vacuus*), in which, when rights are in dispute (*ius controversum*), there would be no judge competent to render a verdict having rightful force. Hence each may impel the other by force to leave this state and enter into a rightful condition." Kant's refusal

If it is true that political philosophy constructs its *polis* out of nature, only to find that nature returns at its frontier, then it is reasonable to think that *that* nature, the one that returns, is in fact the primary problem. This quasi-Aristotelian reversal (for Aristotle too, what came last in the natural process was, in fact, first) implies, with Aristotle, that what is really first in nature, the natural origin, is not what appears first (individuals incapable of sustaining themselves in the state of nature without forming associations). But this reversal also implies, against or beyond Aristotle, that nor is it what appears at the end of the natural process that is, in fact, the origin (the *polis* and its as-if *autarkeia* as end and thus nature of the whole process). What seems to come first here is not the last stage, but the stage after the last, the postultimate stage, which, by an ultra-Aristotelian reversal, will show itself to be the preprimary stage, the origin of the supposedly natural origin. Aristotle says that the *polis*, which comes last in the story he tells, is, in fact, first: I am suggesting that what comes first can only be the state of nature that holds between States, after their supposed *autarkeia* has opened to the outside. Before the *polis*, that comes before the individual, there are relations (and therefore frontiers) between States (that do not yet exist). This possibility, allowed for in the "as if" or "all but" of the supposed autonomy of "the" State, is paradoxical enough to suspend terms such as "first" and "last" and brings with it a temporal complication that we are only beginning to glimpse.

Kant explains this very clearly in the "Universal History" text, still in terms of first and last. Recall the fifth proposition of that text, which claims:

> the highest task which nature has set for mankind must therefore be that of establishing a society in which *freedom under external laws* would be combined to the greatest possible extent with irresistible force, in other words of establishing a perfectly *just civil constitution*. (*KPW*, 45–46)

And the sixth proposition opens on the claim that this highest problem is the last problem: "*This problem is both the most difficult and the last to be solved by the human race.*" Let's read the rest of this famous proposition:

> The difficulty (which the very idea of this problem clearly presents) is this: if he lives among others of his own species, man is *an animal who needs a master*. For

---

of the differend motivates, among other things, his denial of any right to revolt, because in such a case there would be no judge competent to decide between the right of the sovereign and the right of the people. See *KPW*, 81, a passage to which we return in Chapter 4. In Lyotard, the Kantianism of the definition of the differend is tempered by a Hegelianism whereby it *wants* to be expressed, if only as a litigation (see *Le Différend*, §§22–23).

> he certainly abuses his freedom in relation to others of his own kind. And even although, as a rational creature, he desires a law to impose limits on the freedom of all, he is still misled by his self-seeking animal inclinations into exempting himself from the law where he can. He thus requires a *master* to break his self-will and force him to obey a universally valid will under which everyone can be free.[3] But where is he to find such a master? Nowhere else but in the human species. But this master will also be an animal who needs a master. Thus while man may try as he will, it is hard to see how he can obtain for public justice a supreme authority which would itself be just, whether he seeks this authority in a single person or in a group of many persons selected for this purpose. For each one of them will always misuse his freedom if he does not have anyone above him to apply force to him as the laws should require it. Yet the highest authority has to be just *in itself* and yet also a *man*. This is therefore the most difficult of all tasks, and a perfect solution is impossible. Nothing straight can be constructed from such warped wood as that which man is made of. Nature only requires of us that we should approximate to this idea. A further reason why this task must be the last to be accomplished [am spätesten] is that man needs for it a correct conception of the nature of a possible constitution, great experience tested in many affairs of the world, and above all else a good will prepared to accept the findings of this experience. But three factors such as these will not easily be found in conjunction, and if they are, it will happen only at a late stage [nur sehr spät] and after many unsuccessful attempts. (*KPW*, 46–47)

Man's "self-seeking animal inclinations [seine selbstsüchtige tierische Neigung]" bespeak an egoism that is more complex than it might appear (Luc Ferry's French translation has, plausibly enough, "égoïstes" for *selbstsüchtige* here). In the *Anthropology*, Egoism appears right at the beginning (§2), under its learned German name *Egoism*, as a consequence of the very thing that supposedly distinguishes man from natural things (including animals, which means that a self-seeking inclination is already not quite animal)—that is, self-consciousness as an *I*. Given how paradoxical all these relations are in Kant, beyond the paradox they explicitly discuss, it is worth quoting at length:

> While in philosophy we may not call up the judgments of others to confirm our own, as jurists do in calling up the judgments of those versed in the law,

3. In the "Doctrine of Right," Kant shows that the truly political (civil) association cannot be essentially communitarian: "The civil union (*unio civilis*) cannot itself be called a *society*, for between the commander (*imperans*) and the subject (*subditus*) there is no partnership [Mitgenossenschaft]" (*MM*, §41, 85). We will later draw the consequences of this at the level of international politics.

> nevertheless each writer who finds no followers with his publicly avowed opinion on an important topic is suspected of being in error.
>
> For this very reason it is a *hazardous enterprise*, even for intelligent people, to entertain an assertion that contradicts generally accepted opinion. This semblance of egoism is called *paradox*. It is not boldness to run the risk that what one says might be untrue, but rather than only a few people might accept it.—The predilection for paradox is in fact *logical obstinacy*, in which someone does not want to be an imitator of others, but to appear as a rare human being. Instead, a person like this often appears only *strange*. But because every person must have and assert his own thoughts (*Si omnes patres sic, at ego non sic. Abelard*), the reproach of paradox, when it is not based on vanity, or simply wanting to be different, carries no bad connotations.—The opposite of paradox is *banality*, which has common opinion on its side. But with this there is just as little guarantee, if not less, because it lulls one to sleep; whereas paradox arouses the mind to attention and investigation, which often leads to discoveries. (*Anthropology*, 17–18)

This is again the paradox of the legislator (we might say simply the paradox of paradox), but how could we avoid thinking of Kant's own experience after the publication of the first *Critique*? We would need to read here the reflections (which are themselves highly paradoxical) in the *Prolegomena to Any Future Metaphysics That Will Be Able to Come Forward as Science*, and especially in the preface to that text, which presents the task of the *Prolegomena*, which could only come after the *Critique*, as being that of persuading the reader that *critique* "is a completely new science, of which no-one had previously formed merely the thought, of which even the bare idea was unknown, and for which nothing from all that has been provided before now could be used except the hint that *Hume*'s doubts had been able to give."[4] Kant continues imperturbably to formulate the principle of unintelligibility of his work:

> To approach a new science—one that is entirely isolated and is the only one of its kind—with the prejudice that it can be judged by means of one's putative cognitions already otherwise obtained, even though it is precisely the reality of those that must first be completely called into question, results only in believing that one sees everywhere something that was already otherwise known, because the expressions perhaps sound similar; except that everything must seem to be extremely deformed, contradictory, and nonsensical, because one does not

4. Immanuel Kant, *Prolegomena to Any Future Metaphysics That Will Be Able to Come Forward as Science*, tr. Gary Hatfield, rev. ed. (Cambridge: Cambridge University Press, 2004), 11.

> thereby make the author's thoughts fundamental, but always simply one's own, made natural through long habit. (*Prolegomena*, 12)

We might try to formulate the paradox of the paradox of egoism as meaning that it is only in thus exposing oneself to noncomprehension and ridicule that anything nonegoistic (what has recently often been called community) becomes possible. And then generalize further and say that there is communication only in the paradox of this unintelligibility and claim that this is the principle of refutation of all philosophy of a Habermasian type, whether or not it invokes Kant.

Back in the sixth proposition, "*This problem is both the most difficult and the last to be solved by the human race*." The last problem, the most difficult, and thus, in Aristotelian vein, the first problem, the primary problem, the problem of problems, the supreme problem, the highest, *das höchstes*. If this problem were not there to finalize them, the other problems would not even be real problems. So we might be surprised by the beginning of the seventh proposition, which subordinates this supreme problem to another problem, which (at least in the order of the text) follows the last problem, like a postultimate problem that, however, has apparently to be solved before the last problem that we have just quoted:

> The problem of establishing a perfect civil constitution is subordinate to [ist . . . abhängig] the problem of a law-governed *external relationship* with other states, and cannot be solved unless the latter is also solved. (*KPW*, 47)

Obviously, in spite of the order of exposition, this problem must precede the last problem, that of internal political organization. But we can see that this order of priority cannot be simple and that in order to preserve the last problem *as* last problem, Kant opens the perspective of an unthinkable priority of the relations between States over the States themselves. To prepare for a reading of this unthinkable, let's try to explain as simply as possible this problem of the relations between States, whether it be the first or the last, the penultimate or the postultimate, always secondary or preoriginary.

Nature returns, then, at the frontiers of States and, still wanting discord, as Kant has said, spreads antagonism and warfare in a state of anarchy that seems formally identical to the one suffered by individuals in the state of nature. To the extent that this situation ought to push the individual toward civil organization, it would seem that the return of Nature between States ought to push them toward a supranational or international organization that would be the counterpart, on the planetary scale, of the constitution of the individual State, and a super-State of this sort (which would then realize the fantasy not only of every head of state[5] but of political philosophy itself, which talks of The State in the singular, which would like there only to be one) would seem to resolve the problem of frontiers (there would simply be none) and merge again with a certain naturality of the planet, which, it will be remembered, does not present any natural frontiers that cannot be crossed, if only in a ship or on a camel.

The end of nature, according to Kant, is that mankind achieve through discord the full development of all natural faculties. War, which is the form par excellence of this discord, has as its result the dispersion of mankind across the whole surface of the earth,[6] so that they might inhabit even those zones where only natural providence (in the form of moss, reindeer, driftwood, etc.) provides them with the means to live. This movement of violent dispersion is also provoked by the invocation of the prelegal right we discussed, according to which my neighbor must or ought to leave my vicinity if he refuses to enter into a legal association with me: To leave my vicinity, he must be able to go somewhere. One might wonder how this tendency to dispersion is going to lead to the end of nature (i.e., perpetual peace). Why would war not simply continue forever? Or else, why would mankind not continue to disperse indefinitely to avoid war (all the while remaining in the state of nature, for even if they found a provisional peace by fleeing war, war would always threaten so long as that peace was not perpetual, according to the asymmetry of the war-peace couple we pointed out earlier)?

The somewhat surprising reply is to be found in the globe itself, the globe whose form has a quasi-transcendental status in this argument: Dispersion reaches its limit when those fleeing war westward, for example, come back round from the east. As the surface of the globe is finite and continuous, it appears that dispersion has, after all, its limits: "Nature has enclosed them all together within determinate limits (by the spherical shape of the place they live in, a *globus terraqueus*)" (*MM*, §62, 121).

This form of the globe gives Kant a great deal of food for thought throughout his work, and always at moments that touch (if only tangentially)

5. "It is nonetheless the desire of every state (or its ruler) to achieve lasting peace by thus [i.e., by creating a universal monarchy] dominating the whole world, if at all possible" (*KPW*, 113).

6. Recall also the link of violence and dispersion in Aristotle: The separated individual must be a lover of *polemos*. But dispersion, scattering, also happens in order to avoid warfare. There is scatter whether or not there is violence in the narrower sense: archi-violence. This is where we would need to reread in Rousseau the supposedly peaceful scatter of the state of nature.

on the problems that interest us here. Already in the first *Critique*, especially in the chapter on "The Final Aim of the Natural Dialectic of Human Reason," which closes the appendix to the "Transcendental Dialectic," and which vaunts the advantages for theoretical research of admitting the existence of a supreme wisdom, we find the following:

> The advantage created by the earth's spherical shape is well known; but few know that its flattening as a spheroid is the only thing preventing the elevations on the dry land, or even smaller mountains perhaps thrown up by earthquakes, from continuously displacing the earth's axis and perhaps appreciably so in not too long a time; this might happen if the swelling out of the earth at the equator were not such a mighty mountain that the centrifugal force of every other mountain can never noticeably bring it out of place in regard to its axis. And yet without scruples we explain this wise arrangement from the equilibrium of the formerly fluid mass of the earth. (A687/B715n)

Or else, in more complex fashion, but with obvious analogical importance for everything that concerns us here (including the possibility of analogy itself), the following, from the "Discipline of Pure Reason," not by chance under the title "On the Impossibility of a Skeptical Satisfaction [Befriedigung, translated by Tremesaygues and Pacaut[7] as "trouver la paix," finding peace] of Pure Reason That Is Divided against Itself" (we shall come later to the question of perpetual peace in philosophy):

> If I represent the surface of the earth (in accordance with sensible appearance) as a plate, I cannot know how far it extends. But experience teaches me this: that wherever I go, I see a space around me in which I could proceed farther; thus I cognize the limits [Schranken] of my actual knowledge of the earth [Erdkunde, geography] at any time, but not the boundaries [Grenzen] of all possible description of the earth [Erdbeschreibung]. But if I have gotten as far as knowing that the earth is a sphere and its surface the surface of a sphere, then from a small part of the latter, e.g., from the magnitude of one degree, I can cognize its diameter and, by means of this, the complete boundary [Begrenzung], i.e., surface of the earth, determinately and in accordance with *a priori* principles; and although I am ignorant in regard to the objects that this surface might contain, I am not ignorant in regard to the magnitude and limits [Schranken] of the domain that contains them.
>
> The sum total of all possible objects for our cognition seems to us to be

7. Immanuel Kant, *Critique de la raison pure*, tr. A Tremesaygues and B. Pacaud (Paris: Vrin, 1944).

> a flat surface, which has its apparent horizon, comprehends its entire domain and which is called us the concept of unconditioned totality. It is impossible to attain this empirically, and all attempts to determine it *a priori* in accordance with a certain principle have been in vain. Yet all questions of our pure reason pertain to that which might lie outside this horizon or in any case at least on its borderline.
>
> [. . .]
>
> Our reason is not like an indeterminably extended plane, the limits of which one can cognize only in general, but must rather be compared with a sphere, the radius of which can be found out from the curvature of an arc on its surface (from the nature of synthetic *a priori* propositions), from which its content and its boundary [Begrenzung] can also be ascertained with certainty. (A760–62/B788–90)[8]

Now we might wonder whether transcendental-type arguments can find a solid footing on this globe.[9] What if nature, still in dispersive mode, had as its end to send mankind to inhabit other planets? What transcendental difference could there be between crossing the desert on a camel, crossing the ocean in a boat, and crossing interplanetary and even intergalactic space in a spaceship (one imagines Kant: "the camel of space")? More than once, Kant envisages the possibility that there be other inhabited planets in the universe (it was a fashionable subject in the eighteenth century, following Fontenelle's earlier book on the plurality of worlds[10]): "That there could be inhabitants of the moon, even though no human being has ever perceived them, must of course be admitted." Or again:

8. See also the use of the horizon to explain the (only) apparent moral decline of mankind in "Theory and Practice": "It can be shown that the outcry about man's continually increasing decadence arises for the very reason that we can see further ahead, because we have reached a higher level of morality. We thus pass more severe judgments on what we are, comparing it with what we ought to be, so that our self-reproach increases in proportion to the number of stages or morality we have advanced through during the whole of known history" (*KPW*, 89). See the Appendix for a reading of this extended image from the first *Critique* specifically as it resorts to the (unstable) distinction between the concepts of *Schranke* and *Grenze*.

9. We might, for example, invoke the fictitious philosopher de Selby in Flann O'Brien's novel *The Third Policeman*, who shows without difficulty that the world is, in fact, sausage-shaped. See my essay "Introduction to Economics I: Because the World Is Round," in *Bataille: Writing the Sacred*, ed. Carolyn Bailey Gill, 46–57 (London: Routledge, 1995).

10. Bernard de Fontenelle, *Entretiens sur la pluralité des mondes* (Paris: Blargeart, 1686).

> Since, however, even though we might not be able to undertake anything in relation to an object, and taking something to be true is therefore merely theoretical, in many cases we can still conceive and imagine an undertaking for which we would suppose ourselves to have sufficient grounds if there were a means for arriving at certainty about the matter; thus there is in merely theoretical judgments an *analogue* of practical judgments, where taking them to be true is aptly described by the word *faith*, and which we can call *doctrinal faith*. If it were possible to settle by any sort of experience whether there are inhabitants of at least some of the planets that we see, I might well bet all I have on it. Hence I say that it is not merely an opinion but a faith (on the correctness of which I would wager many advantages in life) that there are also inhabitants of other worlds. (A825/B853; tr. mod.)

But if he does indeed often speak of other planets and the possibility that they be inhabited,[11] it seems that Kant never envisages the possibility that mankind might leave the spherical surface of Earth to flee the state of nature (while remaining indefinitely in it) toward space, "the final frontier." For example, still in the sixth proposition of the "Universal History" text, Kant writes in a note:

> Man's role is thus a highly artificial one. We do not know how it is with the inhabitants of other planets and with their nature, but if we ourselves execute this commission of nature well, we may surely flatter ourselves that we occupy no mean status among our neighbors in the cosmos. Perhaps their position is such that each individual can fulfill his destiny completely within his own lifetime. With us it is otherwise; only the species as a whole can hope for this. (*KPW*, 47n)

11. Especially in the precritical text *Universal Natural History and Theory of the Heavens or Essay on the Constitution and the Mechanical Origin of the Whole Universe According to Newtonian Principles* (1755) (in *Immanuel Kant: Natural Science*, ed. Eric Watkins, 182–308 [Cambridge: Cambridge University Press, 2012]), the third part of which develops conjectures as to the inhabitants of the different planets, because, even though Kant is prepared to think that some planets may be uninhabited, or not yet inhabited, he maintains that "most of the planets are certainly inhabited and those that are not will be at some stage" (297). See also §91 of the third *Critique* (to which we return in Chapter 5): "To assume rational inhabitants of other planets is a matter of opinion; for if we could approach more closely to other planets, which is intrinsically possible, we could determine by means of experience whether they exist or not; but we never will come close enough to other planets, so this remains a matter of opinion."

Let us, then, suppose that we try to broaden the limits of the space available to mankind to take in more than the spherical surface of the earth. A transcendental argument ought to be able to accept such a broadening. If this line of argument is to succeed, however, one would have to suppose that, like the earth, the universe as a whole offers a finite space (however vast) to mankind. There is no inevitability in humans' having to form civil associations under the rule of law if they can continue to flee forever without ever returning to their point of departure. Now, such a supposition cannot fail to remind us of the Antinomies of Pure Reason, and more especially the first antinomy that precisely concerns this question of the finitude or infinitude of the universe.

Let me recall as simply as possible the place and principle of the antinomy because, as we shall see, everything here depends on an "analogical" language of nature, frontiers, and violence. Kant takes his time leaving behind the terrain of the understanding in the first *Critique*, for reasons that inspire in him an unusual burst of poetic writing that is worth quoting at length in the context of natural frontiers we are slowly setting up. I will simply emphasize certain expressions:

> We have now not only traveled through the land of pure understanding, and carefully inspected each part of it, but we have also surveyed it, and determined the place for each thing in it. This land, however, is an island, and enclosed in unalterable boundaries by nature itself. [Dieses Land aber ist eine Insel, und durch die Natur selbst in unverändliche Grenzen eingeschlossen.][12] It is the land of truth (a charming [reizender, attractive, seductive] name), surrounded by a broad and stormy ocean [rather than the eminently traversable and driftwood-carrying sea of the political writings], the true seat of illusion, where many a fog bank and rapidly melting iceberg pretend to be new lands and, ceaselessly deceiving with empty hopes the voyager looking around for new discoveries [den auf Entdeckungen herumschwärmenden Seefahrer], entwine him in adventures from which he can never escape and yet also never bring to an end. But before we venture out on this sea, to search through all its breadth and become certain of whether there is anything to hope for in it, it will be useful first to cast yet another glance at the map of the land that we would now leave, and to ask, first, whether we could not be satisfied with what it contains, or even must be

12. Note the naturalism here: We have said that there are no natural frontiers, but an island can give a strong impression that there are anyway (we are going to see how things stand in this regard with a whole planet) and that they are unchangeable and necessary. In spite of himself, Lyotard inherits something of this naturalism when he takes up Kant's description and talks of an archipelago of discursive genres. See *Le différend*, 189ff.

> satisfied with it out of necessity, if there is no other ground on which we could build [we do not yet know]; and, second, by what title we occupy even this land, and can hold it securely against all hostile claims [so it appears we have enemies]. (A235–36/B294–95)[13]

So we are dealing with an island the frontier of which extends indefinitely. The sea around the understanding, beyond the *Grenze* in principle determined from the inside (to talk like the Wittgenstein of the *Tractatus* [4.114; 5.6; 5.61–5.62]), the place of illusion, will be a thick frontier that is never crossed. What will occupy the Transcendental Dialectic (remember that for Kant dialectic is always a "logic of illusion" [*CPR*, A293/B349]) will be this frontier as such, insofar as one cannot avoid trying to understand it as a frontier giving access to something beyond it. It is not by chance that the language of frontiers and territories returns in force here, in the discussion of the transcendental illusion:

> We have to do only with *transcendental illusion*, which influences principles whose use is not ever meant for experience, since in that case we would at least have a touchstone for their correctness, but which instead, contrary to all the warnings of criticism, carries us away beyond the empirical use of categories, and holds out to us the semblance of extending the *pure understanding*. We will call the principles whose application stays wholly and completely within the limits [Schranken] of possible experience *immanent*, those that would fly beyond these boundaries [Grenzen] *transcendent* principles.[14] But by the latter I do not understand the *transcendental* use or misuse of categories, which is a mere mistake of the faculty of judgment when it is not properly checked by criticism, and thus does not attend enough to the boundaries of the territory in which

13. See also the echo of this passage later, in the "Paralogisms of Pure Reason" (but only in the first edition version): "Nothing but the sobriety of a strict but just criticism can liberate us from these dogmatic semblances, which through imagined happiness hold so many subject to theories and systems, and limit all our speculative claims merely to the field of possible experience, not by stale mockery at attempts that have so often failed, or by pious sighing over the limits of our reason, but by means of a complete determination of reason's boundaries according to secure principles, which with the greatest reliability fastens its *nihil ulterius* on those Pillars of Hercules that nature has erected, so that the voyage of our reason may proceed only as far as the continuous coastline of experience reaches, a coastline that we cannot leave without venturing out into a shoreless ocean, which, among always deceptive prospects, forces us in the end to abandon as hopeless all our troublesome and tedious efforts" (A395–96).

14. I look more directly at the complex (and inconsistent) relation between the terms *Schranke* and *Grenze* in Kant's understanding of frontiers in the Appendix.

> alone the pure understanding is allowed its play [die Grenze des Bodens, worauf allein dem reinen Verstande sein Spiel erlaubt ist]; rather, I mean principles that actually incite us to tear down all those boundary posts [Grenzpfähle] and to lay claim to a wholly new territory that recognizes no demarcations anywhere. (*CPR*, A295–96/B352)

So, no more boundaries, either internal or external: We are on the high seas. No more nature here. The reassuring coastline that surrounds the island of the understanding (seen from the inside, from the understanding, it is an island) and separates it from a different element becomes here, seen from the vantage of Reason, already part of the island, a terrain surrounded by fences (and therefore by an eminently artificial, threatened, deconstructible frontier), with what lies beyond it forbidden but, in fact, relatively accessible, and the difference of which from the terrain situated within the fences is no longer naturally clear.[15] What is more, there will now be not only a desire or temptation to go and look at what is on the other side (like the *Seefahrer* who could not resist the call of the high seas[16]) but, in fact, an incitation to escape (or invasion), an incitation that can even be of the order of order itself:

> Hence *transcendental* and *transcendent* are not the same. The principles of pure understanding we presented above should be only of empirical and not of transcendental use, i.e., of a use that reaches out beyond the boundaries of experience [Erfahrungsgrenze]. But a principle that takes away these limits [Schranken], which indeed bids us [gebietet] to overstep them, is called *transcendent.* If our critique can succeed in discovering the illusion in these supposed

15. For the language of enclosure, compare this somewhat incoherent analogy from the "Universal History" essay: "But once enclosed within a precinct [Gehege, an enclosure, a paddock] like that of civil union, the same inclinations [those toward "wild freedom"] have the most beneficial effect. In the same way, trees in a forest [in einem Walde], by seeking to deprive each other of air and sunlight, compel each other to find these by upward growth, so that they grow beautiful and straight—whereas those that put out branches at will, in freedom and in isolation from others, grow stunted, bent and twisted" (*KPW*, 46).

16. But who always might run aground, deliberately or not, like Hume: "Nothing from all that has been provided before now could be used except the hint that *Hume's* doubts had been able to give; Hume also foresaw nothing of any such possible formal science, but deposited his ship on the beach (of skepticism) for safekeeping, where it could then lie and rot, whereas it is important to me to give it a pilot, who, provided with complete sea-charts and a compass, might safely navigate the ship wherever seems good to him, following sound principles of the helmsman's art drawn from a knowledge of the globe" (*Prolegomena*, 11–12).

principles, then those principles that are of merely empirical use can be called, in opposition to them, *immanent* principles of pure understanding. (*CPR*, A296/B352–53)

So the principles in question are *transcendental*, but their use must be no more than immanent. The transcendent use of the transcendental is to be avoided. The principles of pure understanding as such are not to be found *in* experience, but they must be applied only *to* experience, from which they departed only the better to return. The ineluctable character of the transcendental illusion comes from the fact that the transcendental cannot fail to tend to become transcendent, that reason cannot prevent itself not only from crossing the frontier but from *enjoining* us to cross it. We have only just established the limit of the use of the concepts of the understanding (against a certain barbarity),[17] and now here we are wanting to pull down the fence we just put up and charge off into the beyond.

The Antinomy of Pure Reason has a privileged place in the exploration of this frontier, at least for us, because it concerns "the realm of appearances," where there is a world (and a cosmology) and where planets and stars call to us. The Antinomy thus occupies a troubling place with respect to the island (or the planet) of the understanding (of the truth as we know it), because it would seem that only it could claim to establish the frontier of that island or planet, if there is a frontier. And indeed we shall see that the Antinomy is all about the frontier and that all the themes we have picked out of the political writings, where *frontier* seems to have a literal meaning, return, in a way that seems to be analogical, to haunt Kant's text here.[18]

The apparently central position of the Antinomy in the Transcendental Dialectic (between the paralogisms and the ideal, or between the subject and God) is itself a frontier position. The place (and we cannot use this term with impunity, nor indeed terms such as *sphere*, *terrain*, *realm*, *territory*, or even *zone*, because all these terms—and the term *term* itself—are all more or less

17. This is the famous and eminently political story told in the preface to the first edition of the first *Critique*, which give metaphysics the status of a "battlefield," the history of which is hard to organize according to a linear development or teleological fulfillment.

18. It goes without saying that the first *Critique* never stops talking about limits, boundaries, and frontiers, from beginning to end, to the point where it would be pointless to give references; it is precisely this ubiquity of the frontier that we are trying to understand. Let's say for now that Kant is always trying to (de-)limit the limit or draw a frontier on or in the frontier. But if there is one place where the frontier is concentrated, that place is the Antinomy.

mortgaged to the problems we are trying to elucidate) of the Antinomy is that of the world (places, spaces, space, what is spaced in general) as realm of phenomena (*Erscheinungen*, appearances [but not yet illusions]) that must present themselves as being conditioned and that therefore lead one to think that there must be a totality of conditions for a given phenomenon, a totality that, because it is total, must itself be unconditioned. Reason cannot prevent itself from wanting to grasp this totality (which obviously is never given in experience, because everything that is given in experience is necessarily conditioned and therefore limited) and, in so doing, falls into the Antinomy. According to Kant, there are four inevitable antinomies of reason: of the finitude or infinitude of the world, of the simplicity or nonsimplicity of substance, of causality, and of the existence of a necessary being. We are going to look at the first of these, which touches very directly on the problem posed by the status of Kant's argument in the political writings about the sphericity (or at least the finitude) of the terrestrial globe.

The first antinomy, then, concerns the finitude or infinitude, in space and time, of the world (the idea of the totality of all appearances). The thesis of the first antinomy: The world has a beginning in time, and it is finite in space; for if the world did not have a beginning, that would imply that an infinity of time had elapsed before any given moment—but as an infinite series (here that of the successive states of things) is infinite only on condition of never being completed, it follows that this is impossible and that the world must have had a beginning in time. And the world must be finite in space, because if it were not, given that it would not be given to intuition within limits, its size would have to be thought by successive enumeration of its parts, which would require that an infinite time must have elapsed for the world to be thought of as infinite, which is impossible. The antithesis: If the world had a beginning in time, there would have had to be an empty time before this beginning; but as nothing can come from an empty time, the world cannot have a beginning in time. And as for space: If the world were finite, it would have to exist in a limitless empty space; this space could not be part of the world (totality of objects), which would then be in relation with a nonobject, which is impossible.

Even if the antinomies in general do not exactly lead to war, they are certainly not at peace either. Before going into the detail, Kant presents them as jousts, which are not very dangerous but during which one realizes sooner or later that victory always goes to the one who goes last.[19] He then insists, after

19. "These sophistical assertions thus open up a dialectical battlefield, where each party will keep the upper hand as long as it is allowed to attack, and will certainly de-

repeating them, on the fact that they are not for all that a game (*Spielgefechte*) and also that reason cannot simply request or demand peace, because it is implicated in the conflict itself. And yet, we can hope that the conflict rests on a mere misunderstanding, *ein blosser Missverstand*, which would, once dissipated, allow a durable peace to be instituted, a durably calm regime (*ein dauerhaft ruhiges Regiment*), in which reason would dominate the understanding and the senses (*CPR*, A464–65/B492–93).

We were seeking the consequences that would result from extending to the cosmos in general the space into which, fleeing the intolerable state of nature, mankind can disperse to avoid violent confrontation. Just as, on the global scale, Kant needs the finitude of the earth's surface to support his argument that perpetual peace is inevitable, the result of violence itself, here we find that the interest of reason (which would guide me if I absolutely had to take sides in this conflict) is better served, for practical purposes, by the thesis (according to which the world as totality of appearances is finite). It is also on the side of the thesis that we find in the third antinomy the assertion that man is free. It is, however, insufficient to invoke this reassuring convergence, first because what Kant says about the interest of reason is, to say the least, ambiguous, as we shall see, and then because the interest of reason is not in itself sufficient to solve the problem posed by the antinomy.

Let's leave for now (as does Kant himself)[20] the "resolution" of the antinomy and its "political" consequences. Like mankind in the political writings, let's return, after a long detour around the globe, to Kant's arguments in the "Universal History" text. We are getting to the point where we will be able to talk about cosmopolitanism (remember that the title of the text we are reading is "Idea for a Universal History with a Cosmopolitan Purpose").

---

feat that which is compelled to conduct itself merely defensively. Hence hardy knights, whether they support the good or the bad cause, are certain of carrying away the laurels of victory if only they take care to have the prerogative of making the last attack, and are not bound to resist a new assault from the opponent. One can easily imagine that from time immemorial this arena has often been entered, both sides gaining many victories, but that each time the final victory was decisive merely because care was taken that the champion of the good cause held the field alone, his opponent having been forbidden to take up his weapons again. As impartial referees we have to leave entirely aside whether it is a good or a bad cause for which the combatants are fighting, and just let them settle the matter themselves. Perhaps after they have exhausted rather than injured each other, they will see on their own that their dispute is nugatory, and part as good friends" (*CPR*, A422–23/B450–51).

20. "For now we will postpone this fundamental inquiry a little longer" (*CPR*, A465/B493).

We should not believe that the problems addressed by the first *Critique*—problems we have addressed primarily via the apparently analogical language of territories and frontiers—are to be held at a distance from these political questions. On the contrary, Kant himself, in the "Canon of Pure Reason," still talking about the "interests of reason," invokes—the passage is a famous one—the three questions that contain the whole interest of my reason: "What can I know?," "What ought I to do?," and "What may I hope?" Commenting on this passage in *Kant and the Problem of Metaphysics*, Heidegger affirms that these three questions (and therefore the interests of reason) define man not as a natural being but as a cosmopolitan, a citizen of the world, *ein Weltbürger*, and, to that extent, that they "constitute the domain of authentic philosophy."[21] If ever, then, the cosmo-political argument of the "Universal History" text were to prove insufficient, there would be nonnegligible consequences for true philosophy thus defined.

Let's now suppose that natural teleology has exploited discord in order to disperse mankind across the whole surface of the globe, that there are people living in the most inhospitable places, that nature is exercising its providence by providing moss, sending driftwood, and so on. The man who fled west has come back from the east. The quasi-mechanical result of this process of dispersion in a finite space is that frontiers are produced, the state of nature returns at them, and that arrangements must be found, to the extent that flight is no longer possible. Here is Kant in the seventh proposition of his text, the one that poses the preprimary or postultimate problem:

> What is the use of working for a law-governed civil constitution among individual men, i.e. of planning a commonwealth? The same unsociability which forced men to do so gives rise in turn to a situation whereby each commonwealth, in its external relations (i.e. as a state in relation to other states), is in a position of unrestricted freedom. Each must accordingly expect from any other precisely the same evils which formerly oppressed individual men and forced them into a law-governed civil state. Nature has thus again employed the unsociableness of men, and even of the large societies and states which human beings construct, as a means of arriving at a condition of calm and security through their inevitable antagonism. Wars, tense and unremitting military preparations, and the resultant distress [Not] which every state must eventually

21. Martin Heidegger, *Kant and the Problem of Metaphysics*, 5th enlarged ed., tr. Richard Taft (Bloomington: Indiana University Press, 1997), 145. Heidegger also takes up a fourth question ("What is the Human Being?") from the much less reliable text of the *Logic*, which will allow him to embark on what it is tempting to call the anthropologizing drift of the fourth part of the *Kantbuch*.

> feel within itself, even in the midst of peace—these are the means by which nature drives nations to make initially imperfect attempts, but finally, after many devastations, upheavals and even complete inner exhaustion of their powers, to take the step which reason could have suggested to them even without so many sad experiences—that of abandoning a lawless state of savagery and entering a federation of peoples [Völkerbund] in which every state, even the smallest, could expect to derive its security and rights not from its own power or its own legal judgment, but solely from this great federation (*Foedus Amphictyonum*), from a united power and the law-governed decisions of a united will. (*KPW*, 47)

Kant, as we just saw, insists on the analogy between the previous stage of the process (individuals in the state of nature are obliged or constrained to leave it) and this one (States in the state of nature are in an identical situation). But this analogy is not without its problems. We immediately notice an obvious asymmetry: Individuals in the state of nature were faced with a literally intolerable situation—it was quite simply impossible for the individual to subsist without entering into a lawful civil state with other individuals. But one imagines that a State is not exactly in the same situation, for it could in principle survive alone (if we accept the Aristotelian definition whereby the State is defined by its *autarkeia*, or all but), without neighbors. What is more, the State in Kant is defined precisely by the fact that man has left the state of nature, and if he now falls back into it, because of the sphericity of the globe and the inevitability of the formation of frontiers, he cannot be back in it in the same way. Nothing allows us to think that the individual left the state of nature in order to find himself back in it in spite of himself, whereas this is exactly the situation of the State, which finds in spite of itself that the state of nature returns at the frontier.

Let's allow a suspicion to form that this analogy, upon which Kant is so insistent, and which sustains the whole argument in favor of the inevitability of perpetual peace, hides an asymmetry that is troubling for all Kant's thought—or at least his political thought. What is at stake here is at any rate clearly indicated by Kant from the very opening of the "Universal History" text. Given that human actions are neither immediately in conformity with reason (as they would be if humans were true rational cosmopolitans) nor the result of mere instinct (like the actions of animals), they always might present a spectacle of contingency and chaos that would be upsetting for the philosopher (who is here simply a man endowed with reason). To avoid this "dismay" (*Unwillen*, discontent, displeasure, depression), the philosopher must, without strictly theoretical justification but in the interest of reason, suppose that there exists a guiding thread (the natural providence we have been trying to understand from the start). This choice between the rational optimism of the guiding thread and the pessimism of chaos returns in a still more urgent tone in the middle of this seventh proposition, at the moment when the analogy between individuals and States begins to be a problem. But where the preamble suggests a two-branched dilemma (either chaos forever, which is depressing, or else the guiding thread of providence that will lead us inevitably to perpetual peace), here a third possibility seems to be on offer: namely, that perpetual peace arise from chaos by chance, by the pure chaotic action of chaos itself. Before, it seemed undeniable that in chaos there was only chaos, depressing for the philosopher (and therefore for humanity itself considered as rational), and order, if order there were, was hidden; now we have, through philosophical argument and the operator of the guiding thread, found at least some sense of order. The new possibility now invoked by Kant is that this order might in fact be born of the fortuitous action of chaos itself, without our even needing to postulate the existence of the rational guiding thread. The new possibility, troubling for Kant's thinking, is that chaos might order itself in the absence of all teleology. Which is perhaps why Kant dismisses this possibility as soon as he mentions it, so as to return to the two possibilities mentioned in the preamble to the text:

> Whether we should firstly expect that the states, by an Epicurean concourse of efficient causes, should enter by random collisions (like those of small material particles) into all kinds of formations which are again destroyed by new collisions, until they arrive by *chance* at a formation which can survive in its existing form (a lucky accident which is hardly likely ever to occur); or whether we should assume as a second possibility that nature in this case follows a regular course in leading our species gradually upwards from the lower level of animality to the highest level of humanity through forcing man to employ an art which is nonetheless his own, and hence that nature develops man's original capacities by a perfectly regular process within this apparently disorderly arrangement; or whether we should rather accept the third possibility that nothing at all, or at least nothing rational, will anywhere emerge from all these actions and counter-actions among men as a whole, that things will remain as they have always been, and that it would thus be impossible to predict whether the discord which is so natural to our species is not preparing the way for a hell of evils to overtake us, however civilised our condition, in that nature, by barbaric devastation, might perhaps again destroy this civilised state and all the cultural progress hitherto achieved (a fate against which it would be impossible to guard under a rule of blind chance, with which the state of lawless freedom

> is in fact identical, unless we assume that the latter is secretly guided by the wisdom of nature)—these three possibilities boil down to the question of whether it is rational to assume that the order of nature is *purposive* in its parts but *purposeless* as a whole. (*KPW*, 48)

The Epicurean hypothesis, then, is dismissed as soon as it is invoked and already foreclosed by the end of this passage (too improbable a chance, on the one hand; always likely to reproduce barbarity, on the other) in which Kant ends up reformulating his question in the same terms as he did in the preamble.

Now the invocation of Epicurus and chance here does not happen at all by chance. Here we are deciding the problem of universal history in the name of the interest of reason, and almost tautologically: It is reasonable to prefer reason, is what Kant is basically saying, reason should choose itself rather than its other. And yet, the interest of reason is harder to discern when it is invoked on its own account in the first *Critique*, around the antinomy we were just reading, and this is because reason itself is harder to discern. The antinomy, as we recalled, comes about because of the action of reason itself, acting according to its nature, once it crosses the frontier of the understanding to find itself again in its apparently own proper domain or field, that of reason itself, where, however, it turns out to be a bit less than reasonable, at least to the extent that it gives rise to propositions that are perfectly contradictory but apparently irrefutable: about, for example, the question of the finitude of the world. If reason were really rational (if it were reduced to the understanding, the true domain or field of reason that has returned to itself),[22] it would not need to consult its interest to know how to conduct itself. Reason has an interest, then, only to the extent that it is not (yet) fully itself, has not come back to itself, driven as it is to leave on a quest for its systematic circle.[23] The interest of reason in this conflict is therefore not obvious, the more so in that reason in fact has several interests to consider and that these interests are most often themselves in contradiction or at least in competition with each other. Kant, wanting rapidly to characterize the two sides of the antinomy—the

22. "In its speculative use reason led us through the field of experiences, and, since it could never find complete satisfaction for itself there, it led us on from there to speculative ideas, which in the end, however, led us back again to experience, and thus fulfilled its aim" (*CPR*, A804/B832).

23. It is indeed Kant and not Hegel who is speaking: "Reason is driven by a propensity of its nature to go beyond its use in experience, to venture to the outermost bounds of all cognition by means of mere ideas in a pure use, and to find peace only in the completion of its circle in a self-subsisting systematic whole" (*CPR*, A797/B825).

thesis, which is dogmatic (the world is finite; there are simples; there is a causality of freedom; there is a necessary being), and the antithesis, which is empiricist (the world is not finite; nothing is simple; the only causality is natural causality; there is no necessary being)—appeals for the antithesis to the very same Epicurus we have just seen ironically dismissed in the "Universal History" text.

In this part of the first *Critique*, at any rate, there are in fact three interests of reason to be considered: the speculative interest, the practical interest, and the popular interest. The thesis has going for it the practical interest, in that it sustains the "cornerstones of morality and religion," whereas the antithesis robs us of all these supports, "or at least seems to rob us of them" (*CPR*, A466/B494). The thesis can also lay claim to a certain speculative interest, in that the thesis seems to allow for the complete grasp of the chain of conditions for a given conditioned, whereas the antithesis can only perpetually relaunch the search for the unconditioned that it never finds. Finally, it has in its favor the popular interest, which is easily satisfied with "a firm point to which it may attach the reins guiding its steps" (A467/B495). Everything leads one to think that this must be an invincible advantage and that Kant could hardly fail to support the thesis (at least insofar as he is considering the interests of reason), which also seems to be fully in accordance with what we have been reading in the political writings.

The thesis also has a proper name: Plato. The antithesis, which seems defeated in advance, is called Epicurus. Kant repeats that is has no practical interest, because it seems to undermine the bases of morality and religion, but he immediately recognizes that it has a considerable advantage on the side of the speculative interest of reason, if only because it firmly places knowledge in its proper domain, that of experience, where it allows an indefinite extension of conceptual knowledge without ever jumping or crashing through the fence and getting into the field or ocean of the Ideas of Reason. If empiricism limited itself to modest acceptance of its limits, while allowing practical reason to appeal to intellectual presuppositions and to faith (without claiming to have theoretical knowledge of them), all would be well, but it cannot help itself from crossing those same limits to denounce everything beyond them as illusion and fiction.[24]

Why does Kant choose Epicurus to illustrate the empiricism of the antithesis? In fact, the name Epicurus had already figured (again under the sign of exclusion) in this part of the first *Critique*, in the remark on the third antinomy, the one that bears on causality. He is mentioned in discussion of the thesis:

24. See the *Prolegomena*, 7, and the Appendix in this text.

> The confirmation of the need of reason to appeal to a first beginning from freedom in the series of natural causes is clearly and visibly evident from the fact that (with the exception of the Epicurean school) all the philosophers of antiquity saw themselves as obliged to assume a *first mover* for the explanation of motions in the world, i.e., a freely acting cause, which began this series of states first and from itself. For they did not venture to make a first beginning comprehensible on the basis of mere nature. (A450/B478)

Epicurus, then, and the school that bears his name, would be the most empiricist of empiricists, the only true empiricist in fact, or at least the only consistent one,[25] the only one to push empiricism to the extreme consequences enumerated in the antithetic itself. Only Epicurus had the courage to be truly empiricist, to give up the origin. And this is how Epicurus appears regularly throughout Kant's philosophy, often invoked, almost always denounced, a kind of ancient version of Hume, and yet more worrisome than Hume, more present.

The other side, the thesis, is, as we said, associated with Plato. He immediately has an advantage over Epicurus in Kant's presentation, to the extent that it is via a reference to Plato that Kant had presented the very concept (or Idea) of a concept (or Idea) of reason as the very object of the whole Transcendental Dialectic. Epicurus may well have had the merit of recalling the understanding to its proper domain in experience, but he runs the risk of seeming out of place in the dialectic, where Plato is truly at home, to the point that it is from him that Kant borrows the very term "Idea," which is the keystone of the whole discussion of reason here.

Now it is exactly here that Kant makes his remark about legislation in the domain of language and on dead and learned languages, which we quoted earlier. This remark, which will continue to give us food for thought, is followed immediately by another one, no less precious and enigmatic, on the relations between philosophy and philosophical reading (and, indeed, reading in general):

> Plato made use of the expression *idea* in such a way that we can readily see that he understood by it something that not only could never be borrowed from the senses, but that even goes far beyond the concepts of the understanding (with which Aristotle occupied himself), since nothing encountered in experience could ever be congruent to it. Ideas for him are archetypes of things themselves, and not, like the categories, merely the key to possible experiences. [. . .] I do

25. "Epicurus on his part at least proceeded more consistently in accord with his sensual system (for in his inferences he never exceeded the bounds of experience) than Aristotle and Locke" (*CPR*, A854/B882).

> not wish to go into any literary investigation here, in order to make out the sense which the sublime philosopher combined with his word. I note only that when we compare the thoughts that an author expresses about a subject, in ordinary speech as well as in writings, it is not at all unusual to find that we understand him even better than he understood himself, since he may not have determined his concept sufficiently and hence sometimes spoke, or even thought, contrary to his own intention. (*CPR*, A313–4/B370)

So Plato, without exactly understanding what he meant, posited the importance of Ideas. It is perhaps no accident that Kant will defend him not only on the level of practical reason but also, and above all, on that of politics and, in particular, with regard to the *Republic* (the only Platonic text that Kant cites here). For—and this is in line with what we saw in the section on the interest of reason—these Platonic Ideas flourish in the domain of reason itself, where it is most itself (i.e., where it is not entirely reasonable), in its proper domain or field or sphere, beyond the understanding. Not that Plato entirely knew or understood this, which is why we needed an active and well-intentioned reader (i.e., Kant) really to understand what he meant without exactly saying it. Do not, then, make fun of Plato's *Republic* on the grounds that it is impracticable, as does Brucker, but, just where Plato abandons us to such a miserable and shameful reading (*CPR*, A316/B373), take up the baton and think better than Plato what Plato gave us to read and think. The passage that follows (excerpted in *Kant's Political Writings* and described by its editor as "the kernel of his political philosophy" [*KPW*, 15]) indeed contains the essential elements of the fifth proposition of the "Universal History" text, of "Theory and Practice," and the appendix on morality and politics in *Perpetual Peace* (which we shall be reading in detail later):

> The *Platonic republic* has become proverbial as a supposedly striking example of a dream of perfection that can have its place only in the idle thinker's brain; and Brucker finds it ridiculous for the philosopher to assert that a prince will never govern well unless he participates in the ideas. But we would do better to pursue this thought further, and (at those points where the excellent man leaves us without help), to shed light on it through new endeavors, rather than setting it aside as useless under the very wretched and harmful pretext of its impracticability. A constitution providing for the *greatest human freedom* according to laws that permit *the freedom of each to exist together with that of others* (not one providing for the greatest happiness, since that would follow of itself) is at least a necessary idea, which one must make the ground not merely of the primary plan of a state's constitution but of all the laws too; and in it we must initially abstract from the present obstacles, which may perhaps arise not so much from

> what is unavoidable in human nature as rather from neglect of the true ideas in the giving of laws. For nothing is more harmful or less worthy of a philosopher than the vulgar appeal to allegedly contrary experience, which would not have existed at all if institutions had been established at the right time according to the ideas, instead of frustrating all good intentions by using crude concepts in place of ideas, just because these concepts were drawn from experience. The more legislation and government agree with this idea, the less frequent punishment will become, and hence it is quite rational to assert (as Plato does) that in perfect institutional arrangements nothing of the sort would be necessary at all. Even though this may never come to pass, the idea of this minimum is nevertheless wholly correct when it is set forth as an archetype, in order to bring the legislative constitution of human beings ever nearer to a possible greatest perfection. For whatever might be the highest degree of perfection at which humanity must stop, and however great a gulf [Kluft] must remain between the idea and its execution, no one can or should try to determine this, just because it is freedom that can go beyond every proposed boundary. (*CPR*, A316–17/B372–74)

From the point of view of the Ideas, then, of reason itself, it would seem obvious that the interest of reason (at the very least its political interest) would be attached to Plato rather than Epicurus, to the thesis as against the antithesis, just as we saw the "Universal History" text rapidly dismissing Epicurus when it comes to the possibility of peace.

And yet, things are not so simple. Just as Plato can suffer at the hands of too rapid a reading, so Epicurus has been badly served by his readers (and translators). First of all, as one would expect, Epicurus, on the side of the antithesis, has the advantage when it comes to the speculative interest of reason, when reason folds itself back onto the terrain of the understanding, the domain par excellence of reasonable reason, and leaves that terrain only to prevent the understanding from trying to escape its bounds. So once we have recognized the uselessness of empiricism when it comes to the practical interest:

> On the contrary, however, empiricism offers advantages to the speculative interests of reason, which are very attractive and far surpass any that the dogmatic teacher of the ideas of reason might promise. For with empiricism the understanding is at every time on its own proper ground, namely the field solely of possible experiences, whose laws it traces, and by means of which it can endlessly extend its secure and comprehensible cognition. Here it can and should exhibit its object, in itself as well as in its relations, to intuition, or at least in concepts an image for which can be clearly and distinctly laid before it in similar given intuitions. Not only is it unnecessary for the understanding to

> abandon this chain of natural order so as to hang onto ideas with whose objects it has no acquaintance because, as thought-entities, they can never be given; but it is not even permitted to abandon its business and, under the pretext that this has been brought to an end, to pass over into the territory of idealizing reason and transcendent concepts, where there is no further need to make observations and to inquire according to the laws of nature, but rather only to *think* and *invent*, certain that it can never be refuted by facts of nature because it is not bound by their testimony but may go right past them, or even subordinate them to a higher viewpoint, namely that of pure reason. (*CPR*, A468/B496)

So everything seems to be clear, divided up, clearly delimited on both sides of the antithetical frontier: on the one side, Plato and morality; on the other, Epicurus and science. Or, at least, Platonism on the one side, Epicureanism on the other. If we need to extend Plato a little by an effort of reading, one should perhaps do the same for Epicurus:

> Each of the two says more than it knows, but in such a way that the first encourages and furthers knowledge, though to the disadvantage of the practical, the second provides principles which are indeed excellent for the practical, but in so doing allows reason, in regard to that which only a speculative knowledge is granted us, to indulge in ideal explanations of natural appearances, and to neglect the physical exploration of them. (*CPR*, A472/B500)

We know how Plato says more than he realizes, and what that more is, when given a little help from the reader. What about Epicurus? How does he go beyond the obvious or first reading one might be tempted to go in for? Well, by detaching himself, perhaps, from Epicureanism itself. Where Plato goes beyond himself by going beyond experience when it comes to practical reason, and thus confirms and comforts the position of the ("dogmatic") thesis in the antithetic, Epicurus is detached from himself in a way that destabilizes the symmetry of the two sides, which will mean that the antithetical character of the antithetic will be a little disturbed. This happens not so much in the main text but in a footnote called for by the short dramatic paragraph that interrupts the analysis of empiricism (the antithesis, then) after the first two interests of reason (the practical and the speculative), unable to wait for the analysis of the third interest, the popular (whereas nothing of the sort happens on the side of the thesis: no little paragraph, no footnote had interrupted the presentation of the thesis as to all three interests of reason). This little paragraph, a single sentence that sits on the page like a sentence from *Bouvard and Pécuchet*, reads simply: "Dies ist der Gegensatz des Epikureisms* gegen den

Platonisms" (*CPR*, A471/B499: "This is the opposition of Epicureanism* and Platonism").

The élan of this sentence, a summary or dramatic tagline for everything that is being developed in these pages of the first *Critique*, is cruelly interrupted by the footnote asterisk, which refers the reader, even before the end of this clear and decisive sentence, to a long note immediately concerned to separate Epicurus from what is here being asserted. Through an effort of reading perhaps analogous to what was demanded in the case of Plato, we can remove Epicurus "himself" from the antithesis by exempting him from the thesis of the antithesis (because an anti-thesis is still a thesis, it tends to become dogmatic, maintains its clearly defined place on its side of the antithetical fence only by entering into a more or less secret agreement with the thesis as to the proper—thetic—form of its statements). Epicurus himself does not, perhaps, belong on the side of the antithesis, and so perhaps does not become thetic and dogmatic, because he would perhaps not have maintained the thesis of the antithesis as a thesis but only as a *hypo*thesis or working maxim for the conduct of the understanding. And, by saying "perhaps" in this way, by saying it is still a question (whereas in recommending that we read Plato beyond Plato or better than Plato on the side of the thesis, no such hesitation appears, and the remarks on reading have a slightly dogmatic tone, precisely, a thetic tone that brings out the thesis more clearly), Kant, discussing the hypothetical character of Epicurus's thought, himself remains, as is only right, in the hypothetical, without really advancing a thesis about the hypothesis of Epicurus's hypothesis—a hypothesis that, if it were true, would make of Epicurus a true philosopher.[26]

26. Having denounced hypotheses and all that even looks like them in the preface to the first edition of the *Critique* as "forbidden commodities" (Axv), in the "Discipline of Pure Reason," Kant asserts that hypotheses have a role in the exercise of pure reason only as polemical instruments, to be used only to show that the other has as little reason to maintain that his claim is of the order of knowledge as we would to claim it of the opposite. This is precisely what happens in the Antithetic, and in both cases there is a language of endless and unresolved battles and of weapons we should not be afraid of using, precisely in the interests of perpetual peace: "Hypotheses are therefore allowed in the field of pure reason only as weapons of war, not as grounding a right, but only for defending it. However, we must always seek the enemy here in ourselves. For speculative reason in its transcendental use is dialectical *in itself*. The objections that are to be feared lie in ourselves. We must search them out like old but unexpired claims, in order to ground perpetual peace on their annihilation. External quiet is only illusory" (*CPR*, A777/B805). The only true peace of reason is perpetual peace, and we have to pass through the violence of hypotheses in order to achieve it. See too the famous

Here, then, is the note from the dramatic little sentence about Epicureanism and Platonism:

> There is still a question, however, whether Epicurus ever presented these principles as objective assertions. If they were perhaps nothing more than maxims of the speculative employment of reason, then in them he would have shown as genuine a philosophical spirit as any of the sages of antiquity.[27] That in the explanation of appearances one must go to work as though [als ob] the field of investigation were not cut off [abgeschnitten] by any boundary or beginning of the world [we are in the first antinomy]; that one must assume the material of the world as it has to be if we are to be taught about it by experience; that no other way of generating occurrences than their determination through unalterable natural laws, and finally that no cause distinct from the world are to be employed: even now these are principles, very correct but little observed, for extending speculative philosophy while finding out the principles of morality independently of alien sources; if only those who demand that we *ignore* those dogmatic propositions, as long as we are concerned with mere speculation, might not also be accused of trying to *deny* them. (*CPR*, A471n/B499n)

---

comparison with Copernicus in the preface to the second edition of the first *Critique*: "In the same way, the central laws of the motion of the heavenly bodies established with certainty what Copernicus assumed at the beginning only as a hypothesis, and at the same time they proved the invisible force (of Newtonian attraction) that binds the universe, which would have remained forever undiscovered if Copernicus had not ventured, in a manner contradictory to the senses yet true, to seek for the observed movements not in the objects of the heavens but in their observer. In this Preface I propose the transformation in our way of thinking presented in criticism merely as a hypothesis, analogous to that other hypothesis, only in order to draw our notice to the first attempts at such a transformation, which are always hypothetical, even though in the treatise itself it will be proved not hypothetically but rather apodictically from the constitution of our representations of space and time and from the elementary concepts of the understanding" (Bxxii). Kant does not use the word *revolution* about Copernicus here, but as we shall see later, the radical hypothesis does indeed have a revolutionary character that will trouble Kant's analogy between his critical thought and his political thought.

27. "[Die] Weltweisen des Altertums": Norman Kemp Smith's classic 1929 translation (London: Macmillan, 1929) has "philosophers of antiquity" (as indeed does Werner Pluhar's more recent translation (Indianapolis: Hackett Publishing Company, 1996). This would give Epicurus's radical empiricism greater philosophical standing than Kant is strictly allowing—as a specialist of Hume, Kemp Smith might have enjoyed the more eminent status his translation gives to Epicurus, but Kant's term is less committal, making Epicurus a philosopher among "sages" (who are not, perhaps, in general philosophers) rather than among philosophers, and thus maintains the atmosphere of the "perhaps" we are pursuing here.

So Epicurus seems to withdraw a little from the antithetic by resisting the becoming-dogmatic or the becoming-thesis of the antithesis.[28] We advance the hypothesis of the antithesis for the good of theoretical knowledge, according to an *as if* that cannot fail to recall the formulations of the categorical imperative and that troubles the very distinction between speculative and practical interest to the extent that the very concept of an interest of reason already pushes it toward the practical domain, as Kant indeed recognizes. Once they have been taken as hypo-theses, Epicurus's principles leave the practical domain to practical reason (whereas if they are taken as theses, they cannot fail to invade the practical domain and declare it a domain of pure fiction), while allowing the development of the speculative according to an interest that will itself end up being practical too.[29]

28. This privileged position of Epicurus can already be seen in the precritical *Theory of the Heavens*. In his preface, Kant, more *Seefahrer* or astronaut, and less prudent that in the first *Critique* ("I have dared to undertake a dangerous journey on the basis of a slight supposition and already see the foothills of new lands. Those who have the courage to pursue the exploration, will step onto those lands and have the pleasure of bestowing their own name upon them" [194]), envisages, even if only to reject it, the hypothesis that "if the blind mechanism of the powers of nature knows how to develop so magnificently and to such perfection all of its own accord" (ibid.) and says that if this were the case, then, "Epicure [*sic*] lives again in the middle of Christendom" (ibid.). A little later, he accepts some degree of convergence between his own system and Epicurus's, taking his distance on a single point—namely, that Epicurus "was even so impudent that he insisted that the atoms deviated from their straight motion without any reason in order to be able to encounter one another" (198), whereas this very absence of apparent cause, given the order and regularity of the laws of nature, would be the sign of "an all-sufficient highest mind in which the natures of things were designed in accordance with unified purposes" (199). There is a definite proximity here between truth and error that reappears in the Antithetic we are reading.

29. As Kant puts it, "All interest is ultimately practical" (*CPrR*, 102). See also *CPR*, A797/B825 ("If there is to be any legitimate use of pure reason at all [. . .] this will concern not the speculative but rather the *practical use of reason*,") and *CPrR*, 100–2, and more especially the following, which prepares the ground for our discussion of teleological judgment in Chapter 5: "The ultimate aim of nature which provides for us wisely in the disposition of reason is properly directed only to what is moral" (*CPR*, A801/B829). This practical end of reason in general is "*foreign* to transcendental philosophy," which can only tend to pull reason back toward the understanding (ibid.). Kant appends a note to the word *foreign* (*fremd*) to explain that because all practical concepts in the end concern feelings, and therefore pleasure and pain, they do not belong to the domain of transcendental philosophy, which deals with knowledge and not feelings. This motif of the foreign also plays a role in the discussion of this issue in the second *Critique* in a subsection, the title of which proclaims the primacy of the practical over the speculative: "Whether speculative reason, which knows nothing about all that

Is it by chance that Epicurus, the philosopher of chance, should also appear in the antinomy of practical reason? Let's recall that this antinomy, which is as natural and naturally beneficial as that of speculative reason, is born from the Idea of the Supreme Good, the unconditioned in the practical domain, which cashes out into contradictory relations between happiness and virtue. In this antinomy, Epicurus, or the Epicurean, shows up again (as the one who believes that virtue consists in the pursuit of happiness) but is this time opposed not to Plato but to the Stoics, who believe the opposite. And even though the Epicurean position will be dismissed as "altogether false" (*CPrR*, 105), an effort of reading like the one we have noted in the first *Critique* will again be brought to bear in order to separate Epicurus himself a little from his own doctrine or canonic, which also softens the rigor of the antinomy itself:

> For, Epicurus as well as the Stoics extolled above all the happiness that arises from consciousness of living virtuously; and the former was not so base in his practical precepts as one might infer from the principles of his theory, which he used for explanation and not for action, or as they were interpreted by many who were misled by his use of the expression "pleasure" for "contentment"; on the contrary, he reckoned the most disinterested practice of the good among the ways of enjoying the most intimate delight and included in his scheme of pleasure (by which he meant a constantly cheerful heart) such moderation and control of the inclinations as the strictest moral philosopher might require. (*CPrR*, 96–97)[30]

My point is not at all to save Epicurus (who will, in any case, be back to cause more trouble in our reading of the Antinomy of Judgment in Chapter

---

which practical reasons offers for its acceptance, must accept these propositions and, although they are transcendent for it, try to unity them, *as a foreign possession* [wie einen fremden Besitz] handed over to it, with its own concepts, or whether it is justified in obstinately following its own separate interest and, in accordance with the canon of Epicurus, rejecting as empty subtle reasoning everything that cannot accredit its objective reality by manifest examples to be shown in experience, however much it might be interwoven with the interest of the practical (pure) use of reason and in itself not contradict the theoretical, merely because it actually infringes upon the interest of speculative reason to the extent that it removes the bounds which the latter has set itself and hands it over to every nonsense or delusion of imagination?" (*CPrR*, 101). The foreigner in the house of reason is clearly enough the moral law, which is entirely within the paradoxical logic of the legislator. There is legislation only of the foreign.

30. See also the end of the Doctrine of Virtue in the *Metaphysics of Morals*, where the "ever-cheerful heart," recommended by "the virtuous Epicurus," is part of the practice of virtue (§53).

5), or even to vaunt his thinking, but to take this proper name as the index of trouble in Kant, trouble that is perhaps the whole of Kant's thought (once we have decided to make an effort of reading and to continue with this effort even when he deserts us, etc.). This trouble—which here affects the frontier between thesis and antithesis in the antinomy, and thereby the strictly antinomic character of the antinomy, the dialectical character of the transcendental dialectic, and, step by step, the distinction between pure speculative and pure practical reason, etc.—can also be seen under the sign of nature (she wanted the discord), which returns as the (at least potential) violence that lurks along the frontiers of States formed when mankind, now dispersed across the terrestrial globe, is obliged to re-encounter and negotiate this "chaotic" (*KPW*, 49) situation.

Is there in all this a natural process, like the one that is supposed to push human reason beyond all reasonable limit? We can judge this analogically, following natural (here cosmic) teleology:

> The real test is whether experience can discover anything to indicate a purposeful natural process of this kind. In my opinion, it can discover *a little*; for this cycle of events seems to take so long a time to complete, that the small part of it traversed by mankind up till now[31] does not allow us to determine with certainty the shape of the whole cycle, and the relation of its parts to the whole. It is no easier than it is to determine, from all hitherto available astronomical observations, the path which our sun with its whole swarm of satellites is following within the vast system of the fixed stars; although from the general premise that the universe is constituted as a system and from the little which has been learnt by observation, we can conclude with sufficient certainty that a movement of this kind does exist in reality. (*KPW*, 50)

So we judge the natural purposiveness of human affairs according to the analogy of purposiveness in the natural world, that purposiveness itself being freely postulated from the point of view of the human in order to cheer up reason, which does not like chance and finds it dismaying. And yet, the same reason that loves nature and its immutable laws when it comes to phenomena (recall that this is the forte of Epicurean empiricism) runs the risk of allowing natural analogism to settle in a domain that ought in principle to come under the heading of the noumenal rather than the phenomenal—namely, the political history of humanity. We are slowly approaching the thought that "politics" might be the name for the zone in which that analogism cannot be

31. A page earlier Kant states with some confidence that we are "a little beyond the half-way mark" (*KPW*, 49).

decided according to the major Kantian distinctions between phenomenon and noumenon, between speculative and practical reason, and "law" might be the name for the undecidable utterance that is spoken in that place. Thus, for example, just before the passage from the "Universal History" text that seemed to dismiss Epicurus, the explanation in terms of natural purposiveness is shadowed by a troubling mechanistic explanation. Kant has just said that nature pushes the States toward the formation of a Society of Nations:

> However wild and fanciful this idea may appear—and it has been ridiculed as such when put forward by the Abbe St Pierre and Rousseau (perhaps because they thought that its realisation was so imminent)—it is nonetheless the inevitable outcome of the distress in which men involve one another. For this distress must force the states to make exactly the same decision (however difficult it may be for them) as that which man was forced to make, equally unwillingly, in his savage state—the decision to renounce his brutish freedom and seek calm and security within a law-governed constitution. All wars are accordingly so many attempts (not indeed by the intention of men, but by the intention of nature) to bring about new relations between states, and, by the destruction or at least the dismemberment of old entities, to create new ones. But these new bodies, either in themselves or alongside one another, will in turn be unable to survive, and will thus necessarily undergo further revolutions of a similar sort, till finally, partly by an optimal internal arrangement of the civil constitution, and partly by common external agreement and legislation a state of affairs is created which, like a civil commonwealth, can maintain itself *automatically* [so wie ein *Automat* sich selbst erhalten kann]. (*KPW*, 47–48)

This Idea of Mechanical Reason seems to be in every sense the end of nature and the end of politics. There is no nature left in this Idea, insofar as nature puts an end to itself in it or, by the same token, becomes a perfected nature that embraces everything in its mechanics, politics included, which also puts an end to itself here. Nature ends in politics and vice versa. The end of nature is the end of nature; the end of politics is the end of politics. (No) more nature: (no) more politics. The point is not to criticize these propositions of Kant's, because we want to suggest on the contrary that this is the truth of a whole tradition of political thought, which finds itself obliged to think of politics in view of an end that would put an end to it. Political thought is drawn toward the vision of a future in which politics would have disappeared in its self-realization, which would also be the end of nature and the end of history. And by a fatality inscribed in the very form of this thinking, what supervenes when there is no more politics is nature, which, as we have sufficiently seen, is violence itself. So nature, coming to its end in mechanical politics, would have to reappear as absolute violence.[32]

It is the law twice over: We *must* leave the state of nature, and we *ought to* leave it. The States *must* find their external (and thus internal) equilibrium, and they *ought to* find it. Perpetual peace *must* come about, and it *ought to* come about. It is the law. And the coincidence of the two senses of the word *law* is called nature. Opposed to *physis*, *nomos* will always have been called and absorbed by it.

This mechanical language will dominate the end of the "Universal History" text. After the passage in which Epicurus and chance are dismissed, Kant continues (my emphasis except on the last two lines):

> While the purposeless state of savagery did hold up the development of all the natural capacities of human beings, it nonetheless finally [endlich][33] *forced* them [sie nötigte], through the evils in which it involved them, to leave this state and enter into a civil constitution in which all their dormant capacities could be developed. The same applies to the barbarous freedom of established states. For while the full development of natural capacities is here likewise held up by the expenditure of each commonwealth's whole resources on armaments against the others, and by the depredations caused by war (but most of all by the necessity of constantly remaining in readiness for war), the resultant evils still have a beneficial effect. For they *compel* [nötigen] our species to discover *a law of equilibrium* to regulate the essentially healthy hostility which prevails among the states and is produced by their freedom. Men are compelled to *reinforce* this law by introducing a system of united *power* [eine vereinigte Gewalt] hence a cosmopolitan system of general political security. This state of affairs is not completely free from danger, lest human energies should lapse into inactivity, but it is also not without a principle of *equality* governing the *actions and counter-actions* of these energies, lest they should destroy one another. (*KPW*, 49)

This language of force, or rather of forces in the plural that resist each other, of a dynamic equilibrium to be found, gives a certain primacy to the relations between States, even if, as Kant says, this is still happening in view of the internal organization of the State, itself done with a view to the culture and,

32. This is again the principle of science fiction, to which Kant opens the (milky) way.

33. One senses the awkwardness of Kant's position: The state of nature is a state without finality (and thus in a sense not even natural), but finally this finality has to happen to it, though this must above all not happen by chance.

ultimately, the morality of the citizens. For, as we learn from *Religion within the Boundaries of Mere Reason*, we are still in the ethical state of nature even if we have left behind the juridical state of nature.[34] But all of that depends on this mechanical action of the States confined within the finite space of the globe. In the *Perpetual Peace* text, this priority of external relations (whereby the postultimate problem becomes the preprimary problem) is made still clearer and allows us to see what I would like to call the "external abyss" of this argument:

> Even if people were not compelled by internal dissent to submit to the coercion of public laws, war would produce the same effect from outside. For in accordance with the natural arrangement described above, each people would find itself confronted by another neighbouring people pressing in upon it, thus forcing it to form itself internally into a state in order to encounter the other as an armed *power*. (*KPW*, 112)

From the political point of view, one could always start with this mechanical logic, which works in terms of an external force, even though that would mean forgetting the story Kant tells us elsewhere, beginning with the individual in the state of nature. This argument must be valid in general, but if every State were to be formed this way, we would have to refine its logic. Kant is thinking of one virtual State surrounded by already-constituted States, which would make it into a State by pure mechanical pressure. But if we try to think every State was formed in this way, we have to suppose a general "not yet," in which all neighboring States would be formed by the pressure of an absolute exterior that would precede the formation of any State at all. In which case we would no doubt have to look toward catastrophic morphogenesis (or perhaps Epicurean physics) to find a mechanics capable of describing such a situation.

Kant, of course, does not go in this direction. The guiding thread of all this thinking, that of teleological nature, pushes him, rather (in the eighth proposition) to assert that all human history (in this optic chosen by the philosopher to avoid the dismay caused by the spectacle of the empirical chaos of history) can be considered to be the realization of nature's secret design. This is where Kant launches himself into the cosmic analogy we saw, which allows him to see already, in Europe—where commercial relations are tending to replace warfare as the ordinary means of communication between

34. Immanuel Kant, *Religion within the Boundaries of Mere Reason and Other Writings*, tr. Allen Wood and George di Giovanni (Cambridge: Cambridge University Press, 1998), 106–7.

States—the sketch of "a great political body of the future, without precedent in the past," which encourages the thought that one day will see the arrival of "the highest purpose of nature, a universal *cosmopolitan existence* . . . the matrix within which all the original capacities of the human race may develop" (*KPW*, 51).

We shall see in a moment what to think of the "cosmopolitan situation" announced here. Before we get there (it is true that it is starting to keep us waiting), what of this mechanistic teleology of Kant's? We asked whether the state of nature was to be abandoned through obligation or through necessity. It is henceforth obvious that it is both at once, or else (but that is nature) that obligation cashes out as natural necessity. Practical reason, *qua* rational, prescribes cosmopolitan existence as alone worthy of human reason, and natural necessity will make it inevitable. Even if mankind does not care to leave nature for the cosmopolitan automaton out of duty, nature will see to it anyway. What ought to happen will infallibly happen, if at least we follow the guiding thread (which does not give rise to theoretical proof)—but we *ought* to follow it at any rate, and in any case we *must* follow it, because following the guiding thread according to which nature will lead mankind to its end is part of the natural mechanism that leads mankind to its end. We keep our freedom of choice (we can even prefer the Epicurean hypothesis), but the interest of practical reason prescribes that we follow the idea that renders that same prescription pointless, because it will be followed in any case.

We can read this situation in at least two ways. The first reading will find that all is well that ends well, that morality is shored up by the thought that even if humans do not act according to reason, then natural mechanism will, a little slowly it is true, end up doing it for them. But the second reading might not be so sanguine, for a moral end that comes about by necessity is no longer moral at all; the cosmopolitan machine that functions like an automat would leave no place for morality at all. Before the arrival of the cosmopolitan state, the States do not behave morally, for they are constantly waging war on each other. But when war has finally brought about peace in cosmopolitan form, there will be no morality anymore, because that state will maintain itself automatically, in perpetuity. The end of the end is the end of the end.

So it is not for nothing that the text that deals explicitly with the perpetual peace of this cosmopolitan situation should be placed literally under the sign of death:

> "THE PERPETUAL PEACE"
>
> A Dutch innkeeper once put this satirical inscription on his signboard, along with the picture of a graveyard. We shall not trouble to ask whether it applies

> to men in general, or particularly to heads of state (who can never have enough of war), or only to the philosophers who blissfully dream of perpetual peace. (*KPW*, 93)

This perspective of death will turn out to be powerful enough to cast doubt on the whole argumentation we have been following. If the "Universal History" text, which has guided us up until now, closes on hope, and the projection—as freely inevitable, so to speak—of the cosmopolitan situation of perpetual peace, the text bearing that name, the worrying opening of which we have just read, will show us not only that such a peace really is death, and that—contrary to all classical readings of this text—we must do everything to avoid it, but that *all* Kant's frontiers and distinctions are threatened in the very tracing of their line, and that the definition of critique itself will not survive unscathed.

3. Rest in Peace

Cosmopolitanism would, then, be the natural—philosophical—end of politics. But it should not be conceived merely as the determining concept (or rather Idea) for an interesting but ultimately secondary region of Kant's thinking (his political thought) because, as we saw with Heidegger, the interest of reason in general determines philosophy in general as essentially cosmopolitan. Nature, politics, reason, philosophy: Everything converges toward this end, which would also be peace. We philosophize for peace, which implies, as we shall see, that we philosophize so as longer to have to philosophize, to have (perpetual) peace, (eternal) rest.[1] No doubt all philosophical concepts of philosophy are determined by this archeo-teleological schema.[2]

1. Ludwig Wittgenstein, *Philosophical Investigations*, tr. G. E. M. Anscombe (New York: Macmillan, 1973), §133: "The real discovery is the one that makes me capable of stopping doing philosophy when I want to.—The one that gives philosophy peace," where *peace* translates *Ruhe*, rest.

2. This is not to suggest that nonphilosophical (e.g., sociological) concepts of philosophy would escape from this schema. Which is why, while trying to complicate the frontier that passes between a supposed literal sense of the word *frontier* (political frontiers) and a supposedly metaphorical sense (conceptual frontiers), I am not simply proclaiming that "everything is political." It is true that I hope to suggest that, by its use of the word and concept "frontier," philosophy is inseparable from its politics, that there is an irreducible politics of philosophy, but I do not think that the concept of "politics" is adequate to describe what is happening here, for "politics" is a philosophical concept. By showing that "frontier" cannot fail to imply what I (perhaps unwisely) call an "absolute exteriority," I am trying to open the philosophico-political frontier we are exploring to something else again. This "something else" bears some relation, to be analyzed, to what Heidegger calls "thinking" but cannot be identified with it. To show that, it would be necessary 1) to show that Heidegger's thinking of historicality does not entirely escape the teleological schema we have reconstructed, even if it does try

This archeo-teleological schema describes, at any rate, how it is with Kant. In the "Discipline of Pure Reason" in the first *Critique*, the case of philosophy is exactly that of man in the political writings:

> Without this [critique of pure reason], reason is as it were in the state of nature, and it cannot make its assertions and claims valid or secure them except through *war*. The critique, on the contrary, which derives all decisions from the ground-rules of its own constitution [Einsetzung], whose authority no one can doubt, grants us the peace [die Ruhe] of a state of law in which we should not conduct our controversy [unserer Streitigkeit] except by *due process*. What brings the quarrel in the state of nature to an end is a *victory*, of which both sides boast, although for the most part there follows only an uncertain peace, arranged by an authority in the middle; but in the state of law it is the *verdict*, which, since it goes to the origin of the controversies themselves, must secure a perpetual peace [einen ewigen Frieden]. (*CPR*, A751/B779)

Let me formulate bluntly the problem we now need to address. It would seem that in the realization of cosmopolitanism frontiers should simply disappear, allowing everyone to be a citizen of the world, but it turns out that cosmopolitanism makes no sense in the absence of frontiers. A generalized cosmopolitanism (and its generalization is called for by its very concept) falls back into an empty universalism in which the content of the idea of cosmopolitanism disappears, or rather, because we shall see there are nothing but graveyards here, dies out. The cosmopolitanizing of cosmopolitanism would be its death. Cosmopolitanism must not be cosmopolitan if it is to avoid becoming a simple vanishing internationalism. As we shall see, according to a schema that is now familiar to us, the end of cosmopolitanism is the end of cosmopolitanism.

And yet the progress of Kant's argumentation seems continuous and coherent, at least to judge by the summary given in the "Doctrine of Right":

> Hence, under the general concept of public Right we are led to think not only of the Right of a state but also of a Right of nations (*ius gentium*). Since the

---

to delimit it (as, for example, in "The End of Philosophy and the Task of Thinking," in which Heidegger distinguishes forcefully between the "*last* possibility" of philosophy, namely, "the dissolution of philosophy in the technologized sciences," and "a *first* possibility for thinking [. . .] from which the thinking of philosophy would have to start out, but which as philosophy it could nevertheless not experience and adopt") and 2) to establish the real, if complex, links between a "concept" such as *Gelassenheit*—along with everything that refers it to a thinking of the earth and the rootedness of the homeland, or what is proposed under the sign of "country" and repose—with Kant's idea of Perpetual Peace. The nexus of these relations would no doubt still be the figure of man.

> earth's surface is not unlimited but closed, the concepts of the Right of a state and of a Right of nations lead inevitably to the Idea of a Right for all nations (*ius gentium*) or cosmopolitan Right (*ius cosmopoliticum*). So if the principle of outer freedom limited by law is lacking in any one of these three possible forms of rightful condition, the framework of all the others is unavoidably undermined and must finally collapse. (*MM*, §43, 89)

As we saw in the "Universal History" text, for the last problem to be solved, that of the constitution of an internal lawful civil State, we must first, or perhaps at the same time, solve the external problem, that of violent relations along the frontiers. Our question will henceforth be that of knowing if the resolution of the external problem (implying, or so we now suspect, that the inside be exposed to something like an absolute outside, figured in Kant by the starry sky)[3] does not simply liquidate the internal problem, supposedly the last problem. And if this liquidation does not take place in Kant's text, if he does manage to maintain the internal problem even in the perspective of cosmopolitanism, then what of the teleological movement that seemed to go beyond the inside? What are we to think of this movement, first as regards the texts on politics and history but also, via the analogies we have read in the *Critiques*, for example, in Kant's thought more generally, including everything that determines the relations between the critical and doctrinal moments, including in what determines that highly problematic operation that Kant calls judgment?

Let's not get ahead of ourselves. What does that mean here? That we must not get to the end too soon, that the *telos* must await its proper moment, failing which it will not have been the *telos*. In that case, our presentation would be conducted in view of an end we would already know, toward which the point would be to lead the reader via an ordered, methodical path, the right *hodos*, which would give each thing its place and its movement toward the next stage. But (believe it or not) we do not know where we are going, or at least we are going we know not where, a little like a Kantian *Seefahrer* who would set off in spite of Kant's best advice. But we are still going there with Kant, who does know where he is going, or at least—that is the guiding thread—behaves as if he knew.

So let's follow Kant. The "Universal History" text, resolutely "optimistic," seems to lead us or at least direct us toward the perpetual peace of cosmopolitanism. Nature will have pushed us out so that we might develop all our

3. "Two things fill the mind with ever new and increasing admiration and reverence, the more often and the more steadily one reflects on them: *the starry heavens above me and the moral law within* me" (*CPrR*, 133).

faculties through the operation of dispersing discord that will have ended up bringing us back together peacefully and globally, if not cosmically, in the abolition of frontiers, at least as places of violence and nature. However, there is an indication that things are not so simple, to the extent that Kant maintains that the last problem for humanity is the internal problem, which supposes that there are still frontiers to define that inside over against an outside and that humanity is distributed into several different States rather than one big World State. Moreover, Kant recognizes, while announcing the end of violence in the great political body to come, that cosmopolitanism should not imply the pure and simple absence of violence, or at least of opposing forces, and that there must even remain a touch of danger "lest human energies should lapse into inactivity" (*KPW*, 49), lest humankind fall asleep. The danger of cosmopolitanism would then be that of excluding all danger, all violence, all nature. Some danger must remain if we are to avoid the danger of the total loss of all danger, which would, or so one imagines, put humanity back into the ovine slumber of Arcadia, which the whole point was to leave behind. Now this idea that cosmopolitanism might be a dangerous perspective for danger, that absolute peace be the peace of the graveyard, is the idea that dominates the *Perpetual Peace* text, which, as we shall see shortly, can only establish the perpetuity of peace by recognizing that it must at all costs not be perpetual.

So how do things stand in this text as to the idea of a World State without frontiers? Nothing is clear here, because Kant is going to present this idea as being 1) desirable but unfortunately unrealizable; 2) a contradiction in terms; and 3) undesirable but perhaps only too likely. We will need to read patiently to understand how these three judgments are articulated and to see if we can reduce the apparently flagrant contradiction between them.

First argument. We are in the second section of the text, which contains "The Definitive Articles of a Perpetual Peace between States" (we shall come back to the first section, which sets out the "Preliminary Articles" in view of the same end). This second section opens on the definition of the state of nature that gave us food for thought earlier and proceeds by positing as the first definitive article that in every State the constitution must be republican. We shall also return to this. The second article, the one we are immediately interested in here, is formulated as follows: "The Right of Nations shall be based on a Federation of Free States" (*KPW*, 102). It is essentially concerned to explain why such a federation must take precedence not only over the Law of Peoples conceived as a right of war but also over the idea of an International State (one without frontiers, then), which might appear to be the natural *telos* of everything we have seen up until now. This whole article stands under the sign of *contradiction*. Let's first take the end of the article, where the argument seems relatively clear:

> The concept of international right [Völkerrechts] becomes meaningless if interpreted as a right to go to war. For this would make it a right to determine what is lawful not by means of universally valid external laws ["limiting the freedom of each"—the translation here skips the phrase "die Freiheit jedes einzelnen einschränkenden," also qualifying laws] but by means of one-sided maxims backed up by physical force [Gewalt]. It could be taken to mean that it is perfectly just for men who adopt this attitude [the object of the Dutch innkeeper's joke] to destroy one another, and thus to find perpetual peace in the vast grave [dem weiten Grabe] where all the horrors of violence [Gewalttätigkeit] and those responsible for them would be buried. There is only one rational way in which states coexisting with other states can emerge from the lawless condition of pure warfare. Just like individual men [according to the familiar analogy], they must renounce their savage and lawless freedom, adapt themselves to public coercive laws [offentlichen Zwangsgesetzen], and thus form an *international state* [einen Völkerstaat] (*civitas gentium*), which would necessarily continue to grow until it embraced all the peoples of the earth. But [and now an apparent concession to "pragmatic" realism] since this is not the will of the nations, according to their present conception of international right (so that they reject *in hypothesi* what is true *in thesi*),[4] the positive idea of a *world republic* [Weltrepublik] cannot be realised. If all is not to be lost, this can at best find a *negative* substitute [das negative Surrogat] in the shape of an enduring and gradually expanding *federation* likely to prevent war. The latter may check the current of man's inclination to defy the law and antagonise his fellows, although there will always be a risk of it bursting forth anew. (*KPW*, 105)

The *Weltrepublik*, then, the *Völkerstaat* (everything here encourages us to take these two terms as synonyms, or perhaps to understand that the former specifies the form that the latter should take), is the positive idea that is the result of the natural process we have followed, the full realization of which would ipso facto give us perpetual peace (because then there would be no more frontiers, no more enemies, no more nature, and therefore no more violence, etc.). Only the shortsightedness of the constituted States prevents the realization of this idea, or rather its maintenance as an idea to be realized,

4. Explained in "Theory and Practice": "Whatever sounds good in theory has no practical validity. (This doctrine is often expressed as: 'this or that proposition is valid *in thesi*, but not *in hypothesi*.')" (*KPW*, 62); recall the troublesome effects of "hypothesis" in the previous chapter.

and obliges us to fall back on the *Surrogat*, the negative substitute, which is only the federation, the *Bund* that makes war less probable but cannot ward off all danger of war and therefore cannot ensure perpetual peace. If, then, as the very statement of the second article makes clear, the *Völkerrecht* must be based on the federalism rather than the unification of the States, this is because the States themselves, enclosed within their frontiers, cannot liberate themselves from those frontiers and join together at the global level, whether this inability depends on historical contingencies or the very form of their existence.

That is the last paragraph of this second article. Now, its very first paragraph, three pages earlier, had denounced as "contradictory" what is here presented as the positive idea. Still on the basis of the analogy between individuals and States in the state of nature, then, Kant says this:

> Peoples who have grouped themselves into nation states [Völker als Staaten] may be judged in the same way as individual men living in a state of nature, independent of external laws; for they are a standing offence to one another by the very fact that they are neighbours. Each nation, for the sake of its own security, can and ought to [kann und soll] demand of the others that they should enter along with it into a constitution, similar to the civil [bürgerliche] one, within which the rights of each could be secured. This would mean establishing a federation of peoples. But a federation of this sort would not be the same thing as an international state [Dies wäre ein Völkerbund, der aber gleichwohl kein Völkerstaat sein müsste]. For the idea of an international state is contradictory [Darin aber wäre ein Widerspruch], since every state involves a relationship between a superior (the legislator) and an inferior (the people obeying the laws), whereas a number of nations forming one state would constitute a single nation [viele Völker aber in einem Staate nur ein Volk ausmachen würden]. And this contradicts [widerspricht] our initial assumption, as we are here considering the right of *nations* [das Recht der *Völker*] in relation to one another in so far as they are a group of separate states which are not to be welded together as a unit. (*KPW*, 102)

We are dealing with a lot of contradictions here. There is an at least apparent contradiction between the beginning and the end of this part of the text: The end presents as the only true rational solution what the beginning presents as a simple contradiction to be avoided. A contradiction between the end and the contradiction. But it is unclear if this contradiction is supposed to be the result of the very idea of an International State or simply of the relation between this idea and the perhaps limiting frame of International Right. There too, Kant talks of contradiction but seems in that case to be suggesting that this contradiction is not at all final or fatal and concerns merely the self-imposed order of the text, which is here considering International Right as the question of relations between States (which must then remain separate enough to entertain such relations), and which will deal later with cosmopolitan right, which comes just after. In that case the point would be to avoid the passage to the international simply destroying the national, as pointed out by Hegel in the essay on *Natural Law* (1801): The result of universalizing the maxim to defend one's State honorably against its enemies would be that soon there would be neither enemies nor State to defend.[5] In any case, Kant's argument to establish that there is a contradiction in the very concept of an International State seems to be the following: For an International State really to be a State, it would need to have the hierarchical structure proper to every State—namely, the distinction between the legislator and the people. So it seems to Kant that, in an International "State," one member State would have to be in the superior, legislative position with respect to all the others; to that extent it would remain the State that it was and would not, therefore, be absorbed into the new International State supposed to dissolve member State identities. And without this hierarchy, the International "State" would not be a State. It would follow that the International State could not be republican (the *Völkerstaat* could not be a *Weltrepublik* as the end of the section implied) but only monarchical, and tendentially despotic, in its form.

To find a mediation between these apparently contradictory propositions, we need to look, as if by chance, in the central part of this same subsection, just about half way between the two passages we have just read. Once more Kant comes back to the analogy between individuals and States in the state of nature and finally draws the consequences of an asymmetry we pointed out earlier. After the paragraph that we have just quoted, the argument proceeds

5. G.W. F. Hegel, *Natural Law: The Scientific Ways of Treating Natural Law, Its Place in Moral Philosophy, and Its Relation to the Positive Sciences of Law*, tr. T. M. Knox (Philadelphia: University of Pennsylvania Press, 1975), 80: "The maxim of honorably defending one's country against its enemies, like an infinite number of other maxims, is self-canceling as soon as it is thought as a principle of universal legislation; for when so universalized, for example, the specification of country, enemies and defense is cancelled." It might be argued that this Hegelian critique of the operation of the categorical imperative is the matrix of all bad readings of Kant's moral thought, in that it assumes that the *telos* of that thought is to formulate *laws*. Against it (but also somewhat against Kant himself), we might claim that what Kant calls the moral law can only ever give rise to moral decisions that are each time singular: The moral law helps me not so much to formulate moral laws as to decide, each time here and now, if this action I am contemplating is moral or not.

as follows: Just as we despise the lawless condition of savages, one might have thought that the States (the members of which are no longer in the state of nature and should therefore despise it) would be in a hurry to leave that state behind in turn, but in fact they find their glory in that secondary state of nature that is inter-State warfare. So we might be surprised to see the States invoking a supposed right of war (whereas there can be no such right so long as the States do not submit to any external law). The fact that they continue to use the word *right* precisely where there is no right proves, however, that there is, in spite of everything, a moral disposition in mankind, a disposition that could one day show itself more clearly. Now, war itself, while giving rise to this wrong but meaningful use of the word *right*, can never produce a rightful decision. And now the analogy between individuals and States is, if not broken, at least seriously complicated:

> Such a state of affairs cannot be pronounced completely unjust, since it allows each party to act as judge in its own cause. Yet while natural right allows us to say of men living in a lawless condition that they ought to abandon it, the right of nations does not allow us to say the same of states. For as states, they already have a lawful internal constitution, and have thus outgrown the coercive right of others to subject them to a wider legal constitution in accordance with their conception of right. (*KPW*, 104)

So there is indeed a problem here, one that risks interrupting the smooth movement of the teleology that we have followed so far. This is precisely the moment when nature has returned at the frontier. But it turns out after all that the state of nature that reappears here is not directly comparable to that supposed to affect individuals before the formation of lawful associations. This supposedly secondary nature, the double of the primary, true, nature (even though it is the only state of nature one can ever see, for we have always already left the other one), is precisely not such that one must leave it without more ado, because we are no longer here in a lawless state but in a State whose constitutive parts are defined by being already *in* right (even if only imperfectly, in that not all States are republics, far from it) and therefore *within their rights*. It is difficult to see why things would go any further. Why would natural teleology not stop here, at the moment of the frontier and the necessarily violent and unjust plurality of States? And if it were to be interrupted here, before its end, might we not suspect that the teleology had never really worked from the beginning, which would ruin by the same token the very notion of natural teleology, of providence, and, step by step, of rationality itself? If teleology was always going to be interrupted, it was therefore not teleological, or at least was following an a-teleological teleology, and we would have to give up the guiding thread chosen at the beginning of the "Universal History" text to avoid the philosopher's dismay and perhaps even have to take refuge in the "Epicurean" hypothesis that we saw Kant dismiss ironically.

The individual in the state of nature *ought* to leave it, because it is a state without duty, and duty prescribes itself as its own object. One ought to do what one ought to do, and so one ought to leave the lawless state. One owes the law to oneself (on se doit le droit). Having arrived at this moment of a plurality of States, the moment of the frontier, we can see clearly the principle of the "contradictions" of the *Perpetual Peace* text: For here we *ought* to leave the state of nature (but we have already left it!), and we *ought* to enter into a lawful state (but we already have!), and it is hard to see how Kant is going to establish the duty to go further.

This is a formidable problem for Kant: mankind *ought* obviously to leave the state of nature (and has, in fact, done so) but now is back in it without it being obvious where the supplementary duty to leave it again is supposed to come from. The internal law of the State (which for the individual citizens is an external law because it is public) is both sure of itself (in its rights) on its own terrain and yet completely without resource when it exposes itself as it must to the outside. Outside, law is lacking, precisely because inside one is within the law. Providence, which made use of discord to push mankind to the full development of all his rational faculties, risks finding itself blocked here.

This problem is none other than that of radical evil itself. In the *Perpetual Peace* text, Kant invokes it without naming it as such when he speaks of the "depravity [Bösartigkeit] of human nature," which is "displayed without disguise in the unrestricted relations which obtain between the various nations," but which "is largely concealed [sich sehr verschleiert, much veils itself] by governmental constraints in law-governed civil society" (*KPW*, 103), and when he invokes the moral disposition indicated by the use (that more cynically one might call merely cynical) of the word *right* to justify war.[6] But in *Religion within the Boundaries of Mere Reason*, the relation is direct, to the point that we might be tempted to say that radical evil just *is* the

6. See too, again in a relation of *Bösartigkeit* and veiling: "It might be doubted whether any inherent wickedness rooted in human nature influences *men* who live together within a single state, for one might instead (with some plausibility) adduce the deficiencies of their as yet underdeveloped culture (i.e. their barbarism) as the excuse of the unlawful elements in their thinking. But in the external relationships between *states*, this wickedness is quite undisguisedly and irrefutably [ganz unverdeckt und unwidersprechlich] apparent. Within each individual state, it is concealed [verschleiert, veiled] by the coercion embodied in the civil laws, for the citizens' inclination to do violence to one another is counteracted by a more powerful force—that of the government. This not only gives the whole a veneer of morality . . .". (*KPW*, 96)

frontier. In this text, Kant says he can do without a formal proof "that there must be such a corrupt propensity rooted in the human being" (*Religion*, 56) given the abundance of examples drawn from human behavior, all of which turn out to be located along the line of the story Kant has been telling in his political texts. First example: the state of nature, which far from being the Arcadian state invoked by "many philosophers," is, in fact, a state of gratuitous cruelty. And if one hopes to show that human goodness is better revealed in civilization, one will be disappointed, because there we would have to hear a "long melancholy litany of charges against humankind" (56).[7] And yet, says Kant, if that is not enough (the next example will, then, be more telling than the first two),

> we need but consider a state wondrously compounded from both the others [i.e., of nature and civilization], namely that of a people in its external relations, where civilized peoples stand vis-a-vis one another in the relation of raw nature (the state of constant war) and have also firmly taken it into their heads not to get out of it, and we shall become aware of fundamental principles in the great societies we call states directly in contradiction to official policy yet never abandoned, principles which no philosopher has yet been able to bring into agreement with morality or else (what is terrible) suggest [how to replace them with] better ones, reconcilable with human nature: So philosophical chiliasm, which hopes for a state of perpetual peace based on a federation of nations united in a world-republic [ein Volkerbund als Weltrepublik: what Kant himself hoped for in the "Universal History" text but already thinks is contradictory in *Perpetual Peace*, published in 1795, two years after the *Religion* text], is universally derided as sheer fantasy [Schwärmerei]. (*Religion*, 57)

Let us beware of moving too quickly to strictly moral questions, although Kant, in order to be able to continue his argument in the *Perpetual Peace* text, is reduced to invoking them. (Radical evil will, in any case, return to haunt

7. This litany of evils is quite impressive: "Of secret falsity even in the most intimate friendship, so that a restraint on trust in the mutual confidence of even the best friends is reckoned a universal maxim of prudence in social dealings; of a propensity to hate him to whom we are indebted, to which a benefactor must always heed; of a hearty goodwill that nonetheless admits the remark that 'in the misfortunes of our best friends there is something that does not altogether displease us' [La Rochefoucauld]; and of many other vices yet hidden under the appearance of virtue, let alone those of which no secret is made, for to us someone already counts as good when *his evil is common to a class*—and we shall have enough of the vices of culture and civilization (the most offensive of all) to make us rather turn our eyes away from the doings of human beings, lest we be dragged ourselves into another vice, that of misanthropy" (*Religion*, 56–57).

us, in that it is only another name for nature, the frontier, and we may even come around to thinking that it is another name for reason itself: Reason is wicked.)

The interruption of the most obvious destination of natural teleology (the positive idea of a world republic) left a negative surrogate, an association or federation of States. Before the last paragraph of the text, Kant has already presented this surrogate otherwise, in a less negative way, precisely to rule out the "contradictory" idea of a World State. To do so, the same analogy between individuals and States in the state of nature is exploited to the maximum:

> It would be understandable for a people to say; "There shall be no war among us; for we will form ourselves into a state, appointing for ourselves a supreme legislative, executive and juridical power to resolve our conflicts by peaceful means [friedlich]." [So this at the level of individuals coming out of the state of nature.] But if this state says: "There shall be no war between myself and other states, although I do not recognise any supreme legislative power which could secure my rights and whose rights I should in turn secure," it is impossible to understand what justification I can have for placing any confidence in my rights, unless I can rely on some substitute [Surrogat] for the union of civil society, i.e. on a free federation. If the concept of international right is to retain any meaning at all, reason must necessarily couple it with a federation of this kind. (*KPW*, 104–5)

In the last paragraph of this article, which we quoted first, the surrogate (the federation of States in view of peace) was negative, the negative surrogate for the idea of a universal republic; here the surrogate has apparently nothing negative about it—it is the surrogate of the act whereby individuals form a State. It is a surrogate, and no longer an analogon, as a World State would be, because, on the one hand, as we saw, individuals are leaving a state of nature to enter the law, whereas the States, being already in the law but still in a state of nature, cannot realize such a simple exit, cannot cross the frontier with one simple movement; and, on the other hand, a federation does not resemble a State, given the absence of a supreme power to give force to the law.

So the alliance between States, in view of peace, has its own proper and original form, neither quite that of an individual State nor that of a State of States. It is an alliance of "a particular kind," "von besonderer Art," says Kant (*KPW*, 104), particular in that it does not aim to acquire any political power and that it does imply that the members of the alliance "need to submit to public laws and to a coercive power which enforces them, as do men in a state of nature" (*KPW*, 104). An alliance that is not made all at once but that would spread little by little until it embraces all States. This idea, surrogate both for the idea of a World Republic and the constitution of an individual State, that implies the interruption of natural teleology before it has reached its term thus becomes, as it were, a substitute *telos*, but for this idea to be realized (and Kant asserts that one can imagine its real objective realization ["Die Ausführbarkeit (objective Realität) dieser Idee der Föderalität . . . last sich darstellen"]), we must wait . . . for what? For chance, a lucky break, *das Glück*, "good fortune" (*KPW*, 104): With luck this luck will return to us in a moment.

The positive idea that seemed to flow naturally from the teleology now appears to be ruled out. The States, within their rights, are not interested in it. And what is more, this idea involves the internal contradiction we have seen: Because of the necessity in every State that there be a hierarchical relation between legislator and subjects, a supposed World State (a State made up of States) would have to allow one of those States to become the legislator over the others, which would prevent the World State from having the republican form demanded for the individual States, and which would mean that, in fact, it could only be a monarchy. This is the *worst* outcome for Kant, even if it betrays a certain truth about each individual State. As he says in the first Supplement to the text, supposed to show how nature guarantees perpetual peace:

> The idea of international right presupposes the *separate existence* [die *Absonderung*] of many independent adjoining states. And such a state of affairs is essentially a state of war, unless there is a federal union to prevent hostilities breaking out. But in the light of the idea of reason, this state is still to be preferred to an amalgamation [die Zusammenschmelzung] of the separate nations under a single power which has overruled the rest and created a universal monarchy. For the laws progressively lose their impact as the government increases its range, and a soulless despotism, after crushing the germs of goodness, will finally lapse into anarchy. It is nonetheless the desire of every state (or its ruler) to achieve lasting peace by thus dominating the whole world, if at all possible. (*KPW*, 113)

So we need dispersion, or at least separation, to avoid the danger of unification or fusion, which would again be death. Up until now, it had seemed as though nature made use of discord and violence as a provisional means of dispersion in view of a subsequent unification in perpetual peace, whereas now nature is going to maintain the dispersion in dispersion to avoid the terrible consequences of too unified a unification.[8]

8. Following the analogism between the political and the physico-theoretical that is at work in all these discussions, we might want to read this tension of relatively gath-

For there to be the least chance of international right, there must be nations still separated from each other, and so frontiers must subsist, even though we thought they were going to disappear in cosmopolitanism. In the end, which comes before the end, there is cosmopolitanism only in an internationalism that presupposes separate States that are still, however slightly, in a relation of natural violence that is not yet absorbed in cosmopolitanism.

The same holds in Kant's little text on perpetual peace in philosophy, from 1796.[9] Man tends naturally to philosophize and, therefore, to polemicize. This polemic goes as far as "open warfare," but, according to the dialectic we have followed,

> this propensity [. . .] or rather *impulse*, must be seen as one of the benevolent and wise arrangements of nature through which it seeks to avert men from a great misfortune, the putrefaction of the living body. ("Peace in Philosophy," 84)

But, unlike the passage from the first *Critique* we quoted earlier, in which critical philosophy put an end to such warfare by bringing repose and perpetual peace, peace as repose, here that same critical philosophy is still supposed to bring about peace, but a peace that looks like what we were just seeing in restricted cosmopolitan politics:

---

ered dispersion in the light of what Kant says about matter, from at least the *Theory of the Heavens* text through to the *Opus Postumum*. For example, in the latter: "All matter must have repulsive forces, since otherwise it would fill no space; but attractive force must also be attributed to it, since otherwise it would disperse itself into the infinity of space—in both cases space would be empty. Consequently, one can think of such alternating impacts and counterimpacts [as existing] from the beginning of the world, as a trembling (oscillating, vibrating) motion of the matter which fills the entire universe, includes within itself all bodies, and is both elastic and at the same time attractive in itself. These pulsations constitute a living force, and never allow dead force by pressure and counterpressure (i.e. absolute rest inside this matter) to occur" (Immanuel Kant, *Opus Postumum*, tr. Eckard Förster and Michael Rosen [Cambridge: Cambridge University Press, 1993], 25). But also "were repulsion the sole moving force of matter, every matter would dissipate itself into infinity; consequently, space would be empty. But were it attraction alone, all [matter] would coalesce into a single point and space would also be empty. So each quantum of matter can originally fill a space only through the conflict of attraction and repulsion of substances—an action and reaction which is already contained in the concept of a spatial matter, but whose possibility can be made comprehensible by no explanation whatsoever" (ibid., 27).

9. Immanuel Kant, "Announcement of the Near Conclusion of a Treaty of Eternal Peace in Philosophy," tr. Peter Fenves, in *Raising the Tone of Philosophy: Late Essays by Immanuel Kant, Transformative Critique by Jacques Derrida*, ed. Peter Fenves, 83–100 (Baltimore, MD: Johns Hopkins University Press, 1993).

> [Critical] philosophy, which is a permanently armed state (against those who would perversely confuse appearances with things in themselves) and indeed an armed state that thereby also incessantly accompanies the activity of reason—this philosophy opens the prospect of an eternal peace among philosophers [. . .]. This peace has, in addition, the advantage of always keeping alert the powers of the subject exposed to the apparent danger of attacks, thereby promoting by means of philosophy the intention of nature to enliven the subject continually and to guard against the sleep of death [Todesschlaf]. ("Peace in Philosophy," 87)

The only chance for cosmopolitanism, then—and, by analogy, for philosophy itself, *qua* vital activity that preserves us from the death and corruption that would follow from too peaceful a slumber—is that it not be cosmopolitan. Consequently, the federation formed with a view to perpetual peace can subsist only in a frontier tension that must be maintained if the death of planetary peace is to be avoided. Nature thus survives the perspective of its own end, and its providential wisdom turns out to be reticent with regard to the end that everything led us to think really was the end. Nature must, then, prevent nature from fully arriving at its end, hold itself back, short of its most obvious *telos*, and choose a substitute quasi-*telos*, a surrogate that is as positive as it is negative, in which the nature of nature is no longer its own abolition but its maintenance, supposed to favor a peace the name and quality of which have become highly problematic. Thus:

> But *nature* wills it otherwise, and uses two means to separate the nations and prevent them from intermingling—*linguistic* and *religious* differences [Verschiedenheit]. (*KPW*, 113)

Kant inserts a note to the word "religious" to protest that there can be only one religion and, at most, different confessions (*Glaubensarten*), which are of a merely historic interest, contingencies that are all vehicles of the one true religion.[10] This is also the basis of the distinction made in the *Religion*

10. See too *The Conflict of the Faculties*, tr. Mary Gregor (Lincoln: University of Nebraska Press, 1992), 61 (hereinafter *CF*). However uncomfortable the formula here, the teleological determination remains the same: "The euthanasia of Judaism is pure moral religion, freed from all the ancient statutory teachings, some of which were bound to be retained in Christianity (as a messianic faith). But this division of sects, too, must disappear in time, leading, at least in spirit, to what we call the conclusion of the great drama of religious change on earth (the restoration of all things), when there will be only one shepherd and only one flock." See too the more nuanced and complicated argument in the remark "On Religious Sects" (85–109), especially as regards the Jews (95).

book between the visible and invisible church. But this amounts to saying that religion fits into the teleological schema of a unification that the whole point here in *Perpetual Peace* was to stop. It would follow that the only true means nature really has of maintaining human gathering in dispersion is the diversity of languages, which calls for no cautionary statement analogous to the one about religion, whereas we might have expected a remark to the effect that reason is universal and that therefore the diversity of languages is merely a contingent vehicle of it. But Kant says nothing of the sort, and for good reason. Recall a famous but obscure moment in the first *Critique*, at the beginning of the "Transcendental Doctrine of Method":

> It turned out, of course, that although we had in mind a tower that would reach the heavens, the supply of materials sufficed only for a dwelling that was just roomy enough for our business on the plane of experience and high enough to survey it; however, that bold undertaking had to fail from lack of material, not to mention the confusion of languages that unavoidably divided the workers over the plan and dispersed them throughout the world leaving each to build on his own according to his own design. (*CPR*, A707/B735)[11]

Kant now makes a concession to what by now is obvious—namely, that this separation must, according to everything he has said, perpetuate war rather than peace:

> These may certainly occasion mutual hatred and provide pretexts for wars, but as culture grows and men gradually move towards greater agreement over their principles, they lead to mutual understanding and peace. And unlike that universal despotism which saps all man's energies and ends in the graveyard [auf dem Kirchhofe] of freedom, this peace is created and guaranteed by an equilibrium of forces and a most vigorous rivalry. (*KPW*, 113–14)

The peace of the graveyard can always come about, and every State wants it, if we are to believe Kant, to the extent that every State would like to become the only State by annexing all the others. (This is repeated in the immediately following paragraph: "Nature wisely separates the nations, although

11. On these figures of building, see Daniel Payot, *Le philosophe et l'architecte: sur quelques déterminations philosophiques de l'idée d'architecture* (Paris: Aubier-Montaigne, 1982), and Bernard Edelman, *La maison de Kant: conte moral* (Paris: Payot, 1984). On the way that language makes a linear frontier impossible, see also Jacques Derrida, "*Mochlos*—ou le conflit des facultés," in *Du Droit à la Philosophie*, 397–438 (Paris: Galilée, 1990), tr. Jan Plug as "Mochlos, or The Conflict of the Faculties," in *Eyes of the University: Right to Philosophy 2* (Stanford, CA: Stanford University Press, 2004), 83–112.

the will of each individual state, even basing its arguments on international right, would gladly unite them under its own sway by force or by cunning" [*KPW*, 114].) So to have a peace other than the peace of death (a peace that must nonetheless be perpetual if it is to be peace), we need the violence of warlike separation, which, transformed into a balance or equilibrium of forces of emulation or competition, is supposed to guarantee peace. Peace is perpetual only if it perpetually postpones its own mortal perpetuity in favor of a lively balance that still manifestly contains death-dealing and violent elements. If there is to be peace, and perpetual peace, it will therefore not be entirely peaceful.

We may not know where we are going, but it is certain that we are going too fast. This whole part of the argument happens at the level of international right or right of peoples (*Völkerrecht*), which is not yet cosmopolitan or cosmopolitical right (*Weltbürgerrecht*), which, or so we might think, would be the place where we would finally come to the consequences glimpsed in the "Universal History" text. And the third "Definitive Article" of the treaty of perpetual peace does deal with this but already in its titular statement announces a restriction of a right that we had legitimately thought to be without limit (because without frontiers). The statement of this article of the treaty is: "Cosmopolitan Right shall be Limited [eingeschränkt] to Conditions of Universal Hospitality." Why this restriction?

Cosmopolitan right is deduced, once again, from the form of the Earth, which gives to all a "right of communal possession of the earth's surface. Since the earth is a globe, they cannot disperse over an infinite area, but must necessarily tolerate one's company" (*KPW*, 106). The Earth, then, or its sphericity, gives rise both to the insoluble tension of international right and to the apparently more positive content of cosmopolitan right. Kant's clearest statement of the basis of this right comes in the "Doctrine of Right":

> Nature has enclosed them all together within determinate limits (by the spherical shape of the place they live in, a *globus terraqueus*). And since possession of the land, on which an inhabitant of the earth can live, can be thought only as possession of a part of a determinate whole, and so as possession of that to which each of them originally has a right, it follows that all nations stand *originally* in a community of land. (*MM*, §62, 158)

But where we might have thought that this would justify the formation of a World State, Kant specifies that this right is, in fact, a right of relation, a right to enter into relations with the foreigner who remains foreign, a right, then, of the frontier in general:

> A community of land, though not of *rightful* community of possession (*communio*) and so of use of it, or of property in it; instead they stand in a community of possible physical *interaction* (*commercium*), that is, in a thoroughgoing relation of each to all the others of *offering to engage in commerce* with any other, and each has a right to make this attempt without the other being authorized to behave toward it as an enemy because it has made this attempt. (*MM*, §62, 158)

This opposition of *communio* and *commercium*, as the very ambiguity of the concept of *Gemeinschaft* (community or society), is already pointed out, "analogically," in the first *Critique*, precisely around the third analogy of experience. In the totality of appearances, all objects must have relations of a dynamic community (*Gemeinschaft*). This is where Kant points out the ambiguity of the concept:

> The word "community" is ambiguous in our language, and can mean either *communio* or *commercium*. We use it here in the latter sense as a dynamical community, without which even the local community (*communion spatii*) could never be empirically cognized. [. . .] Without community every perception (of experience in space) is broken off from the others, and the chain of empirical representations, i.e. experience, would have to start entirely over with every new object without the previous one being in the least connected or being able to stand in a temporal relation with it. (*CPR*, A213–14/B260–61)

Communio is that of subjective coexistence according to the unity of apperception; dynamic *commercium* is the only way to give that an objective ground and, in the end, ensure the unity of the world as a whole (*die Einheit des Weltganzen*) (A218/B265). This analogy of experience, which is analogical in that it stands in a relation of analogy to the logical unity of concepts, ana-logical with respect to the logical, finds a language not of logic itself (meaning what? the concept of disjunctive community had already appeared much earlier in the *Critique* under the heading of logic: A74/B99 and especially B111–13 recognizes that the category of community "is not as obvious" as other cases in the table of judgments, and that nonobvious character opens the ambiguity we are pursuing here)—not a language of logic, then, but, in a further analogy, the language of political relations. Just as we would have nothing of local *communio* without the global dynamic *commercium*, we would have no State in the singular were it not for the dynamic coexistent multiplicity of all the States. This is the same priority of dynamic rapport over local identity that allows for the remark from *Perpetual Peace*, already quoted, about States being formed by the dynamic pressure of surrounding states (*KPW*, 112). This coexistence of logical, empirical, and political language must itself be understood by analogy with the analogy (of analogy): These three languages here too depend on their dynamic *commercium*. We might say, bluntly, that analogy is (only) analogical, and this must be so well "before" Kant's own analogies between theoretical and practical domains. Reason in Kant is fundamentally and inextricably analogical, in a way that cannot be easily resolved by appeal to any particular *telos*.

Kant did, as it were, foresee this type of reading and tried to forestall it, by describing it (in *The Conflict of the Faculties*) as *abderitism*:

> Since a true stagnation in matters of morality is not possible, a perpetually changing upward tendency and an equally frequent and profound relapse (an external oscillation, as it were) amounts to nothing more than if the subject had remained in the same place, standing still. [. . .] People [. . .] in order to avoid being bound to a single goal, even if only for the sake of variety they reverse the plan of progress, build in order to demolish. [. . .] Inertia (which is here called stagnation [Stillstand]) would be the result of this. It is a vain affair to have good so alternate with evil that the whole traffic of our species on this globe would have to be considered as a mere farcical comedy, for this can endow our species with no greater value in the eyes of reason than that which other animal species possess, species which carry on this game with fewer costs and without expenditure of thought. (147)

See too the third *Critique*, where there is an analogy between (political) *commercium* and natural purposiveness itself: in §65 Kant has just said that the analogy that considers nature as the work of an artist, as "the analogue of art," says too little (for it would assume an artist separate from the work, whereas nature produces itself) and that it would be better to think of nature as an analogue of life. That is still a problem, because one would risk falling into hylozoism (which attributes life to matter as such) or else to appeal to a soul that would be "an alien principle *standing in community* with it [Ein fremdartiges in Gemeinschaft stehendes Prinzip]." Strictly speaking, says Kant, "the organization of nature is therefore not analogous with any causality we know." But this claim calls immediately for a note in which he accepts that an analogy is possible in the other direction, as it were, and it just so happens that this analogy is, again, political:

> One can, conversely, illuminate a certain association, though one that is encountered more in the idea than in reality, by means of an analogy with the immediate ends of nature that have been mentioned. Thus, in the case of a recently undertaken fundamental transformation of a great people into a state,

> the word organization has frequently been quite appropriately used for the institution of the magistracies, etc., and even of the entire body politic. For in such a whole each member should certainly be not merely a means, but at the same time also an end, and, insofar as it contributes to the possibility of the whole, its position and function should also be determined by the idea of the whole. (*CJ*, 246–47)

Cosmopolitan right, then, provides for a right to cross frontiers that remain in place, that can be crossed in order to visit, for people to "present themselves in the society [Gesellschaft] of others," indeed, but in a society still and always defined by what divides it and simultaneously allows it to be thought.

Kant's (hi)story, then involves, on the one hand, an apparently irresistible advance toward the abolition of all frontiers, to the establishment of a World State in which everyone would be a "citizen of the world," and, on the other, a pulling back from this advance moving toward what would in fact be death, a pause or an interruption of this movement at the *inter*-national moment, a moment at which frontiers remain, with the tension they entail, the moment at which we must accept the surrogate, the federation, rather than pure cosmopolitanism. This pulling back emerges very clearly toward the end of "Theory and Practice."

> On the one hand, universal violence and the distress it produces must eventually make a people decide to submit to the coercion which reason itself prescribes (i.e. the coercion of public law), and to enter into a *civil* constitution. And on the other hand, the distress produced by the constant wars in which the states try to subjugate or engulf each other must finally lead them, even against their will, to enter into a *cosmopolitan* constitution. *Or if such a state of universal peace is in turn even more dangerous to freedom, for it may lead to the most fearful despotism* [emphasis added] (as has indeed occurred more than once with states which have grown too large), distress must force men to form a state which is not a cosmopolitan commonwealth under a single ruler, but a lawful *federation* under a commonly accepted *international right.* (*KPW*, 90)

We must then, perhaps, fall short of peace in the interests of peace. There will be no peace (peace that must be perpetual to be worthy of the name peace) except in the inter-national dynamic, in which we still find tension and competition, the violence and contingency of nature, the Babelian non-comprehension of the confusion of tongues, inscribed on the surface of the globe in the form of frontiers that can, of course, be transgressed but which subsist through and for all such transgression. Peace, to be perpetual, must perpetually defer its perpetuity. Peace cannot, then, be declared but only ever announced as perpetually to come, in the form of a promise forever promised and thus never fulfilled.

It will be objected that the fact that perpetual peace cannot be realized takes nothing away from the force of Kant's argument, which is quite ready to accept this impossibility by invoking the distinction between concept of the understanding and Idea of reason. And, indeed, this is what is explicitly stated in the "Doctrine of Right," which summarizes quite calmly what I have been laying out in such agitated fashion:

> Since a state of nature among nations, like a state of nature among individual men, is a condition that one ought to leave in order to enter a lawful condition, before this happens any rights of nations, and anything external that is mine or yours that states can acquire or retain by war, are merely *provisional*. Only in a universal *association of states* (analogous to that by which a people becomes a state) can rights come to hold *conclusively* and a true *condition of peace* come about. But if such a state made up of nations were to extend too far over vast regions, governing it and so too protecting each of its members would finally have to become impossible, while several such corporations would again bring on a state of war. So *perpetual peace*, the ultimate goal of the whole Right of Nations, is indeed an unachievable Idea. Still, the political principles directed toward perpetual peace, of entering into such alliances of states, which serve for continual approximation to it, are not unachievable. Instead, since continual *approximation* to it is a task based on duty and therefore on the Right of men and of states, this can certainly be achieved. (*MM*, §61, 156)

As always, the Idea of reason goes beyond all possible experience, toward a maximum that cannot be presented to intuition for conceptual validation. The object of the Idea is thus beyond phenomenal reality but orients that reality by giving it a sense. Where the "Universal History" text seemed to believe in the future reality (however distant) of perpetual peace, and where the *Perpetual Peace* text still seemed to think that nature would really bring it about one day, here is a more sober and "realistic" assessment: the World State is unrealizable, but it still remains the Idea that guides political judgment and to which the federation of States should approximate as far as possible. Perpetual peace is unrealizable, but we can and ought to approach it infinitely according to the asymptotic curve that is part of Kant's thinking of the Idea.

This (entirely Kantian) response to our analyses is, however, radically insufficient. We have seen that the end (here qualified as unrealizable but nonetheless excellent and desirable) is quite simply death. We cannot therefore want to approach it as closely as possible, because nothing guarantees that a place near that of the World State (necessarily despotic and as close as can be to collapse into the most violent state of nature) is better than a situation very far from it, whether that situation be a federation or not. What our analyses suggest, however, is that the movement toward the Idea can no longer be calibrated or controlled: Because the end is the end, because death is at the end, we can no longer say with any confidence where the good is to be found along the path that starts from the state of nature and leads, beyond all possible experience, to perpetual peace. Even supposing we can always situate ourselves along a line leading from the one to the other, that we can still orient ourselves in thinking (*concesso non dato*), we are still in confusion, we do not really know in which direction we are moving, we can no longer see any endpoint very clearly, nor therefore a possible approach to that endpoint. We no longer really know what "peace" means, to the extent that perpetual peace looks just like death, and that surrogate peace involves war, violence, and danger as essential elements in its definition. So we no longer really know where we are or where we are headed. Here we are, on the frontier, *in* the frontier, looking at the stars no doubt, unless it is their misleading reflection in the muddy water. As the idea of peace is an Idea of Reason, this situation of being in the middle where we can no longer orient ourselves with certainty nor even with any confidence is the very situation of reason seeking its end: for reason itself is only one of its own Ideas.[12]

What if this structure of pulling back, in which the end (that risks really being the end, death) is displaced and comes before the end, not at any fixed point in the process but at some moment at which the end has to (*müssen* and *sollen*) happen, but must above all not be realized—what if this structure (nature, the frontier) were not only that of Kant's natural teleology in general but in fact that of judgment as such? Of judgment as such, namely, in the form of what Kant calls reflective judgment? If we must stop at the frontier, how do things stand, not only with regard to Kant's political thinking, not only with its relations with morality and theory (we are coming to that), but to the system or edifice of Kant's system in general, the relations between the theoretical and practical domains, as these relations are described in the introduction to the third *Critique*, the relations between critique and doctrine, critique and metaphysics? If we manage to establish these analogical links (but as we shall see, what we are tracking here precedes and exceeds, exasperates any analogism), would it not follow not only that we might prefer

12. We would have to say that the understanding is also an Idea of Reason and that therefore the frontier between concept and Idea is as fragile as can be. It would not simply follow that reason is straightforwardly unreasonable but that reason's reason is not that of rationalism.

in Kant the critical moment to the doctrinal moment (and indeed everyone does prefer that) but that, as the doctrinal moment only ever arrives as the death of the critical moment, it never truly arrives, which would leave us forever in the good critical tension? But then we would no longer really understand what critique means, as the concept of critique in Kant draws its content from its teleological determination with regard to doctrine. No critique without doctrine. Without doctrine, no critical step.

Interlude: The Guiding Thread (on Philosophical Reading)

> If one thinks, in the empty space above the earth, a chain, a wire, or a cord, fixed to an immobile point above the earth and stretched by its own weight, one can suppose it to be of such a length respective to the force of its cohesion, that it breaks under its own weight.—I will for the moment call this thoroughly uniform body a thread [Faden], whatever the material of which it is made.
>
> —Immanuel Kant, *Opus Postumum*[1]

Live

Philosophy is above all, perhaps, to do with thinking, but it has not thought very much about the problem of reading (its own reading). Supposing that I know why I read philosophy—or even if I read philosophy in order to figure out why I read it—I still do not know how to read Philosophy (a philosophy, a philosopher, a philosophical text, a philosophical proposition, a philosophical concept?). At any rate, I do read philosophy, somewhat at random, following a movement I could not call "epistemophilic," without really knowing how else to qualify it (not the pleasure of the text, at any rate, or else very rarely, and further still from Barthesian *jouissance*). From what I imagine to be a "traditional" philosophical point of view, I am like Pascal's reader who goes too fast or too slowly, often in an uncomprehending disarray that does not stop me reading, but which puts me undeniably ill at ease.[2]

1. Immanuel Kant, *Opus Postumum*, 7th fascicle, leaf 1, 1 (vol. 22, 4 of the Prussian Academy edition), my translation. This passage and those providing the epigraphs to the next two subsections are not included in the English selections from the *Opus Postumum* (ed. Eckhart Förster [Cambridge: Cambridge University Press, 1993]). They can be found in the French edition by François Marty (Paris: Presses Universitaires de France, 1986), 121, 124. A number of contingent possibilities of reading that were available in the French edition of this book are difficult to maintain in this English version: The standard French translation of Kant's *Leitfaden*, "le fil conducteur," can be taken not only as a "guiding thread" but as a "conductive wire," which motivated the three subtitles of this section (*la phase, le neutre, la terre*) in terms of the three wires in a standard household alternating current cable.

2. "Quand on lit trop vite ou trop doucement on n'entend rien [When one reads too fast or too slowly one understands nothing]," Pascal, *Pensées*, no. 57 (Lafuma), 69

From a book of philosophy, I retain sometimes only the inadequacy of my reading, to the point of practically not daring to admit I have read it. Having read for the first time the *Critique of Pure Reason* years ago, I retained only a handful of details picked up along the way, about space and time, dialectic as logic of illusion, reason always about to run precipitously ahead of itself, a hallucinatory passage on the island of the understanding in the ocean of reason. But what I imagined to be the true substance of the book escaped me entirely. No one told me what was in it, even though I knew that in principle it is a "Copernican Revolution" in philosophy (I never "studied" philosophy, as they say, and even when I know what is supposed to be in this or that philosophical text, as is most often the case, this knowledge is not real knowledge, it does not count, I still understand nothing)—and my ignorance, so to speak, survives my reading. I would have to refer after the fact to books *about* Kant to find out what he "really says," which I then recognize having read (or at least seen) but as though I had to forget my reading and replace it with this second version that I imagine must be the right one, the official one, the one, in any case, I would have to bring in an exam. But, like Proust's narrator finally making it to the Guermantes's dinner table, what I then see that I must have read without reading, what I thought I most wanted to know, is immediately disappointing and loses all interest for me. I was reading Kant in a rather disagreeable tension of incomprehension, and that tension is now resolved into an apparent understanding that seems to have no value.

Which is why I always have to envisage philosophical reading as an urgent invitation to a different rereading. The first time, I read along in order, from beginning to end, dutifully, without really understanding. The second time I must read differently, and the first reading is really only a pretext for this second attempt. This rereading does not know how to proceed, or even where it is going, for, on the one hand, it owes it to itself to be the *right* reading that the first never is (no excuse a second time), but, on the other, it ought to be able to free itself from the linear order of the book to access the text otherwise, in a different order that is not necessarily haphazard for all that (and that might, later, reconstitute a linear order). The point is not to advance toward a triumphant, or even modest, understanding—even if something of the order of understanding might happen along the way. I sense

(Brunschvicg), chosen as the epigraph to Paul de Man, *Allegories of Reading* (New Haven, CT: Yale University Press, 1979). It bears recalling that this is not a straightforward recommendation of "slow" or "close" reading. We shall see in a minute that reading inevitably has to be "too fast" but leaves the question entire as to the appropriate speed at which to read a given text.

that in any case I will never understand. The point is rather to experience or endure something of the order of pure reading, which is as close as can be to stupidity, somewhere between Flaubertian stupor and bedazzlement. And this experience cannot be had simply by reading (it is not about being by the fire with a "good book," far from it), because reading "itself" cannot fail to be disappointing from this point of view. Rather, as they used to say, I have to write my reading, not in order to transcribe something supposedly happening somewhere else (in my head) but to prove by that tracing that the reading I never did in a conscious present, in some inner place of thought, nonetheless took place.

On what conditions does this reading take place? I do not know before seeing it written. (I am writing this not at the end, most definitely not at the beginning, but somewhere in the middle, in the hopes of saving and relaunching my reading that is not done, that seems foggy and confused, congested, rusted up, that feels like I might lose it—like retaining nothing of a dream but its disappearance—but that I do not want to lose.) The reading that will have happened is going on or is still groping around in search of itself through revisions and reorganizations of this text that I am writing in fits and starts, pressed for time (but happy to be pressed for time or obliged by time, because it is impossible to take the time that it takes to read without feeling that time diminish along the way: if one had an infinite time, which is what it would take for a truly philosophical reading, nothing would ever get read, so it always has to go fast, always too fast)—pressed for time, in a hurry to be done, to be rid of it, to be able to return to reading.

This reading may be philosophical in the sense that it is trying very simply and naïvely—as close as can be to stupidity, then—to read what is written in the text. Lack of understanding is necessary if philosophy is to be read. And this lack of understanding has to be precipitate, anticipating from the depths of its confusion the moment when it will write its own inability to understand (philosophical stupidity is not simply idiocy). Many commentaries on philosophical texts presuppose that what is in the text is already known and sorted out, even if they then contest that knowledge. Nothing is more common that the academic gesture that consists in saying: here is what was previously thought to be the content of this text, and now here is the truth of the matter. But if that can help one to get ahead, and if it does seem necessary to pay attention to it, nothing like a reading is opened in this way. And, while dreaming of being accessible to someone who has not read Kant at all (with also some slight ambition to show the most accredited readers of Kant that they have not yet read him), this reading cannot—in spite of its pedagogical ambitions—pretend to be essentially a pedagogical presentation of Kant, cannot claim to replace Kant's text with its content extracted, concentrated, and expressed.

So what is at stake in such a reading? Not simply to be accurate (no doubt that is a condition *sine qua non*, already unrealizable in practice, already of the order of the Kantian Idea, but it cannot be everything). Nor simply—in spite of some appearances—to stand under the reassuring banner of justice (because it is open to the other, all reading would supposedly be immediately ethical and/or political)[3]—unless one gives to the word *justice* a more radical sense that can be given by ethics or politics. Nor, to complete this apparently Kantian trilogy, to appeal to the aesthetic judgment. Reading, as such, cannot be answerable to these three eminently philosophical criteria (truth, justice, beauty) because it opens up their possibility and is always in withdrawal from them, like their shadow or their frontier. Reading is the frontier of thought, whereby the other (the other thought, the unthinkable, the incomprehensible) happens to it.

Trying to show that the structure of the frontier is, literally, inexhaustibly complex, fractal, I am proposing (always for reading, and so beyond any proposition, even speculative) a braid or tress that is made up of at least three threads or strings or wires. First, a partial exposition of Kant; then an argument, a claim about the quasi-concept of "frontier"; and finally a reflection (but one that must exceed any possible reflection, for reasons that will appear in the next sentence) on (philosophical) reading. But as this third thread of the braid is itself the braid (and so on *ad infinitum*), and as this fractally multiplying structure is mostly explained in the second thread, though on the basis of what is given by the first, it seems clear that this structure is not easily presentable.

Neutral

> Now, I can think of this thread as *being nowhere attached*, but floating vertically above the earth in the direction of its weight, in empty space and immensely long (as many miles as you wish), stretched by its weight to an indeterminate length in inverse proportion to the square of the distance from its mid-point:

3. The rapid appeal to "the other," to "difference," and so on, however necessary in politics and elsewhere, has also allowed the formation of a new humanist self-righteousness that only survives by foreclosing everything about the other that really is other (and therefore necessarily other than human). This book is trying to show that any thinking of the other that does not take into account the structure of the frontier cannot fail to produce this self-righteousness.

> there must be a given length of the thread at which, floating freely (attached to nothing) it breaks under its own weight: for as the moment of acceleration of the upper end is smaller than that of the lower, the latter tends to fall more strongly than the former can follow, the strange case would come about that a thread in empty space would break itself without addition of any other force (like two fists hitting against each other).

The fact remains that our point of departure is an attempt to read Kant, who also gave us something (however little) to read about (philosophical) reading.

Kant says that philosophy has to do with discursive concepts, or rather with a discursive use of reason, according to concepts. As opposed to mathematics, in which concepts are constructed and then immediately presented *a priori* to intuition, philosophy cannot construct its concepts but has to have them depend on an always uncertain *a posteriori* validation in experience.[4]

What does this mean? For us, here, that we have to *read* philosophy. It is not presented directly to intuition but goes via discursive "experiences" that we must not *decipher* but *read*. And if we must read philosophy, that means that we always run the risk of getting lost, like Kant in his old age:

> In every discourse I first prepare (the reader or the audience) for what I intend to say by indicating, in prospect, my destination and, in retrospect, the starting point of my argument (without these two points of reference a discourse has no consistency). And the result of this pathological condition[5] is that when the time comes for me to connect the two, I must suddenly ask my audience (or myself, silently): now where was I? where did I start from? This is a defect, not so much of the mind or of the memory alone, as rather of *presence of mind* (in connecting ideas)—that is, an involuntary *distraction*. It is a most distressing feeling, which one can guard against in writing, though only with great labor (especially in philosophical writing, where it is not always easy to look back

4. "Besides intuition there is no other kind of cognition than through concepts. Thus the cognition of every, at least human, understanding is a cognition through concepts, not intuitive but discursive. [. . .] Thinking is cognition through concepts. Concepts, however, as predicates of possible judgments, are related to some representation of a still undetermined object. The concept of body thus signifies something, e.g. metal, which can be cognized through that concept. It is therefore a concept only because other representations are contained under it by means of which it can be related to objects" (*CPR*, A68–69/B92–94). For the distinction between philosophy and mathematics, see especially *CPR*, B743–45.

5. Kant suggests his condition is "a kind of gout that has penetrated the brain" (*Conflict*, 205).

> to one's starting point); but despite all one's efforts, one can never obviate it completely.
>
> It is different with the mathematician [. . .] (*Conflict*, 207)

This passage is part of the concluding part to the third *Conflict*, devoted to "The Power of the Human Mind to Master Its Morbid Feelings Merely by a Firm Resolution." After subsections on sleep and diet, here are some precious pieces of advice about the practice of reading and thinking, in a subsection entitled "On Pathological Feelings That Come from Thinking at Unsuitable Times," which is worth quoting in full:

> Thinking—whether in the form of *study* (reading books) or *reflection* (meditation and discovery)—is a scholar's food; and when he is awake and *alone*, he cannot live without it. But if he taxes himself with a specific thought when he is eating or walking, he inflicts two tasks on himself at the same time—on the head and the stomach or on the head and the feet; and in the first case this brings on hypochondria, in the second, vertigo. To master these pathological states by a regimen, then, all he has to do is alternate the mechanical occupation of the stomach or the feet with the mental occupation of thinking and, while he is eating or taking a walk (restoring himself), check deliberate thought and give himself over to the free play of imagination (a quasi-mechanical activity). But, in the scholar's case, this requires the adoption, in a general way, of a firm resolution to go on a *diet with regard to thinking*.
>
> The practice of occupying oneself with reading or reflecting when dining alone provokes pathological feelings; for intellectual work diverts vital energy from the stomach and bothers it. Reflecting while taking a walk also brings on these feelings, since the work the feet are doing is already draining one's energy.* (The same thing holds true of *studying by artificial light*, if one is not used to it.) However, these pathological feelings arising from intellectual work undertaken at the wrong time (*invita Minerva*) are not the kind that can be eliminated directly and at once by sheer resolution. One can get rid of them only gradually, by breaking the habit through a principle opposed to it. And here we should be speaking only of those that can be mastered immediately.
>
> * [Kant's note] When a man of studious habits goes for a walk alone, it is hard for him to refrain from entertaining himself with his own reflections. But if he engages in strenuous thinking during his walk, he will soon be exhausted, whereas if he gives himself over to the free play of the imagination, the motion will refresh him—the reports of others whom I asked about this confirm my own experience. If in addition to thinking he also engages in conversation while he is walking, he will be even more fatigued, so that he will soon have to sit down to continue with his play of thought. The purpose of walking in the open air is precisely to keep one's attention

moving from one object to another and so *to keep it from becoming fixed* on any one object. (*Conflict*, 199)

This passage is rendered undecidable by its initial figure: from the moment that thinking (reading or meditation) is food, then in its relation to eating we are no longer sure what is the head and what the stomach, what is hypochondria and vertigo, what is mechanical and what is intentional.

—|—

How are we to mitigate this enormous disadvantage of philosophical discourse compared to mathematics (a disadvantage that is nothing other than the necessity of reading).[6] Obviously—Kant does not say anything different—by leaving signposts in the text, milestones, which indicate the direction and meaning to the reader. This direction is immediately double: In reading we have to know not only where we are going but also (Kant seems to think this is harder) where we are coming from.

Any text (of a certain complexity)[7] gives itself at least one reading. Which amounts to saying that any text reads itself, however slightly, or proposes a reading, even an institution of reading, for itself.[8] Kant does not escape this rule any more than anyone else, this rule which flows directly from the discursive nature of philosophy. As such, the philosophical text is a text that tries exhaustively to prescribe the reading appropriate to it and thus to read itself without remainder. As it must (just because it is a text) fail in this endeavor, it makes (a) space or place for the reader, all the while surrounding this place with precautions, trying to forestall readings that it does not want. The most obvious example in this regard would be Hegel's text, which is in a sense no more than the presentation of its own correct reading, the necessity of which is established in part by giving all other possible readings their partial place

6. Here and elsewhere I am indebted to Jean-Luc Nancy's brilliant *Le discours de la Syncope: Logodaedalus*.

7. To be read as in Gödel's theorem. How do we know if a given system is complex enough to give rise to undecidability—by seeing if it gives rise to undecidability. How do we know if a text is complex enough to read itself—by reading it. But as Nancy points out, this value of the undecidable can always simply settle into a new metaphysical term: "It is not enough to say that there is undecidability in a discourse. It is not enough to say it in order to have decided as to the fate, the structure or the potency of the discourse in question. Today, just about everywhere, one finds 'the undecidable' as a solution that some would gladly substitute for the well-worn solutions of such and such a 'truth,' or of Truth itself" (Nancy, *Le discours de la syncope*, 5/1).

8. See Jacques Derrida, "Mochlos ou le conflit des faculties," 422/101.

as moments in the good total reading.[9] Which is why, reading Hegel, one becomes a Hegelian (the text here is in principle already the institution of its own reading, already its own quasi-tautological saturating interpretation). Without getting into that here, what, for Kant, is it to read (Kant)? Even if advice and instructions are not plentiful, Kant says enough to guide us.

There is a notable passage in the *Theory of the Heavens* that, in fact, provides almost all the elements we shall need here:

> In the second part which contains the most essential object of this treatise, I seek to develop the constitution of the universe from the simplest state of nature through mechanical laws alone. If I may dare to suggest to those who are outraged at the boldness of this undertaking that they adopt a certain order in their examination with which they honour my thoughts, then I would request that they read the eighth chapter first, which I hope may prepare their judgement towards a correct insight. If, however, I invite the gentle reader to examine my opinions, then I am rightly concerned that, since hypotheses of this type are usually not held in higher esteem than philosophical dreams, it will be a sour favour for a reader to decide to undertake a careful examination of the histories of nature that I have thought up for myself and patiently to follow the author through the twists and turns by which he avoids the difficulties he encounters, in order finally perhaps to laugh at his own gullibility, like the audience of the London market crier. I can, however, confidently promise that if the reader is hopefully persuaded by the suggested preparatory section to dare to undertake such a physical adventure on the basis of such probable conjectures, he will not encounter as many dead ends and impassable obstacles on his way as he might have originally feared. [. . .]
>
> Finally, I ask to be permitted a short explanation relating to the validity and the presumed value of those propositions which will appear in the following theory and according to which I would wish to be examined by fair judges. The author is properly judged according to the stamp he puts on his wares; I therefore hope that one will not require any more strict responsibility of my opinions in the different parts of this treatise than the value I give to them myself. In fact, the greatest geometrical acuity and mathematical infallibility can never be demanded of a treatise of this kind. If the system is based on analogies and harmonies in accordance with the rules of credibility and a correct way of thinking, it has satisfied all the requirements of its object. [. . .]
>
> If, therefore, in the seventh chapter, enticed by the fruitfulness of the system and the attractiveness of the greatest and most admirable thing we are capable of imagining, and while adhering to the thread of analogy and a reasonable

9. See Derrida, *Glas*, 258–59/231–32.

> credibility, I extend the results of our doctrine as far as possible; if I represent the infinite nature of all creation, the formation of new worlds and the decline of the old ones and the unlimited realm of the chaos of the imagination: I hope the reader will grant the charming attractiveness of the object and the pleasure one experiences in seeing the agreement of a theory in its greatest extension, sufficient consideration so as not to judge it according to the greatest geometrical strictness, which does not in any case have any relevance in this type of consideration. It is precisely this fairness I expect in the third part. Nonetheless, the reader will find somewhat more than mere arbitrariness but somewhat less than undoubtedness in it. (*Theory of the Heavens*, 203–4)

And in a later example, reading Plato, in a famous passage we have already had occasion to quote, Kant posits rules for reading that are absolutely worthy of the interest of Kant's reader:

> Plato made use of the expression *idea* in such a way that we can readily see that he understood by it something that not only could never be borrowed from the senses, but that even goes far beyond the concepts of the understanding (with which Aristotle occupied himself), since nothing encountered in experience could ever be congruent to it. Ideas for him are archetypes of things themselves, and not, like the categories, merely the key to possible experiences. [. . .] I do not wish to go into any literary investigation here, in order to make out the sense which the sublime philosopher combined with his word. I note only that when we compare the thoughts that an author expresses about a subject, in ordinary speech as well as in writings, it is not at all unusual to find that we understand him even better than he understood himself, since he may not have determined his concept sufficiently and hence sometimes spoke, or even thought, contrary to his own intention. (*CPR*, A313–14/B370)

Can we still subscribe to this theory of reading today? Yes and no. Yes, especially now at a time of retrenchment when reading itself is being repressed again in the name of a new supposed "objectivity" or a supposed fidelity to the text, which often enough amounts to a simple refusal of reading in the name of "communication." In order to read, one must start from the possibility of understanding better than the author what is written in the text, and it would be easy to show that any (philosophical) reading is based on this presupposition, whether it be admitted or not.

And yet, this opening of reading immediately opens it up to all manner of risks. How are we to avoid the slide into subjectivism, say, once we are no longer held to the strict literality of the text, when we are claiming to improve the text, as it were, in reading it? Kant, at any rate, a little later, as we have seen, does not hesitate to give instructions for exactly this type of situation:

> The *Platonic republic* has become proverbial as a supposedly striking example of a dream of perfection that can have its place only in the idle thinker's brain; and Brucker finds it ridiculous for the philosopher to assert that a prince will never govern well unless he participates in the ideas. But we would do better to pursue this thought further, and (at those points where the excellent man leaves us without help), to shed light on it through new endeavors, rather than setting it aside as useless under the very wretched and harmful pretext of its impracticability. (*CPR*, A316/ B372–73)

What is going to guide these "new efforts"? In Kant, clearly enough, the Idea itself. Plato thought the Idea without fully thinking it, or at least without thinking it through. If we need to read or reread Plato in order to extend his thinking, we must, then, take this idea of the Idea and bring it closer to the Idea of reason itself, according to the Idea of reason itself (i.e., the Idea of reason *qua* Idea). The Idea of the (rational) Idea should be the (rational) Idea of the (rational) Idea. And so on.

We can compare this structure directly with what is said in the "Architectonic of Pure Reason," where the properly teleological nature of this theory of reading is still more clearly expounded and where we can see more clearly how it engages with the very rationality of reason. Knowledge is scientific only if it is systematic. To be systematic, to have the properly organic coherence of an animal body (*CPR*, A833/B861), it must not be rhapsodic but ordered toward an end that gives it its structure and dictates its schema, of which the scientist has an idea:

> Nobody attempts to establish a science without grounding it on an idea. But in its elaboration the schema, indeed even the definition of the science which is given right at the outset, seldom corresponds to the idea; for this lies in reason like a seed, all of whose parts still lie very involuted and are hardly recognizable even under microscopic observation. For this reason sciences, since they have all been thought out from the viewpoint of a certain general interest, must not be explained and determined in accordance with the description given by their founder, but rather in accordance with the idea, grounded in reason itself, of the natural unity of the parts that have been brought together. For the founder and even his most recent successors often fumble around [herumirren] with an idea that they have not even made distinct to themselves and that therefore cannot determine the special content, the articulation (systematic unity) and boundaries of the science.[10] (*CPR*, A834/B862)

10. Follow throughout these pages the interferences between figures and analogies from the natural world (the animal body, seeds, the fact that systems often seem in fact to be born like maggots, through *generatio aequivoca*) and those that seem more directly

What gives Kant's theory of reading its enormous—insufferable—confidence and self-assurance is its certainty of knowing (or rather of having an Idea about) what reason is and where it is going (where it *ought* to be going, in the right line of a certain rightness we shall come across again later).[11] And as it is also going toward its end, this is also the reason why we *have to* refuse, or at least modulate, this theory of reading and all it brings with it.

Does Heidegger do so in the famous passage from the *Kantbuch* in which he invokes problems of "interpretation"?[12] This important passage is worth quoting in full, including its own long inner quotation from Kant:

> Thus the fundamental intention of the present interpretation of the *Critique of Pure Reason* was to make visible in this way the decisive content of this work and thereby to bring out what Kant "had wanted to say". With this procedure, the laying-out [Auslegung] creates a maxim of its own which Kant himself would have wanted to know had been applied to the interpretation of philosophical investigations and which he put in the following words at the end of a reply to the critique by the Leibnizian Eberhard:
>
>> Thus the *Critique of Pure Reason* may well be the proper *apologia* for Leibniz, even in opposition to his adherents who elevate him with dishonorable words of praise, as it can also be for various older philosophers about whom many writers of the history of philosophy, with all their praise, still let themselves speak nonsense. They do not discover the intentions of these philosophers while they neglect the key to all interpretations [Auslegungen] of the pure products of reason on the basis of mere concepts, the critique of reason itself (as the common source for all), and while they cannot see, beyond the etymology of what their predecessors have said, what they had wanted to say.

called for by the idea of an architectonic itself, of buildings and ruins: "an architectonic to all human knowledge, which at the present time, since so much material has already been collected or can be taken from the ruins of collapsed older edifices, would not merely be possible but would not even be very difficult" (*CPR*, A835/B863).

11. The same schema rules the principles of Biblical exegesis given in *The Conflict of the Faculties*: "If a scriptural text contains certain *theoretical* teachings which are proclaimed sacred but which *transcend* all rational concepts (even moral ones), it *may be* interpreted in the interests of practical reason; but if it contains statements that contradict practical reason, it *must be* interpreted in the interests of practical reason" (*CF*, 65).

12. The book was already written when Michel Lisse's admirable work *L'expérience de la lecture: 1. La soumission* (Paris: Galilée, 1998) appeared. Lisse also reads this passage from Heidegger (63ff), and I note with satisfaction the ways in which our readings converge.

> Certainly, in order to wring from what the words say, what it is they want to say, every interpretation [Interpretation] must necessarily use violence. Such violence, however, cannot be roving arbitrariness. The power of an idea which shines forth [vorausleuchtenden Idee] must drive and guide the laying-out [Auslegung]. Only in the power of this idea can an interpretation risk what is always audacious, namely, entrusting itself to the concealed inner passion of a work in order to be able, through this, to place itself within the unsaid and force it into speech. That is one way, however, by which the guiding idea, in its power to illuminate, comes to light. (*Kant and the Problem of Metaphysics*, 141)

Heidegger appears to be subscribing unreservedly to Kant's theory of reading, which seems to be identical here to the one we read in the first *Critique*. But the passage from Kant that Heidegger chooses to quote, apparently agreeing with it, perhaps has some resources that are different from those of the passage about Plato we were quoting. The passage on Plato certainly did prescribe that one read Plato in the sense of reason, but especially against his detractors who were too quick to mock the apparently unrealistic nature of Plato's political doctrine. Here, Kant is rather reproaching the admirers of the philosophers he mentions, or at least the historians of philosophy, who clearly do not know how to read. This reference complicates things quite a lot, in that the remark quoted by Heidegger comes in the context of a defense of the first *Critique* against a bad reading (so we are looking at a defense of the very text that contains the passage on Plato that we quoted and that Eberhard, to whom Kant is replying in the passage given by Heidegger, has in principle at least already read). Whence the sense that Kant is irritated: The historians of philosophy are bad readers, and the best proof of this is that they have the people they are talking about say pure nonsense. In fact, the first *Critique* is less distant from Leibniz than the Leibnizians, who have no idea what Leibniz meant, which must be what Kant said, because Kant, in practicing the critique of pure reason, is presenting the very form in which all concepts must present themselves, and those concepts must include Leibniz's concepts to the extent that they do no fall outside the bounds of pure reason. Leibniz and the others will therefore always have meant what Kant said, and their "intention" must be the same as Kant's to the extent that they are in reason and that Kant is merely explicating that reason.

This irritation of Kant's against the historians of philosophy is made clearer in the *Prolegomena*, a text provoked, as is well known, precisely by the fact that the first *Critique* was so badly read (or at least so little read).[13] Kant's argu-

13. We would need to read the whole appendix to the *Prolegomena*, where Kant explains in sum that to judge the first *Critique* the standard of judgment has to be . . . the

ment is complex in that even though it indeed seems to confirm a certain teleologism of rational reading, it posits two different ways of presenting this reading. Two passages will suffice to show this.

First, the second paragraph of the text, in the preface:[14]

> There are scholars for whom the history of philosophy (ancient as well as modern) is itself their philosophy; the present prolegomena have not been written for them. They must wait until those who endeavor to draw from the wellsprings of reason itself have finished their business, and then it will be their turn to bring news of these events to the world. Otherwise, in their opinion nothing can be said that has not already been said before; and in fact this opinion can stand for all time as an infallible prediction, for since the human understanding has wandered over countless subjects in various ways throughout the centuries, it can hardly fail that for anything new something old should be found that has some similarity with it. (*Prolegomena*, 5)

The historians of philosophy, then, who send news reports of what is happening in the land of philosophy, always report that nothing is happening, because nothing can happen, everything already having been said. For them, reading comes down to finding an ancient precedent for every apparently new proposition.

The second passage, at the very end of the preamble, which follows the preface: These scholars, who must be quite erudite, great readers (even if they are poor readers of contemporary philosophical texts) in that they do manage to find in ancient texts everything that can be said today, are not, in fact, such great readers, because, in reality, they depend secretly on the new texts to find out what was in the old ones, which they are unable to read before they have read the new ones. The historians, who seem to be imposing order in philosophy by finding old precursors for the new philosophers, are going backward, because they only find out after the new what was in the old. For it is not false that one can find old analogies for the newest ideas: Is not my very own biggest idea, says Kant, that of the division of judgments into synthetic and analytic, already to be found in Locke?

---

first *Critique*. One can judge what gives the principle of judgment only according to its own principle of judgment. It is clearly this problem, already abyssal in the first *Critique*, that will return in the third, according to a movement that is, as I shall try to show later, anything but teleological.

14. I recall that the *Prolegomena*, apparently entirely oriented toward future metaphysics but in fact turned toward the past (in the form of the first *Critique*, precisely), have a "Preface" (*Vorrede*), then a "Preamble" (*Vorerrinnerung*: a pre-memory, which concentrates the structure we are interested in). I analyze the structure of the *Prolegomena* in greater detail in "Towards a Criticism of the Future," *Legislations*, 229–39.

> I find a hint of this division already in *Locke's* essays on human understanding. [. . .] But there is so little that is definite and reduced to rules in what he says about this type of cognition, that it is no wonder if no one, and in particular not even *Hume*, was prompted by it to contemplate propositions of this type. For such general yet nonetheless definite principles are not easily learned from others who have only had them floating obscurely before them. One must first have come to them oneself through one's own reflection, after which one also finds them elsewhere, where one certainly would not have found them before, because the authors did not even know themselves that their own remarks were grounded on such an idea. Those who never think for themselves in this way nevertheless possess the quick-sightedness to spy everything, after it has been shown to them, in what has already been said elsewhere, where no one at all could see it before. (*Prolegomena*, 22–23)

So this does not mean simply that the historians are necessarily wrong to find analogies with what has already been said, simply that they do not understand that what these analogies reveal is what is *new* in the new.

Kant will not disagree that nothing is more common than to see old ideas presented as though they were new:

> We have long been accustomed to seeing old, threadbare cognitions newly trimmed by being taken from their previous connections and fitted out by someone in a systematic garb of his own preferred cut, but under new titles; and most readers will beforehand expect nothing else even from this critique. Yet these *Prolegomena* will bring them to understand that there exists a completely new science, of which no one had previously formed merely the thought, of which even the bare idea was unknown, and for which nothing from all that has been provided before now could be used except the hint that *Hume's* doubts had been able to give. (*Prolegomena*, 11)

This gesture is complex, and it is easy to get lost between the old and the new, the apparently new and the apparently old. See too, in a note to "What Is Orientation in Thinking," just after the passage quoted above batting off an accusation of Spinozism, Kant continues:

> Similarly, another scholar detects *skepticism* in the *Critique of Pure Reason*, although the whole intention of this work is to reach firm and definite conclusions on the scope of our *a priori* knowledge. He likewise detects a *dialectic* in these critical investigations, although their whole aim is to resolve and eliminate for good that dialectic in which pure reason inevitably becomes trapped and entangled when everyone uses it in a dogmatic manner. The Neo-Platonists, who called themselves Eclectics because they managed to discover their own

> conceits throughout the works of earlier authors after they had themselves imported them into these, proceeded in exactly the same way; so in this respect, there is nothing new under the sun. (*KPW*, 246–47n)

On the basis of what is new, one realizes after the fact that it is perhaps not all that new, even if, if truth be told, it had never been properly thought out before. So Locke never really thought out the distinction between analytic and synthetic judgments, even if the distinction is stated in his text, as we realize after reading Kant.

So one can read Kant's theory of philosophical reading two ways. First, we read upstream, as it were, according to reason that determines teleologically what will have been said by Plato or Leibniz, for example. We can figure out what Plato "meant" by his idea of the Idea, in spite of the obscurity of his writing, by reading according to the order of reason, which wants "Idea" to mean what Kant says it means in reading Plato in this way. But, second, this is possible only if Kant had already found, *sponte sua*, independently of Plato or anyone else, what is truly said by the word *Idea*, only to realize after the fact that the other had, obscurely it is true, thought and said it before him. The historian of philosophy goes wrong by thinking that, because it has been said before, nothing new has been said now, which it has insofar as it has been said *anew*; but it would also be a mistake to think that one can do completely without the history of philosophy and only read the new, because it is that history that bequeaths us a language that is still obscure but whose obscurity can be pierced by the double movement of philosophical reading.

How could one not agree?[15]

But does Heidegger, in taking up this theory of Kant's, say anything new? This is a complex situation: Kant has bequeathed to us a way of understanding

15. It is not surprising to find exactly this schema at work in the Hegelian or Lacanian reaction to deconstructive work. It is loudly announced that this work brings nothing new, because everything it says (when read, badly, as a critique of Hegel or Lacan) is supposedly already there in Hegel or Lacan. So, for example, it is asserted that Derrida produces a bad reading of Hegel, then to attack a falsely teleological version of Absolute Knowing in the name of a "differance" that turns out, supposedly, to have been already thought by Hegel himself. One finds that Hegel, when read in a certain way, is already the thinker of differance, etc., forgetting that Derrida is not claiming anything other when he *reads* in Hegel (it is "in" Hegel, to be read) something no one could see there before. It could be shown that this is an *a priori* structure of misrecognition (of misreading) that defines historicism as such.

the relation of philosophy to its past, according to which the new is said anew. So we might expect that Heidegger, in taking up anew this new "anew," would do so *anew*. If the passage we quoted does introduce something new into these tangled relations, it seems to be the motif of *violence*. Reading Kant according to Kant's Idea, according to Heidegger, would not happen without violence. But this violence is not simply violence, to the extent that it is guided or channeled by "the power of an idea which shines forth." Under the influence of an Idea (which is not itself violent), violence mutates into power, still with an element of risk and audacity, because the idea of the work is not stated in the work, all the while constituting its "concealed inner passion [verborgenen inneren Leidenschaft]." The inner passion gives the idea, which is confirmed by its capacity to illuminate the inner passion.

And yet, in spite of what seems new in this idea of violence, this Heideggerian reading of Kant's theory of reading remains Kantian: The transformation of brute violence into ideal light constitutes the very movement of Kant's thought, the very idea of its idea as sense-giving Idea. And this reading of Heidegger's reading of Kant's reading of reading again confirms the strange *nachträglich* logic we saw in the *Prolegomena*, because it is without a doubt Heidegger's reading that allows us to uncover in Kant the thought of the aftereffect that allows us to claim that Heidegger is confirming Kant, etc.

While recognizing all that is powerful and indispensable in this schema, especially when it comes to the refutation of the historian's reading of philosophy, we need to pursue the privilege still granted by Heidegger to the Idea itself. This idea of the Idea (as guiding or inspiring) that confirms the Platonic heritage, which Kant, as we saw, was the first to acknowledge, still remains the guiding Idea of Heidegger's remarks here. Which, of course, agrees with Heidegger's own insistence on the repetition at play in his reading.[16]

16. The last words of this third section of the *Kantbuch* (followed immediately by the fourth section that inscribes this motif of repetition in its title): "The laying of the ground for metaphysics grows upon the ground of time. The question concerning Being, the grounding question for a laying of the ground for metaphysics, is the problem of *Being and Time*. This title contains the guiding idea of the preceding interpretation of the *Critique of Pure Reason* as a laying of the ground for metaphysics. The idea, however, attested to through this interpretation, provides an indication of the problem of a fundamental ontology. This is not to be grasped as something supposedly 'new,' as opposed to the allegedly 'old.' Rather, it is the expression of the attempt to adopt in an original way what is essential in a laying of the ground for metaphysics, i.e., to aid in the ground-laying through a repetition [Wiederholung] of its own, more original possibility" (*Kant and the Problem of Metaphysics*, 141–42).

The guiding idea is the guiding idea, and this idea, even if it does not go without some violence, nonetheless places violence on the path of its retro-teleological justification.

Can we (ought we) escape from this very potent model of philosophical reading, that remains proudly, virilely, metaphysical through and through? Would we then, in laying claim to a certain violence of reading but trying to withdraw that violence from the perspective of the Idea (and therefore from interpretation in the strict sense and, *a fortiori*, from intended meaning, even if it were unconscious or secret)—would we then be allowing ourselves to venture into what Heidegger calls "roving arbitrariness"? Or, if we violently transpose this question into the vocabulary of this book, can we read, in violence, outside the perspective of (perpetual) peace, without losing meaning and ending up in "pure nonsense"? In other words, is there meaning that is not in the end that of reason? This is clearly the question that will have been not on the horizon of this book, but between every sentence, in every punctuation sign.

So we cannot here prejudge that question. But even supposing that we manage, after our passage through this theory of philosophical reading (which there is no question of simply refusing), to think a reading that is not ruled by the perspective of the Idea of the Idea of Reason, it would not do to rush too rapidly to the thought that we could read without ever appealing to a guiding thread. For even supposing that reading begins when repetition and recitation stop, even supposing that reading must at a certain moment abandon the text without immediately knowing which way to turn, how is it to orient itself?[17]

If these questions are unavoidable with respect to any text (how do we read once we *read*, once we are no longer content with more or less erudite commentary and even interpretation—for the opening to reading we are talking about must *de jure* precede any erudition, which tends to operate the authoritarian foreclosure of that opening), we might suspect that they take on a peculiar complexity when the text to be read (supposing that we can fix its bounds and limits) is signed by Immanuel Kant. For as we happily appeal to the notions of guiding thread and orientation, we cannot for long ignore the fact that these notions are to a certain extent themselves Kantian, signed with

17. It would not be difficult to show, on the basis of "What Is Orientation in Thought?," that this very question only really arises in situations where orientation is impossible. Thought seeks to orient itself only when the Orient (the origin) has been definitively lost.

Kant's name. Even if we are wary of the idea of the Idea of reason, we must nonetheless seek in the text for a guiding thread (or run the risk of not reading at all). But this guiding thread risks at every moment getting entwined with the guiding thread (*der Leitfaden*) itself, the (as always discursive) concept or figure of guiding thread that runs throughout Kant's text.[18]

To avoid getting tangled up, then, perhaps we should simplify things for a while and take as a provisional guiding thread for reading Kant the guiding thread itself, which he has left behind in the labyrinth of his work to help the reader find his way.

What is the guiding thread? Kant does not present it directly in the context of his discussion of reading. He appeals to it rather in situations in which an empirical complexity risks overwhelming the philosopher who wants to get a clear view of things, to the point, as in the opening of the "Universal History" text, of provoking his dismay. The guiding thread will help one to find one's way out of the labyrinth of the empirical (the figure of which is always diversity and dispersion) precisely by providing guidance, or at least an orientation, toward the exit. The guiding thread, which is indispensable in philosophy, is always a technical aid designed to help its user find the way out.[19]

The guiding thread initially accompanies the adventurer, who does not have a clear sense of where he is going or of what he might find when he gets

18. It has become common to find and even follow the *Leitfaden* in the third *Critique* and the political writings, but the term *Leitfaden* appears very early in the first *Critique*, in the title of the subsection entitled "Von dem Leitfaden der Entdeckung aller reiner Verstandbegriffe," translated as "On the Clue to the Discovery of All Pure Concepts of the Understanding" (*CPR*, A66/B91).

19. Empiricity always retains something of the character of matter in general—i.e., of *chaotic dispersion*, such as that from which Kant has the cosmos emerge in *Theory of the Heavens*: "I assume that when all matter of which the spheres that constitute our solar system, all the planets and comets, consist, was dissolved into its elementary basic material at the beginning of all things, it occupied the entire space of the universe in which these formed bodies now orbit. This state of nature, even if one considers it in and for itself without regard to any system, appears to be the simplest that could follow upon nothingness. At that time, nothing had formed yet. The arrangement of heavenly bodies distant from one another, their distance moderated by attraction, and their shape that derives from the equilibrium of the assembled matter, are a later state. Nature as it bordered directly on creation, was as raw, as unformed as possible. However, even in the essential properties of the elements that make up chaos, the characteristic of that perfection can be felt that they have from their origin, in that their essence is a consequence of the eternal idea of divine reason. The simplest, the most universal properties that

there. Not only does the one who carries the end of the guiding thread not entirely know where he is going, but he knows that the guiding thread will not help him find out. If he carries the thread, it is to leave a trail or trace behind him, an inscription of the path he will have taken. This trace has a double function: On the one hand, the point is for the adventurer to be able to retrace his path in the other direction, to escape after the more or less hazardous encounter he risks having in the labyrinth, if he gets to the center, if it has a center; but on the other hand, this trace is useful to those who come after, either to bring help if he does not return after a certain length of time (but how long, exactly?) or to try again to bring off the adventure he may not have brought to a successful conclusion (how are we to know, if he has not come back?).

In the first case, one breaks a path that was closed or unknown until now. Here the guiding thread is of no immediate use and does not help to determine the path to take. At most one can use it to retrace one's steps after a trip that went nowhere, and perhaps leave it there to mark the path *not* to

appear to have been designed without any intention, matter that seems to be merely passive and in need of forms and arrangement, has, in its simplest state, an endeavour to form itself into a more perfect state by a natural development. However, *the difference in the kinds of elements* contributes the greatest part to the regulation of nature and the formation from chaos by which the state of rest that would prevail under a universal equality among the dispersed elements, is eliminated and the chaos in the points of the more strongly attracting particles begins to form. The species of this basic material are without doubt infinitely varied judging by the immeasurability nature shows in all directions. For that reason, those with the greatest specific density and attractive force, which, on their own, occupy less space and are also less common, will, with the same distribution throughout the space of the world, be more widely dispersed than the lighter types. Elements of 1,000 times greater specific mass are a thousand, perhaps a million times more dispersed than those lighter by the same measure. And since these gradations have to be thought of as being as infinite as possible, the former type of dispersed elements will be distant by a so much greater distance from one another as the latter, just as there can be bodily constituents of one type that exceeds another in density in the same measure as a sphere that has been described with the radius of the solar system does another that has a diameter of one thousandth of a line./ In a space filled in such a way, universal rest lasts only a moment. The elements have essential forces to put each other into motion and they are a source of life for themselves. Matter immediately endeavours to form itself" (*Theory of the Heavens*, 227–28). *Mutatis mutandis*, the pure manifold of sensation in the first *Critique* retains something of this character of dispersion, as does the potentially "rhapsodic" character of perceptions that would not be unified into experience by being my experience (*CPR*, A156/B195) or indeed of disorganized philosophical exposition (A81/B106; A832/B860).

take next time, until one finds the path (a path) that leads . . . where, exactly? To the end? That is, a specific place one knew of in advance and at which one hoped to arrive? Or perhaps (necessarily, in fact) the place where, after the fact, having arrived, one finds an end whose existence or nature one did not know, or that one did not know *was* the end.

This venturesome sense of the guiding thread is the one that is dominant (without being named as such) in, for example, the opening to the preface of the second edition of the first *Critique*:

> Whether or not the treatment of the cognitions belonging to the concern of reason travels the secure course of a science is something which can soon be judged by its success. If, after many preliminaries and preparations are made, a science gets stuck as soon as it approaches its end, or if in order to reach this end it must often go back and set out on a new path; or likewise if it proves impossible for the different co-workers to achieve unanimity as to the way in which they should pursue their common aim; then we may be sure that such a study is merely groping about [herumtappen], that it is still far from having entered upon the secure course of a science; and it is already a service to reason if we can possibly find that path for it, even if we have to give up as futile much of what was included in the end previously formed without deliberation. (Bvii)[20]

This whole preface is written under the sign of the path to be broken or traced. Whereas logic, mathematics, and physics have entered on the correct path, metaphysics has not yet found it. Metaphysics, which must find its own path for itself (be its own pupil, says Kant), has not got there yet, even though it is older than the other sciences just named, and even though it would survive "even if all the others were swallowed up by an all-consuming barbarism [in dem Schlunde einer alles vertilgenden Barbarei gänzlich verschlungen werden sollten]" (*CPR*, Bxiv; this *Schlunde* or yawning chasm is again what we are calling "frontier").

But once the correct path has been found, the point is to leave the guiding thread in place so that everyone can follow. In the case of speculative reason, where hypotheses become apodictic demonstrations, in principle all the reader has to do is hold on tight to the guiding thread and follow along,

20. See too the *Prolegomena*, which are proposed as being "the plan and guide [als Plane und Leitfaden] for the investigation, and not the work itself," that is, the first *Critique*, which "abandons all the usual paths and adopts a new one" (*Prolegomena*, 131, 130). The motif of the *Herumtappen* is the object of a remarkable analysis by Diane Morgan in *Kant Trouble: The Obscurities of the Enlightened* (London: Routledge, 2000).

however difficult the path may be at times. From time to time one might stop with the guide to admire the scenery or to look back at the ground covered. Sometimes one might even listen patiently to stories of the misadventures of other travelers, and one might especially remember the story of a certain *Seefahrer* whose fate we envied a little in spite of everything. But in principle, by reading on along the guiding thread, we will eventually reach the end.

This way of thinking about the guiding thread has, then, two distinct moments: that of the adventurer who more or less heroically finds the right path and that of the reader who does not have to seek in this way but simply to follow the guide. And yet, this is not how Kant explicitly uses the figure of the guiding thread. If we are indeed dealing with a situation in which one is faced with an empirical confusion, a disorganized space that at first sight does not offer a clear path to follow (so this space can be a desert or an ocean as well as a labyrinth, and perhaps especially a desert or an ocean, where the trace of the path taken by ship or camel disappears more or less rapidly, making it harder to retrace it later),[21] the guiding thread is used in situations where one will never arrive at the certainty of having followed the right path, where the hypothesis will never be transformed into apodictic certainty. Where, before, the guide could with absolute certainty indicate the right path that had been found at last, now he can only suggest a path to the reader without ever establishing that it is the only one possible. Here the guiding thread is chosen among others that are possible. It surely leads somewhere (for there are no *chemins qui ne mènent nulle part*),[22] but one does not know exactly where it goes before getting there, and nothing guarantees arrival. Here the adventure is radicalized: Where, before, it ended up opening a sure path whence adventure was henceforth excluded, except in the form of the more or less hair-raising tales of others' misadventures, we are now following a guiding thread in which we can never place our full confidence but on which we must depend all the more because it is our only resource where we are, always somewhat lost in nature.

We choose to have confidence in the guiding thread because we have no

21. See Jorge Luis Borges's story "The Two Kings and the Two Labyrinths," where the desert turns out to be the ultimate labyrinth. Recall Kant's admiration for the camel as "ship of the desert."

22. "Chemins qui ne mènent nulle part" is the title of a poem written in French by Rilke (number 31 of the *Quatrains valaisans* [1924]) and is used, without being attributed as such, for the title of the French translation of Heidegger's volume *Holzwege*. I exploit the literal meaninglessness of the idea of a road leading nowhere in the more elaborated reading of Frege's distinction between *Sinn* and *Bedeutung* in *Frontiers*, 320–21.

choice if we want to find our way out. The thread can mislead, be a poor guide, but we cannot but follow it. So the guiding thread is a strange concept (?) in Kant, and one that immediately doubles up. The guiding thread reassures us that there must be a guiding thread. It promises that there is a way out (from nature), and this way out turns out to be the promise that there is a way out. At the end of the guiding thread we find the guiding thread. It is the third *Critique* that makes this arresting and vertiginous logic most explicit:

> This agreement of nature with our faculty of cognition is presupposed *a priori* by the power of judgment in behalf of its reflection on nature in accordance with empirical laws, while at the same time the understanding recognizes it objectively as contingent, and only the power of judgment attributes it to nature as transcendental purposiveness (in relation to the cognitive faculty of the subject): because without presupposing this, we would have no order of nature in accordance with empirical laws, hence no guideline [Leitfaden] for an experience of this in all its multiplicity and for research into it. (*CJ*, 72)

According to this logic, the guiding thread is always a guiding thread that leads to the guiding thread. This could take some time. This thread has, properly speaking, no end, and we can, and even must, follow it indefinitely. Its *end* is that there must be an end, but we can approach this end only without end.[23]

Ground

> How would it be if an iron thread pulled by magnetic force were to break under its own weight?

If, then, in order to read Kant, we could only take the guiding thread as our guiding thread (according to a contingent necessity that we are trying to think through), we would read nothing but the guiding thread without end. So we must absolutely choose a guiding thread other than the guiding thread itself if we really want to read. According to a supplementary fold of necessity and contingency, this choice (but the term "choice" will not do, for we are as far as can be from the subjectivity implied by such a concept) must necessarily be contingent and must be made *for* contingency, in the name of contingency. In this book, we have indeed chosen a guiding thread that, as we are slowly coming to see, names contingency itself (i.e., the frontier). Our working hypothesis is that Kant, whose entire philosophy is an attempt to

23. So we should have to say that in Kant *all* purposiveness is without purpose, or that the purpose of purposiveness is its very purposiveness (without purpose).

think the frontier as bound or limit[24] (or as the frontier between bound and limit: we dwell at length on Kant's distinction between *Grenze* and *Schranke* in the Appendix), never manages to think the frontier itself, while thinking of nothing but that. Kant *limits* the frontier.

Clearly, such a guiding thread is not even a guiding thread if "guiding thread" always implies, as we have just suggested, its own endless hypothetico-teleological confirmation. Because *frontier* names that which will inevitably cut any such thread, or perhaps the weight of the thread that will inevitably stretch it to breaking point. And so our reading, which set off to follow the guiding thread of the frontier, on the basis of texts where it seems it must be thought of literally and directly (i.e., the "political" texts, and especially the *Perpetual Peace* text that is, as it were, our guiding text), ends up sooner or later with the end of the thread in its hand. But this end, where the fibers of the cord are beginning to unravel, where the dis-tress begins, this end that must be somewhere, is at no determinable place on the *Seekarte* of Kant's system. This uncertainty, which we think is radical (or more than radical, as there is no root to dig up here), is that of the frontier itself, which is never a simple line and always has a thickness, an abyssal zone where one finds oneself between . . . what and what? We do not know. In no-man's-land.

Happily for us, the frontier (which as such is pure space or spacing, the priority of space—the "final frontier"—over time) cannot be pure and must cash out into plural and heterogeneous frontiers (which is why *frontier* is not a proper noun, not a concept or even an idea). In Kant, the frontier can be said to be nature, violence, warfare, radical evil, contingency, but also providence, critique, or peace. By allowing what is no longer a guiding thread to spread and disperse in this way, we are tending in our reading of Kant's universe to follow a movement that can seem to be the converse of the one Kant imagines at the origin of the universe. Encouraging a certain dispersion, we are of course laying claim to a certain "materialism." But this materialism (which is "immaterial," as Lyotard might say)[25] is not on its way (retro-teleologically, as it were) to any terminal dispersion, which would be merely the negative

24. See Jacques Derrida: "Kantianism is not only a powerfully organized network of conceptual limits, a critique, a metaphysics, a dialectic, a discipline of pure reason. It is a discourse that presents itself as an essential project of *delimitation*: a thinking of the limit as *positing* the limit, foundation or legitimation of judgment with respect to these limits" (*Du droit à la philosophie*, 89/54; tr. mod.).

25. This book bears the traces of unpaid and unpayable debts: to recent readings of Kant by Jean-François Lyotard (that I also contest here or there), by Jean-Luc Nancy (unsurpassable), and by Jacques Derrida, whose importance for this book is beyond calculation and obviously is not limited to his work explicitly on Kant.

image of some absolute knowledge. If matter cannot gather itself enough to *be* matter without immediately idealizing itself (according to Hegel's demonstration in the Introduction to the *Philosophy of History*)[26] no more can it be absolutely dispersed (because all absolutes come down to the same). The stuff of our reading, then, is held in a partial dispersion, partially gathered, sufficiently (or so we hope) to give some access to the intelligibility and rationality it can only also contest.

It is obvious that such a dispersing reading sits uncomfortably with the linear order of the book. The guiding thread gives a sense of order, but what cuts it goes against that order. This text is made up of cuttings of Kant, cuttings that are juxtaposed, gathered up, scattered again.

---

26. "Matter possesses gravity in virtue of its tendency toward a central point. It is essentially composite; consisting of parts that exclude each other. It seeks its Unity; and therefore exhibits itself as self-destructive, as verging toward its opposite. If it could attain this, it would be Matter no longer, it would have perished. It strives after the realization of its Idea; for in Unity it exists ideally" (G. W. F. Hegel, *The Philosophy of History*, tr. J. Sibree [Mineola, NY: Dover, 1956], 31). See too Derrida's commentary in *Glas*, 29–30/22–23.

4. Radical Nature

> This reveals to us a strange and unexpected pattern in human affairs (such as we shall always find if we consider them in the widest sense, in which nearly everything is paradoxical). A high degree of civil freedom seems advantageous to a people's *intellectual* freedom, yet it also sets up insuperable barriers to it. Conversely, a lesser degree of civil freedom gives intellectual freedom enough room to expand to its fullest extent.
>
> —Immanuel Kant, "What Is Enlightenment?"

One might wonder: Where is politics according to Kant? What is its place in the great rational systematics?

Neither in the Architectonic of the first *Critique*, nor in the preface to the *Groundwork for the Metaphysics of Morals*, nor in the introduction to the third *Critique* does Kant make an explicit place for politics. Recall that the great division of the system (once logic has been separated out) into philosophy of nature and moral philosophy (*CPR*, A840/B868) sets up the conflict we will be examining: The political moralist will place politics on the side of nature; the moral politician, in principle at least, on the side of morality. We might expect that the introduction to the *Metaphysics of Morals* would decide, when it makes a distinction, within moral laws, between juridical laws and properly moral laws (the distinction that will motivate the division into a Doctrine of Right and a Doctrine of Virtue); but we shall see that only the political moralist thinks politics is entirely on the side of right, because the mere legality of an action decides nothing as to its political morality, and this is also the case in what Kant calls moral anthropology. Especially in his doctrinal texts, Kant does tend to try to keep politics in the realm of right. But we shall see that he regularly recognizes that politics is political only to the extent it does not remain simply in that realm. Which is why politics finds a certain truth in illegality, and especially in the absolute illegality of revolution.

So to the question "Where is politics?" we reply (because Kant does not reply): On the frontier, or, rather, *in* the frontier, in the transitional spaces, between the great divisions of the system. As politics in Kant's descriptions depends on a remainder of violent nature inscribed along frontiers, a remainder that cosmopolitanism does not absorb, politics will be inscribed as a frontier in Kant's text every time he draws a frontier in it. "Political" will be, then, the frontier between nature and *Sitten*, between critique and doctrine, between understanding and reason, between concept and idea, between determinative judgment and reflective judgment, etc.

The frontier in its "proper" sense subsists, then, in international and even cosmopolitan right, whether as the most visible sign of the evil rooted in mankind or as the index of a vital tension in the equilibrium of nations. This peaceful equilibrium of States, which, as we saw, becomes the substitute *telos* in the face of the mortal perspective of a World State, may be based on a federation and, therefore, not be quite the same as a simple "balance of power." But it seems that power and balance there still must be, and, we might be tempted to say against Kant's explicit intention, risk of catastrophic collapse of the sort that appears at the end of the "Theory and Practice" text:

> Nowhere does human nature appear less admirable than in the relationships which exist between peoples. No state is for a moment secure from the others in its independence and its possessions. The will to subjugate the others or to grow at their expense is always present, and the production of armaments for defence, which often makes peace more oppressive and more destructive of internal welfare than war itself, can never be relaxed. And there is no possible way of counteracting this except a state of international right [einem allgemeinen Völkerstaat], based upon enforceable public laws to which each state must submit (by analogy with a state of civil or political right among individual men). For a permanent universal peace by means of a so-called *European balance of power* is a pure illusion, like Swift's story of the house which the builder had constructed in such perfect harmony with all the laws of equilibrium that it collapsed as soon as a sparrow alighted on it.[1] (*KPW*, 91–92)

How are we to understand Kant's hesitations around cosmopolitanism? Reading these texts, we do not really know what to think about it anymore. On the one hand, it must be admitted as the only *telos* worthy of reason, like

1. In this 1793 text, Kant still seems to believe in the International State: The theory of right "recommends to us earthly gods the maxim that we should proceed in our disputes in such a way that such an *allgemeinen Völkerstaat* [and not *Völkerbund*; the translation here reverts for no textual reason to 'a universal federal state' to translate what just a few lines earlier was 'a state of international right,' which is also misleading as it suggests a *Zustand* rather than what is here explicitly a *Staat*] may be inaugurated, so that we should therefore assume that it is *possible* (*in praxi*)" (*KPW*, 92). It is only really in *Perpetual Peace* itself that the clearer (though still far from clear) distinction between the International State (as Idea of reason) and the realizable Federation (as negative surrogate) is put in place.

a state that one *ought to* realize and that providential nature *will* realize even against our will. On the other hand, we have to see in it the greatest danger, because a World State could only be a monarchy that would inevitably become despotic and fall into anarchy and renewed violence. And if we fall back on the idea of a federation of states in view of peace, no longer as the preliminary sketch of what a true cosmopolitan State of the World will be, not even as its negative surrogate but as the only way to realize perpetual peace, between the state of nature and the peace of the graveyard, then we must accept that cosmopolitan right be restricted and that tension and danger, and therefore nature and frontiers, be maintained, in a precarious equilibrium that a sparrow always might destroy in truly catastrophic fashion.

The frontier on which we are perched here, more or less balanced, more or less exposed to danger, is most obviously the frontier that passes between morality and politics. Or rather, given that we are claiming that politics is itself a frontier, between morality and mechanical necessity. This means that we are situated at the center of the great Kantian division between mechanism and freedom, necessity and obligation, and this is why Kant will add a long appendix (*Anhang*) to the *Perpetual Peace* text to demonstrate that there can be no conflict between politics and morality, insofar as the former is merely the "applied branch" (*KPW*, 116) of the latter. It is indeed a question of frontiers:

> The frontier-god [der Grenzgott] of morality does not yield to Jupiter, the frontier-god of violence [Gewalt], for even Jupiter is still subject to fate. In short, reason is not sufficiently enlightened to discover the whole series of predetermining causes which would allow it to predict accurately the happy or unhappy consequences of human activities as dictated by the mechanism of nature; it can only hope that the result will meet with its wishes. But reason at all times shows us clearly enough what we have to do in order to remain in the paths of duty, as the rules of wisdom require, and thus shows us the way towards our ultimate goal [Endzweck]. (*KPW*, 116; tr. mod.)

The fact remains that these relations are extremely complex. We thought we had understood that there could be no disagreement between politics and morality to the extent that they were respectively practical and theoretical, but the topography in question turns out to be more complicated. Kant has just posited an absolute superiority of morality over politics; so it is not that "honesty is the best policy" (it often is not) but rather that "honesty is better than any policy" (*KPW*, 116), which complicates any theory/practice distinction. For even if morality is theoretical, it is theoretical only by being immediately practical also (the moral law is a chimera if it is not in principle applicable, practicable). And if politics is assuredly practical, it must not for all that simply take morality to be its theory. Because the practical man (*der Praktiker*) can very well recognize morality *qua theory*, and even as *practical theory* (recognize, that is, that we *can* do what we *ought to do* [*selbst bei eingeräumtem* Sollen *und* Können]), but still object that we do not *want* to do what we ought and can do (namely, that which will lead to perpetual peace). We would then have to admit that right (public right, at any rate) rests on a *coup de force* (because the people do not want right), which immediately opens a space between right and politics, theory and practice, and seems to make politics into a domain the theory of which cannot be fully theoretical but which must accept that it draws its maxims from the real world as it is. This argument gives rise to the political moralist to whom Kant, in a famous argument, is going to oppose the moral politician. The point is not to separate morality and politics but to separate two ways of conceiving of their relation. As we shall see, Kant has the greatest difficulty drawing the frontier (necessary for all this thinking) between these two positions.

Let me briefly summarize what distinguishes these two characters. The political moralist sees the world as ruled purely by mechanical force-relations, or as a nature. It follows that for him politics consists in using this mechanism to govern people with a view to defined goals (which might even be praiseworthy goals, even perpetual peace itself) and that morality is essentially just a rhetoric designed to facilitate this mechanical activity. The model for the political moralist is, curiously enough, the professional jurist (i.e., one for whom the law is a career, work [*Handwerk*] and not a question of legislation—it is not easy to imagine a professional legislator . . .), who leaves his profession to enter politics. As such, the jurist is concerned not with legislation but with the application of existing laws, whatever they be. This application is, then, mechanical in that the laws are being thought of on the model of the laws of the physical world.[2] Kant has nothing against this, to the extent that, as we have seen, civil laws are necessarily accompanied by force (without which they would not be applicable in the face of the opposite force—natural violence—that humans put up against the law, *qua* natural and therefore selfish individuals) and, consequently, function like a nature ruled mechanically. But those jurists who then feel justified in leaving this quasi-mechanical sphere

2. We can see more clearly how that never could be moral by keeping in mind Jean-Luc Nancy's pithy formulation, according to which in Kant "the [moral] law is the law *to make the law*" (*L'impératif catégorique* [Paris: Flammarion, 1983], 16). But as I suggested above, this "law to make the law" cannot project its end in a *law made* and must always be law *in the making*.

to reflect on law in general, to cross the frontier between the administrative application of the law and politics proper,

> cannot take this step except in a spirit of chicanery, for they will follow their usual procedure of applying despotically formulated coercive laws in a mechanical manner, even in a sphere where the concepts of reason only allow for lawful coercion, in keeping with the principles of freedom, which alone makes possible a rightfully established political constitution. (*KPW*, 119)

The political moralist will set goals and then seek technical means to reach them; he knows in advance where he wants to go and then, taking account of empirical circumstances (including what he believes he knows about human nature and the current and historical practice of politics), calculates how to get there, all the while inventing a pragmatic morality to justify himself. The political moralist makes use of shady practices (*Praktiken*: underhanded methods) rather than true *praxis* (*Praxis*).

Over against the political moralist, then, the moral politician. One senses that Kant will have a hard time defining him: If he is too moral, we will no longer be in the domain of politics, which is what we are discussing; if he is too political, we will fall back into natural mechanism. The moral politician believes that "the principles of political expediency" ("die Prinzipien der Staatsklugheit," more literally: the principles of political prudence), which are not the same as moral principles, can be reconciled with morality, which has an absolute priority. A moral politics cannot be *simply* moral but must be moral above all else. It cannot ignore the quasi-mechanical world of existing laws but must not think about it either. It must not treat the practical world as a mechanical world but must treat it as if it were a mechanical world, or rather as an *as-if* mechanical world.

To make the separation he needs (and in so doing, because this is crucial, "ensure that practical philosophy is at one with itself"), Kant takes up again from a great height a distinction that rules over his whole philosophy—namely, the distinction between the material and the formal:

> To ensure that practical philosophy is at one with itself, it is first necessary to resolve the question of whether, in problems of practical reason, we should begin with its *material* principle, i.e. its *end*, as an object of the will, or with its *formal* principle, i.e. the principle which rests on man's freedom in his external relations [äussern Verhaltnis] and which states: "Act in such a way that [handle so, dass] you can wish your maxim to become a universal law (irrespective of what the end in view may be)." (*KPW*, 121–22)

On the side of the material principle, we have the political moralist, who has an end in view (perhaps even a praiseworthy end) and who calculates according to mechanical laws how to get to it; on the side of the formal principle (which is really just the categorical imperative), we have the moral politician. This principle may well (and, in fact, must) encourage the advent of perpetual peace but must not be invoked as though perpetual peace were its goal. But there is a paradox here that is going to trouble the distinction between politics and morality and, therefore, between political moralist and moral politician: It turns out that the moral politician, who does not have his eyes fixed on the goal (perpetual peace), is better at moving toward that goal than the other guy, who does not take his eyes off it. The reason is that the political moralist, for whom bringing about perpetual peace is a technical task and who needs to make crafty prudential calculations about natural mechanism, is unable to ground his calculus in necessity. History gives examples of all sorts of political arrangements giving rise to all sorts of results, in fact. Where we thought we might be in the domain of necessity (nature envisaged as a mechanism), we find ourselves in the domain of contingency and uncertainty, and where we might have thought we were far from reality, in the domain of pure morality, we are apparently, and a little magically, more realistic. The reason for this (although Kant does not lay it out in this way) is that the position taken influences the way things turn out. The political moralist, just by trying to calculate according to natural mechanism, in fact breaks that mechanism, whereas the moral politician, who has no regard for the mechanics of it, in reality favors the goal he does not have in view but that he will achieve as though it were a bonus prize:

> For morality, with regard to its principles of public right (hence in relation to a political code which can be known *a priori*), has the peculiar feature that the less it makes its conduct depend upon the end it envisages (whether this be a physical or moral advantage), the more it will in general harmonise with this end. And the reason for this is that it is precisely the general will [allgemeine Wille] as it is given *a priori*, within a single people or in the mutual relationships of various peoples, which alone determines what is right among men. But this union of the will of all [diese Vereinigung des Willens aller], if only it is put into practice in a consistent way, can also, within the mechanism of nature, be the cause which leads to the intended result and gives effect to the concept of right. (*KPW*, 123)[3]

3. See too in the eighth proposition of the "Universal History" text: "In the present case, it is especially hard to be indifferent, for it appears that we might by our own rational projects accelerate the coming of this period which will be so welcome to our descendants" (*KPW*, 50).

The very fact of looking anywhere but at the goal can become a cause for the goal to be realized. And conversely, for the theory of the political moralists, who attempt to show that the mechanical behavior of mankind in society outplays moral goals:

> Such theories are particularly damaging, because they may themselves produce the very evil they predict.[4] For they put man into the same class as other living machines, which only need to realise consciously that they are not free beings for them to become in their own eyes the most wretched of all earthly creatures. (*KPW*, 123)

The moral politician, then, who is not concerned about the efficacy of his position, is by that very fact more efficacious than the efficacy man, the political moralist. Above all do not look where we are going, and we will get there all the sooner. The natural mechanism cannot fail to mislead you if you rely on it but will serve you if you do not think about it. Think not about what you want to bring about, because nature will not help you, but about what you *ought* to bring about, independently of any realism, and, voilà, it will get done thanks to this same natural mechanism. That is the problem of political wisdom (*Staatsweisheitproblem*) that characterizes the moral politician, whereas the political moralist is concerned with mere political prudence (*Staats-Klugheitproblem*).

Let's pause for a moment over this value of prudence, *Klugheit*. Kant's whole moral philosophy is based on excluding it, apparently without appeal. For example, in the first *Critique*:

> In the doctrine of prudence the unification of all ends that are given to us by our inclinations into the single end of happiness and the harmony of the means for attaining that end constitute the entire business of reason, which can

4. This is also an insistent theme of *The Conflict of the Faculties*: "How is a history a priori possible? Answer: if the diviner himself creates and contrives the events which he announces in advance./ It was all very well for the Jewish prophets to prophesy that sooner or later not simply decadence but complete dissolution awaited their state, for they themselves were the authors of this fate. [. . .] So far as their influence extends, our politicians do precisely the same thing and are just as lucky in their prophecies. We must, they say, take men as they are, not as pedants ignorant of the world or good-natured visionaries fancy they ought to be. But in place of that 'as they are' it would be better to say what they 'have made' them—stubborn and inclined to revolt—through unjust constraint, through perfidious plots placed in the hands of the government; obviously then, if the government allows the reins to relax a little, sad consequences ensue which verify the prophecy of the supposedly sagacious statesmen" (*CF*, 143).

> therefore provide none but pragmatic laws of free conduct for reaching the ends recommended to us by the senses, and therefore can provide no pure laws that are determined completely a priori. (*CPR*, A800/B828)

And the second *Critique* makes of prudence the very mark of what is most clearly opposed to morality—namely, self-love: Following the maxims of prudence leads one to seek one's personal happiness rather than follow universal reason. To ground morality in prudence would ruin its simplicity and accessibility to all:

> The maxim of self-love (prudence) merely *advises*; the law of morality *commands*. But there is a great difference between that which we are *advised* to do and that to which we are *obligated*.
>
> What is to be done in accordance with the principle of the autonomy of choice is seen quite easily and without hesitation by the most common understanding; what is to be done on the presupposition of heteronomy of choice is difficult to see and requires knowledge of the world; in other words, what *duty* is, is plain of itself to everyone, but what brings true lasting advantage, if this is to extend to the whole of one's existence, is always veiled in impenetrable obscurity, and much prudence is required to adapt the practical rule in accordance with the ends of life even tolerably, by making appropriate exceptions. But the moral law commands compliance from everyone, and indeed the most exact compliance. Appraising what is to be done in accordance with it must, therefore, not be so difficult that the most common and unpracticed understanding should not know how to go about it, even without worldly prudence. (*CPrR*, 33)

The fact remains—and again it is Epicurus who comes along to trouble Kant's thinking—that it is not impossible that prudence might encourage us to choose the moral law, although the moral law ought to be its own motive:

> Now, so many charms and attractions of life may well be connected with this incentive that even for their sake along the most prudent choice of a reasonable Epicurean, reflecting on the greatest well-being of life, would declare itself for moral conduct; and it can even be advisable to connect this prospect of a cheerful enjoyment of life with that motive which is supreme and already sufficiently determining of itself; but this connection should be made only to counterbalance the allurements that vice does not fail to display on the opposite side, and not so as to place in this the proper moving force, not even the smallest part of it, when it is a question of duty. For that would be tantamount to wanting to taint the pure moral disposition in its source. The majesty of duty has nothing to do with the enjoyment of life; it has its own law and also its own court, and even though one might want to shake both of them together

> thoroughly, so as to give them blended, like medicine, to the sick soul, they soon separate of themselves; if they do not, the former will effect nothing at all, and though physical life might gain some force, the moral life would fade away irrecoverably. (*CPrR*, 75)

So that prudence, which defines Epicurean morality ("for the [Epicurean], *prudence* was equivalent to morality" [*CPrR*, 93; see too *CPrR*, 106–7n]) becomes the touchstone for the crucial distinction between self-love and morality, a frontier question: "So distinctly and sharply drawn are the boundaries of morality and self-love that even the most common eye cannot fail to distinguish whether something belongs to the one or the other" (*CPrR*, 33). So not only is there a clear-cut frontier between prudence and morality, but everyone immediately sees that there is; it is impossible to be mistaken about this unless one's head is muddled by the schoolmen to the point that one has become insensible to the heavenly voice of morality. And this is how our appendix takes things up again from the beginning:

> Hence there can be no conflict between politics, as an applied branch of right, and morality, as a theoretical branch of right (i.e. between theory and practice); for such a conflict could occur only if morality were taken to mean a general *doctrine of prudence* [allgemeine *Klugheitslehre*], i.e. a theory of the maxims by which one might select the most useful means of furthering one's own advantage—and this would be tantamount to denying that morality exists. (*KPW*, 116)[5]

So nothing is clearer or more crucial for Kant than this distinction between morality and prudence.[6] And yet (perhaps this is precisely the mark of poli-

5. To maintain consistency with the ethical writings, I have here and elsewhere translated *Klugheit* as "prudence" rather than "expediency" or "opportunism," although *Klugheit* definitely carries a connotation of cleverness and even craftiness that "prudence" does not quite capture.

6. This does not mean that prudence has no place in Kant. See, for example, in the first *Critique*, Kant's appeal to prudence in a context that, as chance would have it, recalls our opening discussion of Frege: "Above, in the presentation of the table of the categories, we spared ourselves the definitions of each of them, on the ground that our aim, which pertains solely to their synthetic use, does not make that necessary, and one must not make oneself responsible for unnecessary undertakings that one can spare oneself. This was no excuse, but a not inconsiderable rule of prudence [eine nicht unerhebliche Klugheitsregel], not immediately to venture a definition and seek or pretend to completeness or precision in the determination of the concept if one can make do with one or another of its marks, without requiring a complete derivation of everything that constitutes the entire concept" (*CPR*, A241; this passage is deleted in the second edition).

tics), in this same appendix this crucial distinction will start to become problematic. For in the passage that introduces our two characters, and that we have already quoted, Kant says the moral politician is the one who "conceives of the principles of political prudence [Staatsklugheit] in such a way that they can co-exist with morality" (*KPW*, 118). One might perhaps see in the hyphen added when the term reappears in the passage we are now quoting (*Staats-Klugheitproblem*) a clarification on Kant's part, wishing perhaps, after describing the "practices" of the political moralist, to give a more restrictive determination of the term, having initially used it in a broader sense in which it is not excluded that it be compatible with morality. But we shall see that this uncertainty shakes, however slightly, the watertight nature of the distinction between political moralist and moral politician. Because this happy situation, according to which the best politics would be morality itself (Kant's motto for the moral politician is "Seek ye first the kingdom of pure practical reason and its *righteousness*, and your object [the blessing of perpetual peace] will be added unto you" [*KPW*, 123]), is not without its complications. For, even if prudence is firmly placed on the side of the political moralist, the moral politician has to appeal to it in turn: the advantage of political wisdom is that it "leads straight to its goal [führt gerade zum Zweck]" (*KPW*, 122), but by that very fact runs the risk of going to its goal too fast, in a precipitation that can only be violent because it is too direct. Moral zeal must, then, be restrained, and this is done not exactly by returning to prudence but by remembering prudence: "leads straight to its goal, so long as we prudently remember [doch mit der Erinnerung der Klugheit] that it cannot be realized by violent and precipitate means [ihn nicht übereilterweise mit Gewalt herbeizuziehen], but must be steadily approached as favourable opportunities present themselves [sondern sich ihm nach Beschaffenheit der günstigen Umstände unablässig zu nähern]" (*KPW*, 122).[7]

So the moral politician must not be simply or purely moral, because being purely moral would mean being too moral (so to speak, because that is hard to reconcile with a thinking of unconditional morality), given that here morality, in what pushes it to excess, risks falling into the very violence it is supposed to avoid. Just as perpetual peace always might be brought about in the worst violence (the soulless despotism that falls back into natural an-

7. The potentially deathly quality of the position of the moral politician is brought out more starkly still in Kant's association of it with the "proverbial saying *fiat iustitia, pereat mundus* [let justice be done though the world should perish]," which Kant himself discreetly (prudently) softens by translating it as "let justice reign, even if all the rogues in the world must perish" (*KPW*, 123).

archy; the peace of the graveyard), the (overly) moral politician risks trying to impose morality *now*, without taking into account the natural contingencies that must *de facto* delay the advent of morality in politics. Perpetual peace is good, but to get it one must wait, and wait more specifically for natural contingencies to lend themselves to it, again by chance. With luck, one can be moral in politics. This was already a problem in the initial statement of the principle of the moral politician, which immediately blurs the distinction it is trying to establish:

> The moral politician will make it a principle that, if any faults which could not have been prevented are discovered in the political constitution or in the relations between states, it is a duty, especially for heads of state, to see to it that they are corrected as soon as possible; it should be ensured that these political institutions are made to conform to natural right, which stands before us as a model in the idea of practical reason, and this should be done even if selfish interests have to be sacrificed. It would be contrary to all *political prudence, which in this case agrees with morality* [aller, hierin mit der Moral einhelligen, Staatsklugheit zuwider ist], to destroy any of the existing bonds of political or cosmopolitan union before a better constitution has been prepared to take their place. And while it would be absurd to demand that their faults be repaired at once and by violent measures,[8] it can still be required of the individual in power that he should be intimately aware of the maxim that changes for the better are necessary, in order that the constitution may constantly approach the optimum end prescribed by laws of right. (*KPW*, 118; emphasis added)

Let's try to understand. There is apparently a *Staatsklugheit* that is not yet axiologically determined, and one can have two conceptions of it. The first, the moral politician's, believes it to be compatible with morality, and this compatibility gives rise to *Staatsweisheit*, political wisdom. The other conception, that of the political moralist, believes it to be distinct from morality

8. In the first *Critique*, Kant argues that the proper conduct of critique must be independent from any anticipated positing of what comes after the critique, which positing could only be dogmatic and thereby violent. Critique should to that extent not know in advance where it is going. Which means that it is never exactly critique, if the meaning of "critique" is provided teleologically by its relation to a doctrine to come. The point of the work done in this book is to show how Kant, a little in spite of himself, leads us to an experience of interrupted teleology that, by the same token, interrupts the received definitions of critique. It follows, among other things, that this reading cannot be another "critique of Kant." It seems to me that a very plausible name for this "critique" radicalized *qua* critique by this inhibition or interruption with respect to doctrine might be "deconstruction."

because of natural necessities, and this conception will give rise to a limitative determination of *Staatsklugheit* as mere *Klugheit*, mere calculative prudence that is not at all moral. But the champion of *Weisheit* must remain attentive to *Klugheit*, not forget about it at any rate, to avoid moral politics going too fast and too violently. So it would be prudent not to be too wise in politics, wise to be a bit prudent, and this too is compatible with morality. Morality prescribes that one not be too moral in politics, and the reason is that a purely moral politics would paradoxically collapse into political moralism—by demanding that all vices be immediately corrected, the moral politician would have to take that correction as a goal and calculate technical means to reach it, which would turn him into a political moralist. To avoid this catastrophic reversal, to avoid turning into a political moralist, the moral politician has to become, preventatively, a bit of a political moralist, inoculate himself with a dose of prudence to avoid his supposed wisdom turning into destructive terror.

In Kant's difficulty maintaining this crucial but evanescent distinction, we can see the outline of nothing less than the problem of the revolution, which is, as has often been said, the keystone of all Kant's political philosophy. One risks making revolution if one is too moral in politics, and nothing in politics is as immoral as revolution or insurrection. Before reading what *Perpetual Peace* will say about this, let's see how the "Doctrine of Right" establishes the constitutive illegitimacy of that temporal frontier, the revolution.

As always in the practical sphere, Kant will appeal to the value of contradiction in grounding the law, and this is what we shall follow here.[9] There ought not be revolution, because it would be contradictory. This argument has two stages (bearing respectively on the executive power and the legislative power), which are not always adequately separated and that Kant himself may on occasion confuse. First, from the point of view of law, the supreme legislative power of the State belongs to the people, or at least to its unified will. The executive power, the agent or regent of the State, must be kept separate from it, on pain of despotism (we shall return to this). This executive power is subordinate to the legislative power, which can nominate it, depose it, but not punish it. For, once there is a supreme executive power in the State, it cannot be punished, because such punishment would have to be an executive

9. For Kant, "whatever the content of our cognition may be, and however it may be related to the object, the general though to be sure only negative condition of all our judgments whatsoever is that they do not contradict themselves; otherwise these judgments in themselves (even without regard to the object) are nothing" (*CPR*, A150/B190).

act: one cannot constrain (by law) the one who by definition has all power of (lawful) constraint, because that would be a contradiction (*MM*, §49, 94).

However, unlike Rousseau, for whom the people is directly the sovereign,[10] for Kant the people must have a head to represent itself to itself. This supreme head is not the executive regent, on pain of despotism. The people, according to a mechanism that, in spite of certain appearances, is not entirely Hobbesian, makes itself sovereign by bowing to the supreme power it gives to its head. The people is sovereign only if it sees its sovereignty embodied in its head, in whom the people sees itself to be sovereign and to which it is thus subjected. That there be such a head is inscribed in the rational idea of the State and is therefore not a historical contingency. But there are irreducible historical contingencies in every State, because States are not *de facto* formed according to the Idea of Reason, which merely provides the yardstick to measure the rationality of the State that exists and that owes its factual existence to mechanical and contingent causes. As we saw, the exit from nature cannot happen simply according to law, which is *de facto* laid down in nature (and therefore violence) and which is thus never entirely lawful, never simply right.[11] That there be a head of State (a singular legislator) is inscribed in reason, but that there be *this* head of State is each time a singular contingency. The head of State one has cannot by definition (just because he is an empirical individual) be adequate to the Idea of supreme power that alone gives him his real power, whence the permanent and worrisome possibility that his legitimacy might be contested. Any given (contingent) head of State is constitutively both legitimate according to reason and potentially illegitimate according to history, whence the temptation, sternly denounced by Kant in the name of the legitimacy of legitimacy, legitimacy itself, to undertake historical research to cast into doubt (or even to shore up historically) the legitimacy of the powers that be. As soon as one has the head of State that one has (i.e., as soon as there is a State), this head really does represent the people, which can only see itself represented in its head, who is legitimate by the very fact of being the head. According to reason,

10. See my book *Dudding: des noms de Rousseau* (Paris: Galilée, 1991) for an analysis of the aporias of sovereignty in Rousseau, which give rise to the (necessarily aporetic) theory of the legislator.

11. "A right line (*rectum*), one that is straight, is opposed to one that is *curved* on the one hand and to one that is *oblique* on the other hand" (*MM*, introduction §E, 26). Recall the Lutheran image of the warped wood that man is made of according to the "Universal History" text. Our own reading here is probably more oblique than curved. See too Jacques Derrida, *Du droit à la philosophie*, 77–81; tr. Jan Plug as *Who's Afraid of Philosophy? Right to Philosophy 1*, 45–48.

the head of State, who is never adequate to the Idea of Reason, always in fact put in place in violence and therefore illegality, is by virtue of that very fact perfectly legitimate according to reason.

Historical research into the origin of this power is, therefore, futile ("for savages draw up no record of their submission to law; besides, we can already gather from the nature of uncivilized men that they were originally subjected to it by force" [*MM*, §52, 111–12]). If one undertakes such research, this can only be with a subversive aim, because casting doubt on the legitimacy of the supreme legislative power (represented by this or that head of State) already suspends his supremacy and is therefore already a crime even if the head of State is behaving in the most corrupt manner (*MM*, §49, Remark A; §52).[12]

This crime is again signaled by a contradiction. For the supreme power to be legally contestable, it would have not to be supreme:

> Therefore a people cannot offer any resistance to the legislative head of a state which would be consistent with right, since a rightful condition is possible only by submission to its general legislative will. There is, therefore, no right to sedition (*seditio*), still less to rebellion (*rebellio*), and least of all is there a right against the head of a state as an individual person (the monarch), to attack his person or even his life (*monarchomachismus sub specie tyrannicidii*) on the pretext that he has abused his authority (*tyrannis*). —Any attempt whatsoever at this is high treason (*proditio eminens*), and whoever commits such treason must be punished by nothing less than death for attempting *to destroy his fatherland*

12. According to Kant's logic, here we would have to say that there is always abuse of supreme power: Just because supreme power is always (transcendentally) legitimate, it is by that same fact (empirically) abusive. As in many of the situations we are analyzing (and exemplarily that of perpetual peace), this means that it is insufficient (but necessary, of course) to say that the legitimate State is simply an Idea of Reason to be approached asymptotically. Kant's famous note on regicide (*MM*, 97n) concerns a crime that is in some ways simply the extension of the crime of asking the question of the sovereign legitimacy of the head of state. In a way that is not unlike Hegel's famous analysis of enlightenment and terror in the *Phenomenology*, the attempt to shed light on the legitimacy of legitimacy leads to violence in that it cannot fail to render legitimacy illegitimate. This is what Kant, in the note, calls "a chasm that irretrievably swallows everything [ein alles ohne Wiederkehr verschlingender Abgrund]" (*MM*, 132). This chasm opens as soon as someone (for example, Kant) asks the question of the legitimacy of the head of state: He thus becomes a bit of a regicide, whence certain consequences we will follow a little later. This chasm or abyss (another version of the frontier) might also be connected to one of the privileged figures of the sublime in the third *Critique* (see, for example, *CJ*, §29, 153) but also to the *Unübersehbare Kluft* said to separate the world of nature and the world of freedom in the introduction to that work (*CJ*, 63).

> (*parricida*). The reason a people has a duty to put up with even what is held to be an unbearable abuse of supreme authority is that its resistance to the highest legislation can never be regarded as other than contrary to law, and indeed as abolishing the entire legal constitution. For a people to be authorized to resist, there would have to be a public law permitting it to resist, that is, the highest legislation would have to contain a provision that it is not the highest and that makes the people, as subject, by one and the same judgment sovereign over him to whom it is subject. This is self-contradictory [welches sich widerspricht], and the contradiction is evident as soon as one asks who is to be the judge in this dispute between people and sovereign (for, considered in terms of rights, these are always two distinct moral persons). For it is then apparent that the people wants to be the judge in its own suit. (*MM*, 96–97)

Let the people merely ask the question of the sovereignty of the sovereign (the sovereign that in a certain sense it itself is) and everything will start to come undone. So the factually violent origin of the State must remain veiled to the people as such, in the name of reason itself, if reason is to have any chance of prevailing in politics.

Let me give the fuller context of this argument:

> A people should not *inquire* with any practical aim in view into the origin of the supreme authority to which it is subject, that is, a subject *ought not to reason subtly* for the sake of action [werktätig vernünfteln] about the origin of this authority, as a right that can still be called into question (*ius controversum*) with regard to the obedience he owes it. For, since a people must be regarded as already united under a general legislative will in order to judge with rightful force about the supreme authority [Staatsgewalt] (*summum imperium*), it cannot and may not judge otherwise than as the present head of state (*summus imperans*) wills it to. Whether a state began with an actual contract of submission (*pactum subiectionis civilis*) as a fact, or whether power came first and law arrived only afterward, or even whether they should have followed in this order: for a people already subject to civil law these rationalizations are altogether pointless and, moreover, threaten a state with danger. If a subject, having pondered over the ultimate origin of the authority now ruling, wanted to resist this authority, he would be punished, got rid of, or expelled (as an outlaw, *exlex*) in accordance with the laws of this authority, that is, with every right. (*MM*, 95)

So the subject (here Kant) who raises these questions in spite of everything, even to say that they should not be raised (and even if he tries hard to draw casuistical distinctions between reasoning and reasoning "subtly," between calling something into doubt and calling it into doubt "in a practical way"), is as close to illegality as can be, insofar as he is divulging the secret that grounds political power in law. We shall see a little later that there is an intractable tension in Kant between the resolutely public character of right and its veiled, secret ground.[13]

This is why:

> A law that is so holy (inviolable) that it is already a crime even to call it in doubt *in a practical way*, and so to suspend its effect for a moment, is thought as if it must have arisen not from men but from some highest, flawless lawgiver; and that is what the saying "All authority is from God" means. This saying is not an assertion about the *historical basis* of the civil constitution; it instead sets forth an Idea as a practical principle of reason: the principle that the presently existing legislative authority ought to be obeyed, whatever its origin. (*MM*, 95)

Nowhere is the entanglement of force and law so clear. For if the head of State is the supreme head, this is because he has force on his side. This force is *de facto* limited and finite, of course; but *de jure*, this force is irresistible. So that law can always rightfully appeal to supreme force to enforce itself. The law must be stronger than any force, stronger than force itself. This is where the distinction between legislative and executive powers begins to tremble a little, because it is clear that the (absolute) force of law may be called in and even guaranteed by the legislator but can only be exercised by the executive. In

13. To be compared to the secret at the basis of religion as described in *The Conflict of the Faculties*: "The biblical theologian as such cannot and need not prove that God Himself spoke through the Bible, since it is a matter of history [. . .] [Treating it] as a matter of faith, he will therefore base it—even for the scholar—on a certain (indemonstrable and inexplicable) *feeling* that the Bible is divine. But the question of the divine origin of the Bible (in the literal sense) must not be raised at all in public discourses directed to the people; since this is a scholarly matter, they would fail completely to understand it and, as a result, would only get entangled in impertinent speculations and doubts" (35–37). This would be the place to reread the analysis of the "mystical foundation of authority," in Derrida's "Force of Law," and especially the following: "Since the origin of authority, the foundation or ground, the position of the law can't by definition rest on anything but themselves, they are themselves a violence without ground. Which is not to say that they are in themselves unjust, in the sense of 'illegal.' They are neither legal nor illegal in their founding moment. They exceed the opposition between founded and unfounded, or between any foundationalism or anti-foundationalism. Even if the success of performatives that found law or right (for example, and this is more than an example, of a state as guarantor of a right) presupposes earlier conditions and conventions (for example in the national or international arena), the same 'mystical' limit will reappear at the supposed origin of said conditions, rules or conventions, and at the origin of their dominant interpretation" (34/14).

both cases, as we have seen, law, in the name of noncontradiction, forbids any rebellious or revolutionary violence, but here, when we are dealing explicitly with the limits of power, contradiction (again invoked by Kant) seems to be as close as can be to the heart of the constitution itself, and Kant's argument, which in this transitional paragraph between the one that posits the illegality of resistance against the executive and the one we have just quoted on the illegality of resistance against the sovereign legislator, is as awkward as can be:

> Indeed, even the constitution cannot contain any article that would make it possible for there to be some authority in a state to resist the supreme commander [obersten Befehlshaber] in case he should violate the law of the constitution, and so to limit him. For someone who is to limit the authority in a state must have even more power [Macht] than he whom he limits, or at least as much power as he has; and, as a legitimate commander [Gebieter] who directs the subjects to resist, he must also be able to protect them and to render a judgment having rightful force in any case that comes up; consequently he has to be able to command resistance publicly. In that case, however, the supreme commander in a state is not the supreme commander; instead, it is the one who can resist him, and this is self-contradictory [welches sich widerspricht]. (*MM*, 96)

Where is the contradiction here? In the fact of thinking that one can place a (legal) limit on (supreme) power. But this contradiction is double: first, in order to limit a force, one must have at one's disposal a force of resistance at least equal to the force one is trying to limit; translated into discourse, into claimed rights, these two forces will literally contradict each other. But that there be two forces thus contradicting each other is (second, then) a contradiction with respect to the Idea of the State, which involves the Idea of one supreme head, whereas in this case there would be two supreme heads (that of power and that of the power limiting that power) contradicting each other, which therefore destroys the very idea of law. This is why Kant will vigorously criticize the (English) model of a "moderate" constitution that might appear to give the limitative power to the people itself but which turns out to be an "absurdity" (*Unding*): "Instead of belonging to right it is only a principle of prudence" (and so, we might say, a principle for the political moralist), which allows for undue influence on government in the named of a supposed popular opposition.

Revolution, consequently, is strictly illegal, even if it is carried out in the name of the purest morality, especially if it is carried out in the name of the purest morality. The illusion of revolution consists in believing itself to be justified or justifiable in the name of the most moral morality. In this sense, the apparently most moral revolution, the purest in its republican (and therefore peaceful) intentions, would be the least moral and the most violent, just because it presented itself as moral. Because the revolution breaks absolutely all constituted legality and can only reinstate a legality after a *hiatus*, "the silence of the laws,"[14] which is none other than the state of nature, pure illegality.[15]

So it is in the name of morality itself that the moral politician must avoid rushing in a revolutionary way toward the *telos* of a republican State in conformity with the Idea of Reason. To the extent that we have such an Idea, thanks to reason, we must avoid making it a goal to be attained by some programmed action, failing which we will fall back into political moralism. In order to be a moral politician, one must look away from the rational goal and have eyes only for the formal principle of law, which absolutely forbids that one could ever ground in law a radical attempt to realize the law. So the moral politician will be more political than the political moralist (who thinks he is being so very political) by refusing to exploit politics to supposedly moral ends. Being "more political" here means waiting for opportunities to arise to give a little nudge, make a little improvement, according to a wisdom that looks as close as can be to simple political prudence. In this perspective, one can let revolutions come (and in a certain secret way, the very fact of asking the question of law cannot fail to call for them to come) as further opportunities that allow some progress toward the goal one must, above all, not have directly in view, because after the revolution, once we have passed through the abyssal hiatus of the state of nature that it comprises, once we have crossed the temporal frontier, a new regime will have been installed if chance is on the side of the revolutionaries, a necessarily legal regime that cannot legally be overturned on the pretext of restoring the old order.[16] For

14. See Maurice Blanchot, "L'insurrection, la folie d'écrire," in *L'entretien infini* (Paris: Gallimard, 1969), 336. I read Kant and Sade together as regards the revolution in "Forget to Remember: Remember to Forget: Sade *avec* Kant," in my *Open Book / Livre ouvert*, 93–108 (CreateSpace, 2005).

15. See too in "Theory and Practice," where there is also insistent appeal to the value of contradiction: "It is clear that these peoples [who have risen up in revolution] have done the greatest degree of wrong in seeking their rights in this way. [...] For such procedures, if made into a maxim, make all lawful constitutions insecure and produce a state of complete lawlessness (*status naturalis*) where all rights cease at least to be effectual" (*KPW*, 82).

16. This structure whereby, having crossed the frontier, one enters a new regime also has a more clearly negative aspect brought out in "What Is Enlightenment?": "A revolution may well put an end to autocratic despotism and to rapacious or power-

the moral politician, whose wisdom consists in a nonmechanistic quasi-prudence, the revolution is the very example of luck, of the opportunity to be grasped, the natural opportunity that prefigures the natural end of politics that must, above all, not be transformed into a goal to be attained mechanically. The moral politician, then, will let things come to him, according to the laws of this quasi-prudence, laws that in a note Kant calls "permissive laws" of reason:

> These are permissive laws of reason, which allow a state of public right to continue, even if it is affected by injustice, until all is ripe for a complete upheaval [Umwalzung] or has been prepared for it by peaceful means. For any *legal* constitution, even if it is only in small measure lawful, is better than none at all, and the fate of a premature reform would be anarchy. Thus political wisdom [die Staatsweisheit, not "political prudence" as the translation now misleadingly has it], with things as they are at present, will make it a duty to carry out reforms appropriate to the ideal of public right. But where revolutions are brought about by nature alone, it will not use them as a good excuse for even greater oppression,[17] but will treat them as a call of nature to create a lawful constitution based on the principles of freedom, for a thorough reform of this kind is the only one which will last. (*KPW*, 118–19n; tr. mod.)

So in what does the moral character of the moral politician consist, finally? In a softening of the moral imperative, or at least in a political patience that will welcome even illegal and immoral events (revolutions) with a view to the end that must not be rushed and that must not even really be aimed for or taken as an end. This is also why, in external relations too, one must wait for the right moment and not try to bring about perpetual peace too soon:

> But as for the external relationship between states, no state can be required to relinquish its constitution, even if the latter is despotic (and hence stronger in relation to external enemies), so long as this state is in danger of being engulfed at any moment by other states; hence while plans must be made for political

---

seeking oppression, but it will never produce a true reform in ways of thinking. Instead, new prejudices, like the ones they replaced, will serve as a leash to control the great unthinking mass" (*KPW*, 55).

17. A little earlier in the main text: "If, however, a more lawful constitution were attained by unlawful means, i.e. by a violent revolution resulting from a previous bad constitution, it would then no longer be permissible to lead the people back to the original one, even although everyone who had interfered with the old constitution by violence or conspiracy would rightly have been subject to the penalties of rebellion during the revolution itself" (*KPW*, 118).

> improvement, it must be permissible to delay their execution until a better opportunity arises. (*KPW*, 118)

What is this moral-political "wisdom" that is neither strictly moral nor strictly political? What is its secret, the play of its veils? Who gets to have it or practice it?

Having established to his satisfaction that there can be no objective conflict between politics and ethics, on the grounds that once we have recognized the absolute authority of the concept of moral duty "it is patently absurd to say that we *cannot* act as the moral laws require" (*KPW*, 116), Kant turns to a transcendental analysis of public (and therefore political) right. What makes public right public is the transcendental character of publicity (*Publizität*). No matter the material content of the law, for it to be public it must have the form of publicity or publicness, and the same goes for the right of peoples (i.e., international law, which is law only insofar as it can be founded on the possibility of making public the maxims of any proposed political action without the fact of publication *ipso facto* making that action inoperative). It is "easy," then (as moral knowledge always is in Kant), to know whether an action is in conformity with public or international law: It suffices to run its maxim through the test of publicity understood in this way.

We can begin here to get a sense of what, for Kant, is supposed to distinguish morality from politics: In morality, one can assess whether a proposed action is moral by running its maxim through the test prescribed by the categorical imperative, to see if this maxim can without contradiction be taken as a universal law. This does not require publicity in any normal sense. But in public law, the categorical imperative prescribes a test slightly displaced from that of morality itself, one which gives the "transcendental formula" of public right: "All actions affecting the rights of other human beings are wrong [unrecht] if their maxim is not compatible with their being made public" (*KPW*, 126). First, the domain of this principle is restricted to the political sphere (or at least the sphere in which my freedom externally confronts that of others); second, what is the proof in this test is not formal noncontradiction (as in the moral categorical imperative) but compatibility with making this same maxim public. This compatibility (*Verträglichkeit*) is measured in more complicated fashion than the simple test of noncontradiction that grounds ethics, because here one must take into account a possible resistance or opposition of others to what I propose to undertake:

> For a maxim which I may not *declare openly* without thereby frustrating my own intention, or which must at all costs be *kept secret* [*verheimlicht* werden muss] if it is to succeed, or which I cannot *publicly acknowledge* without thereby inevitably arousing the resistance of everybody to my plans, can only have stirred up this

> necessary and general (hence *a priori* foreseeable) opposition against me because it is itself unjust and thus constitutes a threat to everyone. (*KPW*, 126)

This principle, says Kant, is purely negative in that it identifies what is unjust rather than what is just.[18] As such, this principle is "like any axiom, valid without demonstration and [. . .] *easy* to apply" (*KPW*, 126; emphasis added). As if by chance, the two examples Kant gives to illustrate this principle are, for internal right, insurrection, and, for external right, various forms of international relations: what we have called the temporal frontier of revolution, where one regime is in discontinuous temporal transition into another in the same place, and the spatial frontier of the state, where one regime is in discontinuous spatial transition into another at the same time.

First example: There can be no right to insurrection, even in an obvious case in which the people's rights are being violated by the sovereign, because the maxim of such an action could not be publicly declared. First by reason of contradiction, as we just saw: the contract that binds the people to the head of state could not contain a right allowing the people to use violence against that head, for in that case the head of state would not in fact be the head of state—which is a contradiction. But this contradiction is brought out by noting that if one were to declare publicly the maxim of the action of rising up against the head of state, the point of the insurrection would by that very fact be compromised ("the maxim would therefore have to be kept secret" [*KPW*, 127]), whereas the corresponding maxim of the head of state (to punish by death any attempt at rebellion) would not at all have to be kept secret: The head of state knows that he (at least in principle) "possesses *irresistible* supreme power" and so "does not have to worry that his own aims might be frustrated if his maxim became generally known" (*KPW*, 127).

Kant seems less sure of this position, however, in *The Conflict of the Faculties*:

> Why has a ruler never dared say publicly that he recognizes absolutely no *right* of the people opposed to him, that his people owe their happiness solely to the

18. It might be possible to argue for a similar reading of the categorical imperative itself: Rather than look forward to the formulation of laws, the import of the categorical imperative would, on this view, remain each time singular, always a purely formal test of *this* action and its maxim. On such a reading, the Hegelian objection from the *Natural Law* essay mentioned previously would simply become irrelevant. Pursuing this line of thought might bring Kant closer to Derrida, who argues for a radicalized version of duty such that not only is it morally insufficient to act in conformity with duty but even acting for the sake of duty, as Kant requires, still falls short. On Derrida's view we must act *out of* duty (i.e., beyond duty) with an element of invention or contingency that is very germane to everything being argued here. See my essay "Deconstruction and Ethics," in *Interrupting Derrida* (London: Routledge, 2000), 34–46.

> beneficence of a government which confers their happiness upon them, and that all presumption of the subject to a right opposed to the government (since this right comprehends the concept of permissible resistance) is absurd and even culpable? The reason is that such a public declaration would rouse all of his subjects against him; although, as docile sheep, led by a benevolent and sensible master, well-fed and powerfully protected, they would have nothing wanting in their welfare for which to lament. (*CF*, 155–57n)

Which complicates somewhat the relation between secret and publication. This extra move in the play of the veil, which keeps what is no secret secret all the while letting something of it be seen (and which we might suspect just is politics), is registered a little further on in this same text, with regard to the British constitution. Kant has just briefly repeated the transcendental argument in favor of publicity. But states in fact do not stop at banning publicity, which is, however, required for the rational progress for which Kant is arguing. There is something worse than such an interdiction, or at least something other, and here is where the veil will hide itself, veil itself, and in so doing perhaps show itself for what it "is."

What is worse—or at least other—than the interdiction of political publicity? A disguise, and this time a legal disguise, of the nature of the Constitution itself. This disguise, as Kant will say immediately, is not very effective as a disguise, but we might be tempted to say that it works all the better for that fact. And that is the veil, in its mysterious transparency:

> Another disguise, which is easily penetrated indeed, but is one to which a nation, nevertheless, is legally committed, is that pertaining to the true nature of its constitution. It would be an insult to its majesty to say of the British nation that it is an *absolute monarchy*: some rather maintain that a constitution *limiting* the will of the monarch through the two Houses of Parliament, acting as representatives of the people, is supposed to exist; and yet everyone knows perfectly well that the monarch's influence on those representatives is so great and so certain that nothing is resolved by the Houses except what he wills and purposes through his minister. The latter then probably even proposes resolutions in connection with which he knows that he will be contradicted, and even arranges it that way (for example, with regard to slave-trade) in order to provide a fictitious proof of the freedom of Parliament. This representation of the nature of the case has something delusive about it so that the true constitution, faithful to law, is no longer sought at all; for a person imagines he has found it in an example already at hand, and a false publicity [eine lügenhafte Publicität] deceives the people with the illusion of a *limited* monarchy in power by a law which issues from them, while their representatives, won over by bribery, have secretly subjected them to an *absolute monarchy*. (*CF*, 163)

This disguise is worse than the interdiction of publicity, because it is legal, and it remains in place in spite of, and by means of, publicity itself. Publicity, whose—transcendental—principle appeared to be clear and infallible, and to keep the secret out of politics, can nonetheless allow this secondary disguise with respect to the true nature of the constitution to come about. What is the secret? The fact that by means of a pseudo-transcendental publicity, or by means of a transcendental pseudo-publicity, the public believes that it is in the presence of the thing itself, "the true and rightfully established constitution," whereas this is not at all the case. Kant claims that this disguise of the true nature of the British constitution is easy to see through: There is a veil in the sense of a misleading cover, and it must be torn or penetrated for the truth to be discovered. One senses Kant's impatience and even irritation faced with the British imposture: The British are proud of having already realized a constitution in conformity with the transcendental principles of right; well, we had better disabuse them immediately, and that will not be difficult. Kant does not even deign to do so in the main text and relegates the task to a footnote:

> A cause, the nature of which one does not directly understand, makes itself known through the effect which unfailingly attaches to it. What is an *absolute* monarch? He is one at whose command, if he says, "war is necessary," a state of war immediately exists [es soll Krieg sein, sofort Krieg ist]. What is a *limited* monarch, on the other hand? He who must first consult the people as to whether war is or is not to be; and the people say, "there is to be no war," so there is no war [es soll nicht Krieg sein, so ist kein Krieg]. For war is a situation in which *all* political power must be at the disposal of the sovereign. Now the British monarch has conducted wars aplenty without seeking the consent for them. Therefore, this king is an absolute monarch who ought not to be one, of course, according to the constitution; but he is always able to bypass it because precisely through those political powers, namely, that he has it in his power to dispense all appointments and posts, he can consider assured the assent of the representatives of the people. In order to succeed, however, this system of bribery must certainly not be publicized [muss . . . nicht Publicität haben]. Hence it remains under the highly transparent veil of secrecy [Es bleibt daher unter dem sehr durchsichtigen Schleier des Geheimnisses]. (*CF*, 163n)

What is the conceptual status of this rather seductive "highly transparent veil"?[19] Such a veil is not content simply to let something show through:

19. "One wonders, too, where to have clothing commence. Where a *parergon* begins and ends. Whether any garment would be a *parergon*. G-strings and the like. What to do with absolutely transparent veils. And how to transpose the statement to painting.

It does not hide that it is not hiding anything, or it lets see that it is letting everything be seen. But, by letting it be seen in this way that it is letting everything be seen, with a wink of connivance, as it were, does it not hide even more effectively what it is supposed to be letting one see? The veil always also unveils or promises an unveiling, but that promise, and the prospect of finally seeing what is behind it, are also part of the veiling. What the veil is really veiling is that the promise of unveiling and revelation is part of the seductive game of politics. For what "is not known to the public" is not any kind of content: The king does not bother to ask the people's opinion, not so that he can simply hide what he intends to do, to make a secret of it, but because he can count on public approval and thereby the connivance of the public in the structure of secrecy itself. What is hidden in this apparent transparency is its "system"—namely, the structure of the veil itself, given no publicity because it is hiding in plain sight as publicity itself. All supposed political "transparency" is at risk of producing the same effect of "corruption" through the action of what is, apparently, publicity itself, the appearance of publicity as appearance itself. The disguise is easy to pierce because there is not even really a disguise; the veil is transparent, and even very transparent, there is no secret—and just that is its whole mystery. This system cannot be known to the public as such, because it defines publicity or publicness itself as a transcendental structure. The so-called public space as such is always veiled to itself, never entirely available to itself as itself. The truth in politics is not available in politics. There is no secret except the absence of any secret—and that is the secret that the philosopher must try to get out.

Second example: International right is necessarily a public right that "implies by definition that there is a general will which publicly assigns to each that which is its due" (*KPW*, 127; tr. mod.). So if, for example, the question arises of knowing whether a State can break a promise made to another State (under the pretext of its internal responsibilities), or if it is permissible for less powerful States to attack a neighbouring State that has become powerful and threatening, or if a small State can be subjected to a larger State whose territorial continuity it interrupts, then one can immediately discover that these actions would be unjust because the fact of publishing their maxims could not fail to make the proposed actions unrealizable by virtue of forewarning the other State.

Here we find at work again all the ambiguity of the political moralist and

---

For example, Cranach's Lucretia holds only a light band of transparent veil in front of her sex: where is the *parergon*?" (Jacques Derrida, *The Truth in Painting*, tr. Geoffrey Bennington and Ian McLeod [Chicago: University of Chicago Press, 1987], 57; tr. mod.).

the moral politician, exacerbated by the fact that Kant's supposed "solution" to what he here calls "the antinomy of politics and morals" merely makes the antinomy in question more antinomic, perhaps beyond the form of antinomy itself. For, according to the principle of publicity of maxims, in each case listed above the injustice of the action in question is proved by the fact that making the maxim public would render it ineffective. We know it is unjust because it would not work if made public. The transcendental injustice of political prudence (which is just politics itself, however) is seen in the fact that it would miss its aim if it did not keep its maxims secret.

How does the secret work here? Everything that Kant wants to say implies that (public) right does not like the secret, that the secret is on the side of (moralizing) politics, that it suffices to dissipate the secret to be on the right track when it comes to politics and morality and their relationship. It is not that every maxim made public is by that fact made moral (for, as Kant recognizes as though in passing, "the person who has decisive supremacy has no need to conceal his maxims [seiner Maximen nicht Hehl haben darf]" [*KPW*, 129], so that revealing the secret can also be a power play) but that, according to this negative test, no maxim that does not pass the test of publicity can be considered moral. There are no secrets for the moral politician, everything must be declared, unveiled, brought to light. But this righteous doctrine of nonsecrecy encounters two distinct problems: First, it makes sense only in the very situation whose advent it is supposed to help along—namely, perpetual peace. For there to be a politics compatible with morality, and which by that fact could lead to perpetual peace, we would already have to have perpetual peace (and thus there would be no need for politics at all, because, as we have said, the end of politics is the end of politics). Politics can finally be moral when it no longer needs to be politics; we can have perpetual peace when we've got perpetual peace; transparency can reign when transparency reigns.

This much we could have deduced from our earlier arguments. But there is a second problem that is worse for Kant. Moral politics does not tolerate the secret. But, according to Kant himself, moral politics itself is based on a secret. As we shall see, this secret is even the secret of the secret, the secret itself, the very secret that allows for the possibility of a moral politics in the first place. This secret is so secret that one must not even try to find out what it is. In saying so, Kant immediately violates the secret that he has just put in place as the very foundation of moral politics. And by blowing the secret of the State (of any State) in this way, Kant, according to his own doctrine, is guilty of the highest treason and risks exile and death. This is the political price of philosophy, or perhaps its political secret. To avoid this consequence, the secret of the secret must be re-established, its violation must be kept secret; but as this (philosophical) violation of the (political) secret is absolutely indispensable if politics is to have a chance finally of being moral, this secret violation of the political secret must be made public, but somehow made public secretly.

Which is why we have not yet breathed a word about the second supplement to the *Perpetual Peace* essay, between the first supplement (which concerns the natural "guarantee" of perpetual peace) and the appendix on the relations between morality and politics that has been exercising us. This second supplement is indeed entitled "*Secret* Article of a Perpetual Peace [Geheimer Artikel zum ewigen Frieden]" and was added to the second edition of Kant's text in 1796. This little supplement takes to a certain limit the logic we have been following thus far. We have seen that the secret, the need for secrecy, is sufficient proof of the immorality of a political maxim, and this is what Kant duly recognizes at the beginning of the article. The secret is objectively contradictory in public right but can perhaps be justified subjectively. What does this mean? That the identity of the author of the secret, or of the one who dictates it (*die ihn diktiert*), can remain secret:

> But in subjective terms, i.e. in relation to the sort of person who dictates it, an article may well contain a secret element, for the person concerned may consider it prejudicial to his own dignity to name himself publicly as its originator [Urheber]. (*KPW*, 114)

So if there is a secret article, what is, or should remain, secret is not so much the article itself or its content but the name of its author. The secret article makes a secret of its signature. But in fact there is only one secret article of this kind (where the "subjective" secret is justified), and that secret article is as follows, openly declared by Kant, written out in quotation marks, emphasized, without forgetting the signature (for *Perpetual Peace* was not published anonymously and had Kant's name on the title page):[20]

> *"The maxims of the philosophers on the conditions under which public peace [öffentlichen Friedens] is possible shall be consulted by states which are armed for war."* (*KPW*, 115)

How is this a secret? In that such an article could never be admitted to by its authors, namely the heads of State, who must hide their invitation to the phi-

20. From the first edition of *Perpetual Peace*, the title page indeed reads: "Zum ewigen Frieden. Ein philosophischer Entwurf. Von Immanuel Kant." Like Rousseau, Kant was proud of the fact that he signed his work. See *The Conflict of the Faculties*, 11: "I sign my name to all my writings, so that I cannot be accused of using underhanded means."

losophers to discuss such questions behind a general authorization allowing the philosophers to debate everything "freely and publicly." The States, then, wanting to consult the philosophers, who are mere subjects (Untertanen), cannot do so openly, because that would compromise the dignity of the supreme legislative authority of the State ("to which," Kant adds with a hint of irony made hollow by the gravity of the problem here, "we must naturally attribute the highest degree of wisdom [die grösste Weisheit]" [*KPW*, 115]) to have to ask advice from someone who cannot, by definition, have the same degree of wisdom. The secret is here guaranteed by publicity itself: The State pretends to be generously allowing a freedom, an openness, publicity, where in fact it is secretly hoping to learn something in secret. The article is, then, secret and, in fact, doubly secret: both within the State, where the head of state will not admit to his subjects that he is seeking counsel from some of them (the philosophers), and without, in relations between States, where the heads of State will not want to admit to each other that they are all looking for counsel from mere philosophers. This article can be so secret that there is no need for it even to appear in the perpetual peace treaty being signed by the States entering into the federation of States (the "surrogate" solution to the issue of perpetual peace), because everyone's agreement on this point "already lies in the obligations imposed by universal human reason in its capacity as a moral legislator" (*KPW*, 115).

So there is no need to make public the article of publicity itself: In fact, it must remain forever secret in its self-evident rationality, for fear of compromising the dignity of the supreme authority of the State, and it *can* remain forever secret, because in any case it is a universal rational obligation, which will to that extent already be known and about which the states can have mutual confidence in each other, because this secret can be a secret for no one in that it emanates from universal reason. What remains secret, then, is not the fact of publicity (everybody, all subjects, can hear and read, freely discussing among themselves, the philosophers to whom the States concede that freedom) but its end (to give counsel to the states armed for war).

What is Kant doing in formulating and signing this secret article? Obviously betraying the secret by publishing it. Not only is he already using the freedom he is also demanding in so doing, but he is making the publication even more public by revealing its secret (and therefore not straightforwardly moral) purpose. He makes public the secret purpose of publicity itself. Kant reveals the true but hidden address of his whole text (the head of State) and thereby too his political ambition (to dictate to that head of State), or at least the inextricable entanglement of his moral thought and its being compromised by the kind of subjective "prudence" he so forcibly denounces elsewhere. But is this revelation (namely, that revealing the secret, as when in the *Rechtslehre* he reveals the secret violent origin of the state that the subjects are supposed never to know, obviously making the philosopher guilty in the eyes of public right) not still harboring a further secret?

What exactly is going on in this publication of the secret? Kant says in his secret article (that he is thus dictating to its author, namely, the head of State, whose dignity is compromised here not so much by being the author of the article in question but by the very fact of having to have it dictated to him by one of his subjects, the fact of not even being its author, of having the structural stupidity of the sovereign revealed) that the philosophers must be consulted by the head of state. But this consultation looks odd, because if the head of State allows the philosophers to express themselves publicly so he can secretly be informed as to what reason itself dictates to mankind in general, this is not exactly in order to act accordingly but just in order to hear. The philosopher must simply be "given a hearing [daßs man ihn *höre*]" (*KPW*, 115). The head of State does not exactly *listen* to the philosopher, for fear of indignity, but one might hope he *hears* the philosopher. The head of State needs to do this just because the philosopher has no political power at all: In politics, it is not the philosopher's but the jurist's judgment that makes the law. However, as in the case of the political moralist (who "does not deserve a hearing [verdienen sie kein Gehör]" [*KPW*, 123]), that judgment, which is content merely to apply the law to the case, is by definition hand in glove with the powers that be. In applying the law, the jurist by definition has right on his side, with all the overwhelming force without which it would not be right. But according to an inevitable effect of corruption and usurpation, the force of law (without which the law would not be the law) will always win out over law itself, meaning that, in Kant's words, the jurist, having taken as symbols the scales and the sword, does not hesitate to throw the sword into the balance when the scales are not coming down on his side (*KPW*, 115). However, in order to decide, not the cases under the law but the case of the law itself,[21] this force must be absent. The right of right must then be spoken secretly by the philosopher from beyond the boundaries of force and, indeed, of right—which is why the philosopher cannot be king and rather tends to join the legislator in his exile, *ex lex*, outlawed from the City, structurally sentenced to death, from which secret position he hopes to make himself heard, knowing that he cannot exactly be listened to.

This secret place of exile for the philosopher, which is nonetheless a pub-

21. See Jean-Luc Nancy, "*Lapsus judicii*," in *L'impératif catégorique*, 35–60 (Paris: Aubier-Flammarion, 1983).

lic place and even the place from which what is public can be defined—for philosophy is intrinsically public, rationally speaking it should have no secrets—this secret but radically open and thereby exposed place is exactly what we are calling the frontier: It is always on the edge of the "mechanical" system of right (which is always perfectly and necessarily right, because the law is the law), the zone of transition between existing systems of right (figured by the revolution in time and the frontier of the State in space). This secret place, which is neither simply spatial nor simply temporal, and which tendentially fills the whole space and time of politics, like a fractal curve, this place from which the philosopher (the critical philosopher at least) makes himself heard without being listened to can nonetheless just about be recognized and named by right, if only the better to locate it and keep it safely out in the margins or the marches.

In the introduction to the *Rechtslehre*, having separated out the domain of right from the domain of virtue (the former considering the limitation of my freedom by that of others as a question not of virtue but solely of constraint and thus able to be formulated "by analogy with the possibility of free movement of bodies within the law of the *equality of action and reaction*" [*MM*, 26]), Kant nonetheless recognizes a frontier zone that, although it does not come under morality, is also separated from the domain of law while still appealing to it for decision. This zone is presented through discussion of two cases that appear to be diametrically opposed and that limit the domain of right rather as contradiction and tautology limit the domain of logic in Wittgenstein's *Tractatus* (5.101). We will no longer be surprised to find that, as is so often the case in Kant whenever trouble is brewing, these cases are presented with reference to Epicurus:

> But without making incursions into the province of ethics, one finds two cases that lay claim to a decision about rights although no one can be found to decide them, and that belong as it were within the *intermundia* of Epicurus.—We must first separate these two cases from the doctrine of right proper, to which we are about to proceed, so that their wavering principles will not affect the firm basic principles of the doctrine of right. (*MM*, 26)

The *intermundus* or *metakosmion*[22] is, from the point of view of right at any rate, the place of ambiguity or equivocation (*ius aequivocum*), placed, margin-

22. Posited by Epicurus in the letter to Pythocles, as quoted by Diogenes Laertius in book 10 §§88–89) of *The Lives and Opinions of Eminent Philosophers*: "A world is a circumscribed portion of the universe, which contains stars and earth and all other visible things, cut off from the infinite, and terminating in a boundary which may be

ally, in an appendix to the introduction. The two cases in question are not just any cases but run the risk, if one is not careful, of taking over the whole domain of right. One case is equity and the other the right of necessity.[23]

Equity pulls right toward morality, the right of necessity toward mere natural mechanism (we might want to say that the whole domain of public right—of politics—just is the *intermundus*, the frontier, between these two domains):

> An authorization to use coercion is connected with any right in the *narrow* sense (*ius strictum*). But people also think of a right in a *wider* sense (*ius latium*), in which there is no law by which an authorization to use coercion can be determined.—There are two such true or alleged rights, *equity* and the *right of necessity*. The first admits a right without coercion, the second, coercion without a right. It can easily be seen that this ambiguity really arises from the fact that there are cases in which a right is in question but for which no judge can be appointed to render a decision. (*MM*, 26–27)

The argument from equity arises when the strict application of right produces injustice, as judged according to a criterion that cannot be presented to any tribunal and that cannot, therefore, give rise to a legal judgment. According to equity, in Kant's example, one ought *not* to respect the equal distribution of profits in a case where one partner has done more work and thereby suffered greater losses that the others: His disproportionate loss *ought* to be compensated, but according to the law, one *must* respect the contract that demands equality. According to equity, someone who receives a payment due to him in a currency that has meantime been devalued is due a supplementary payment that no tribunal, however, is in a position to accord. Equity is a "mute divinity who cannot be heard [*eine stumme Gottheit*]" (*MM*, 27) but

---

either thick or thin, a boundary whose dissolution will bring about the wreck of all within it, in an exterior which may either revolve or be at rest, and be round or triangular or of any other shape whatever. All these alternatives are possible: they are contradicted by none of the facts in this world, in which an extremity can nowhere be discerned. That there is an infinite number of such worlds can be perceived, and that such a world may arise in a world or in one of the *intermundia* (by which term we mean the spaces between worlds) in a tolerably empty space and not, as some maintain, in a vast space perfectly clear and void" (tr. R. D. Hicks [Cambridge, MA: Harvard University Press, 1925], 617–19).

23. Having mentioned these pages in a note, Derrida says: "No need to insist: what is at stake in the three pages that follow is quite simply vertiginous" (*Du droit à la philosophie*, 87n/199n: to my knowledge, Derrida nowhere develops a reading of these pages, however).

who incites one to push cases before a tribunal when they can, according to Kant, be heard only by the *court of conscience*. Kant does not contest the *truth* of what he calls equity's motto ("the strictest right is the greatest wrong [*summum ius, summa injuria*]") but simply the ability of right to remedy that wrong, which it inevitably produces in its very righteousness.

Second case: the supposed right of necessity (*ius necessitatis*). Kant deals with it even more rapidly, under the sign of contradiction, because here there would supposedly be a right where there is no injustice. I invoke the right of necessity not when the other has attacked me and I have killed him to save my own life but when, without it being his fault, I would die if I did not kill him. After the shipwreck, I push the only other survivor off the single piece of floating wreckage in order to use it to save myself. Here I am acting under a certain constraint, but right cannot be involved, says Kant, because there could be no penal law to punish this case (it would make no sense to threaten me with death for taking by force the last floating plank, "since a threat of an ill that is still *uncertain* [death by a judicial verdict] cannot outweigh the fear of an ill that is *certain* [drowning]" [*MM*, 28]). This does not mean that the action is *just* (for I have caused someone to die without legal justification) or even *legal*: It is not that I am not guilty (I am) but simply not punishable. Invoking necessity changes nothing, because "there could be no necessity that would make what is wrong conform with law" (*MM*, 28).

In both cases, then, there is equivocation. In the case of equity, subjective right (as exercised by reason) justifies me whereas objective right (as practised by a tribunal) can only find that I am in the wrong; in the case of necessity, subjective right says I am wrong where the objective right of the tribunal finds me in the right or at least cannot punish me even though I am not innocent. In both cases, the proper exercise of right leaves a residue of injustice that belongs to the *intermundus*, or the frontier, in the sense that it concerns right (neither of these cases is purely a moral matter and in both cases the question is that of a possible legal judgment by a tribunal).

In order to put forward a doctrine of right, Kant has to get rid of the problem of equity, even though it clearly can show up at any moment in the exercise of right, and even though in fact it *must* show up in every case, each time right is rendered in pure legality, to the extent that the more right is right, the less just it is. Perfectly right right, analogically mathematical or mechanical, always runs the risk, by its very rightness, of being merely right, pure constraint without justice, force of law become simple force, and thus absolutely unjust. And even though the case of necessity seems as though it would show up less often (on the basis of Kant's example or the tradition he is following here), it is no less important, in that the very possibility of such an unjudgeable case (even if there were only one) puts the whole doctrine of right into question.

So it is no accident that this problem of a supposed right of necessity returns in Kant at a crucial point of his political philosophy—namely, the revolution. It is hard not to see the similarity between the shipwreck survivor (guilty but unpunishable) and what happens in revolution, where the revolutionaries are never within their rights but where, once the revolution has succeeded (if it succeeds), they are unpunishable too. And just as, in the case of the shipwreck, the other could have appealed to the same right if he had succeeded in pushing me into the deep, in the case of the revolution, if the people invokes the right of necessity to justify its rebellion, the head of state could just as plausibly invoke it to justify its repression. Right cannot punish this action that suspends right ("Necessity knows no law" because necessity just is the illegal law of nature) and is suspended on it (in the case of revolution, this shows how right originates in a violence that escapes its judgment).[24]

In "Theory and Practice," having established the absolute illegality of revolution, Kant clarifies this argument:

> Nor can a right of necessity (*ius in casu necessitates*) be invoked here as a means of removing the barriers which restrict the power of the people; for it is monstrous to suppose that we can have a right to do wrong in the direst (physical) distress.* For the head of state can just as readily claim that his severe treatment of his subjects is justified by their insubordination as the subjects can justify their rebellion by complaints about their unmerited suffering, and who is to decide? The decision must rest with whoever controls the ultimate enforcement of the public law, i.e. the head of state himself. Thus no-one in the commonwealth can have a right to contest his authority.
>
> *[Kant's note:] There is no *casus necessitatis* except where duties, i.e. an *absolute* duty and another which, however pressing, is nevertheless *relative*, come into conflict. For instance, it might be necessary for someone to betray someone else, even if their relationship were that of father and son, in order to preserve the state from catastrophe. This preservation of the state from evil is an absolute duty, while the preservation of the individual is merely a relative duty (i.e. it applies only if he is not guilty of a crime against the state). The first person might denounce the second to the authorities with the utmost unwillingness, compelled only by (moral) necessity. But if a person, in order to preserve his own life, pushes a shipwrecked fellow away from the plank he grasps, it would be quite false to say that (physical) necessity gives

24. For an analysis of a very particular instance of this case, see my article "'*Ces petits différends*: 'Lyotard and Horace," in *Legislations: The Politics of Deconstruction*, 152–71.

> him a right to do so. For it is only a relative duty for me to preserve my own life (i.e. it applies only if I can do so without committing a crime). But it is an absolute duty not to take the life of another person who has not offended me and does not even make me risk my own life. Yet the teachers of general civil law are perfectly consistent in authorising such measures in cases of distress. For the authorities cannot combine a *penalty* with this prohibition, since this penalty would have to be death. But it would be a nonsensical law which threatened anyone with death if he did not voluntarily deliver himself up to death when in dangerous circumstances. (*KPW*, 81–82)

See too the famous note to §49 of the "Doctrine of Right" on the execution of the sovereign and the abyss it opens up. Here there is a further complication in that Kant recognizes that one might at least understand the people's (illicit) appeal to the right of necessity if they simply force the sovereign to abdicate (and by extension, even if they *assassinate* him): They would have no real right on their side, but the supposed right of necessity would at least provide a pretext for their illegal action. What opens the abyss is the claim to be justified in condemning the sovereign "formally," according to the law (*MM*, 97n).

So if equity appears in every case as the inevitable bending of the right that is always too right (in the sense of straight, *rectus*), its inevitable becoming-oblique, the case of necessity (always an exceptional case) is always at the basis of right. For as Kant insists, all law must have the character of necessity, be it on the side of the laws of nature dictated by the legislative understanding or on the side of the moral law, where the typic that borrows from nature the form of conformity to law (*Gesetzmässigkeit*) also borrows this character of necessity.

That all laws have the character of necessity is a leitmotif of the *Groundwork of the Metaphysics of Morals* and the second *Critique* (see, for example, the whole "Analytic of Pure Practical Reason" [*CPrR*, 17–90]). Moral necessity and natural necessity cannot, of course, be simply identified, and Kant separates them already in the first *Critique* (see, for example: "The *ought* [das *Sollen*] expresses a species of necessity [eine Art von Notwendigkeit] [. . .] which does not occur anywhere else in the whole of nature" [A547/B575]). The fact remains that "law" and "necessity" are to be found on both sides of the great Kantian frontier between nature and freedom and that the relationship between the sense they have on each side remains obscure (the object of an analogy). What is the *law of law* that allows these two senses to communicate? Or what is the *necessity of the necessity* that rules over law in general? It will not suffice simply to invoke the *Kluft* that will be opened in the introduction to the third *Critique*, and the analogical bridge supposed to link its two sides, because we cannot yet presuppose that we are dealing with similar enough situations on each side of the abyss to allow a bridge to make the connection. So it is still obscure to claim that the necessity on each side is of a different species, in that on the practical side necessity seems to be quite radically different insofar as it immediately doubles up: Practical laws are laws insofar as they are practical and immediately determine the will but simultaneously insofar as they are theoretical (known *a priori* to be such). We are still dealing with something like knowledge on the practical side. (The moral law as formulated by Kant obligates us but also informs us: Our relation to the text of the second *Critique* is not immediately practical but theoretical. This problem is difficult enough to motivate Levinas's radical suggestions about "ethics as first philosophy" and "an ethics of ethics." But Levinas also still writes a theory of ethics in spite of himself.) This doubling up seems to allow for the analogy, but in a way that the analogy itself tends to efface, or leaves, precisely, in "equivocation."

The whole enigma (mystery or secret) of Kant's thinking about law is concentrated in this problem, this "equivocation" of a necessity that grounds law, and thus right, but that here immediately undermines the foundations of that same right to the point that, once again, it must remain secret. The secret of the law is that necessity knows no law, whereas all law must know necessity.[25]

This is, again, the secret hidden at the origin of the state, into which the subjects must not even inquire, the very question of which cannot even be raised without right being immediately overrun and provoked into a puni-

25. The other example of Kant's invoking the law of necessity is no less dramatic than the others, to the point of being not only exceptional but about the exception, the state of exception that, according to Carl Schmitt, who is perhaps not as far from Kant as one might suppose, is definitional of sovereignty as such. Again in the "Doctrine of Right," Kant is justifying, *contra* Beccaria, the use of the death penalty for murderers and their accomplices but stumbles on the possibility of having to execute everybody: "If, however, the number of accomplices (*correi*) to such a deed is so great that the state, in order to have no such criminals in it, could soon find itself without subjects; and if the state still does not want to dissolve, that is, to pass over into the state of nature, which is far worse because there is no external justice at all in it (and if it especially does not want to dull the people's feeling by the spectacle of a slaughterhouse), then the sovereign must also have it in his power, in this case of necessity (*casus necessitatis*), to assume the role of judge (to represent him) and pronounce a judgment that decrees for the criminals a sentence other than capital punishment, such as deportation, which still preserves the population. This cannot be done in accordance with public law, but it can be done by an executive decree, that is, by an act of the right of majesty which, as clemency, can always be exercised only in individual cases" (*MM*, 107–8).

tive paroxysm. This is the same secret that Kant is betraying, *ex lex*, when he secretly tries to denounce secrecy in *Perpetual Peace* and when he banishes our two equivocal cases to the Epicurean *intermundus* in the introduction to the "Doctrine of Right," only to see these two ghosts return phantomatically to haunt the entire text, emerging from the abyss of regicide or coming down from the heights of revolutionary violence.[26] Exactly here, on the frontier of right, torn between pure justice and natural necessity, is the place of the philosopher-politician, undecidably moral and moralistic, in the right and yet always radically equivocal, with his wisdom that is also always mere prudence, his claim to *parrhesia* that is still always perhaps a rhetorical ploy, his wholly public secrets and totally transparent veil. This properly equivocal position, this frontier position, where law trembles, gathers together the quasi-concepts we have been following in Kant. Nature is again one possible name for this, to the extent that, since Heraclitus, nature has loved to hide, fold on itself, double and veil itself, make itself secret. In spite of certain appearances, this frontier as such (but in truth it is nothing and can have no quiddity) is no more political than it is conceptual, no more practical than it is theoretical, but rather the "dynamic" division of these putative domains. Which is why we cannot avoid crossing Kant's final frontier—namely, that of judgment.

26. In "What Is Enlightenment?," just before the "paradox" of a lesser civil freedom allowing for a greater intellectual freedom: "But only a ruler who is himself enlightened and has no fear of phantoms, yet who likewise has at hand a well-disciplined and numerous army to guarantee public security, may say what no republic would dare to say: Argue as much as you like and about whatever you like, but obey!" (*KPW*, 59).

5. The Abyss of Judgment

> [Space] is (like time) limitless (not infinite).
>
> —Immanuel Kant, *Opus Postumum*
>
> *Wahrscheinlichkeiten fallen hier gar weg, wo es auf Urteile der reinen Vernunft enkommt.*
>
> —Immanuel Kant, *Critique of Judgment*

We still do not know what a frontier is, or even what its nature is, except to be of nature. And we could even say that just that is the frontier: not knowing. We trace frontiers in order to know, but we will know nothing of the frontier itself. Kant is less interested in knowledge per se, *pace* the neo-Kantians, than in its frontier, where knowledge fails.

If there were in Kant a faculty of the frontier, it would clearly be the faculty of judgment. The success of the operation might be disputed, but the aim of the third *Critique* seems clear enough: that of throwing a bridge over the abyss that has opened between the world of experience and the world of freedom, between speculative and practical reason.[1] The abyss is, it would seem, again what we are here calling the frontier, in a peculiarly exacerbated or exasperated form. But judgment would be the faculty allowing it to be crossed, or at least allowing the two sides to be joined. Judgment would then be reason itself being rational, the pure faculty of relations that are both singular and analogous. But it will turn out, following a fractal logic that has been appearing regularly along our path, that the frontier, and therefore judgment itself, is merely the layered multiplication of its own collapsing structure.

Let's put this suggestion to the test of reading. We must first note a certain complication in the treatment Kant reserves for judgment. For example, in the first *Critique*, just where he explains the discursive character of human

1. As Derrida points out, the bridge is a figure of analogy, an analogy for analogy itself, just as analogy is a bridge that, being thrown over the abyss, also throws us into a kind of mise en abyme: "The abyss calls for analogy—the active recourse of the whole Critique—but analogy plunges endlessly into the abyss as soon as a certain art is needed to describe analogically the play of analogy" (*The Truth in Painting*, 36).

knowledge, Kant draws from it a primordial place for judgment. The understanding is not an intuitive but discursive faculty, because, unlike mathematics, it gives rise to a knowledge by concepts that it does not construct. But all the understanding can do with concepts is to judge with them:

> Now the understanding can make no other use of these concepts than that of judging by means of them. [. . .] Judgment is therefore the mediate cognition of an object, hence the representation of a representation of it. In every judgment there is a concept that holds of many, and that among this many also comprehends a given representation, which is then related immediately to the object. We can, however, trace all actions of the understanding back to judgments, so that the *understanding* in general can be represented as a *faculty for judging* [ein Vermögen zu urteilen]. For according to what has been said above it is a faculty for thinking. Thinking is cognition through concepts. (*CPR*, A68–69/B93–94)

To think is to know via concepts; for us, those concepts have a discursive use; so we use them in order to judge. What is proper to the act of judgment is the fact of identifying, for a concept, a case of that concept, a case that will be subsumed under that concept. Judgment always has to do with cases, whence, a little further along in the first *Critique*, a more detailed description of its operation, at the very beginning of the chapter entitled "Of Transcendental Judgment in General," where "judgment" now translates *Urteilskraft*. As the understanding is the faculty of rules, judgment is the power of subsuming under those rules (i.e., of recognizing cases). General logic cannot contain rules for judgment because (according to a formula Wittgenstein would later make famous) there would have to be a further rule for the application of rules, and then a rule for the application of *that* rule, and so on *ad infinitum*. Judgment is an innate capacity that cannot be taught, the *Mutterwitz* that no knowledge can provide or do without.[2]

What distinguishes transcendental judgment is that it seems that it can give itself its cases *a priori* and thus find its object without exposing itself to the risk that *Mutterwitz* will fail. Given that it deals only with the relation to an object in general, transcendental logic as such presupposes that its case is given, without having to subsume it each time. As there is transcendental logic only insofar as a possible object in general is given, this logic cannot fail to presuppose that object. But as, according to a formula Kant constantly

2. This is why much later, and equally famously, Kant will say that philosophy cannot be learned (except historically) and that at best we can learn to philosophize (*CPR*, A837/B865). One can become erudite without making up the failure of judgment that Kant calls simply *Dummheit*, stupidity, and this would be the basis for his objections against the historians of philosophy we read earlier.

repeats, our knowledge is limited by the bounds of possible experience, even this apparently certain judgment is oriented toward empirical judgments as alone giving it possible content. Judgment as such, then, cannot avoid the singular case, and this is what will give it its peculiar status in Kant: For judgment is presented both as a faculty and as the "faculty" of any possible distinction between faculties, the faculty of their frontiers.[3]

According to the definitive introduction to the third *Critique*, judgment has no place in doctrine, in the achieved system of a metaphysics, but only in critique. So it seems there is something properly critical about judgment. From the point of view of doctrine, there are only two types of concepts—of nature, on the one hand; of freedom, on the other. In the system, judgment, situated between these two domains, can be attached to either of these two faculties as needed. Having repeated and justified the division of philosophy into two in its first section, the introduction pulls back to consider "The Domain of Philosophy in General," "Vom Gebiete der Philosophie überhaupt." This is where we encounter a famous passage that tries to draw frontiers in this domain, which contains all objects of any possible application of concepts:

> Concepts, insofar as they are related to objects, regardless of whether a cognition of the latter is possible or not,[4] have their field [ihr Feld], which is determined merely in accordance with the relation which their object has to our faculty of cognition [Erkenntnisvermögen] in general.[5]—The part of this

3. Jean-François Lyotard provides perhaps the most sustained reading of this position of judgment in Kant (see especially *Leçons sur l'analytique du sublime* [Paris: Galilée, 1991]). However, I am wary of the temptation to seek in the Analytic of the Sublime the place of the political in Kant. I shall rather be attempting what might appear to be a rehabilitation of the teleological judgment, but as radically cut from its *telos*. This does not simply return us to the famous "purposiveness without purpose" or "finality without end" of the aesthetic judgment (as brilliantly expounded by Derrida in *The Truth in Painting* [83–118]) but rather to something of the order of the end of the end, a purposiveness without purposiveness or a finality without finality.

4. The term *Erkenntnis* does not necessarily imply knowledge of a theoretical kind but refers to a relation to the object in general. But there is some hesitation in Kant on this matter, marked here by the fact that philosophy in general, according to the title of this section of the introduction, has a "domain," whereas what is more properly called a domain (that of theoretical knowledge) will later be circumscribed within that general domain.

5. So the field is the zone within the general domain where there is an as yet indeterminate relation between concept and object; that there be this relation constitutes a kind of cognition prior to knowledge. Kant does not say whether the general domain of philosophy extends still further out, but one might imagine that general logic would

> field within which cognition is possible for us is a territory [Boden, a ground] (*territorium*) for these concepts and the requisite faculty of cognition. [So the territory is situated within the field, is smaller than it.] The part of the territory [following a concentric progression, then] in which these are legislative [gesetzgebend] is the domain [Gebiet, the same word as for the whole space of philosophy in general: as with all legislation, what irrupts in the center is also the absolute outside] (*ditio*) of these concepts and of the corresponding faculty of cognition. Thus empirical concepts do indeed have their territory in nature, as the set of all objects of sense, but no domain (only their residence [Aufenthalt], *domicilium*) [so we are to imagine that the part of the territory that does not fall within the domain is the residence or can give rise to a residence]; because they are, to be sure, lawfully generated, but are not legislative, rather the rules grounded on them are empirical, hence contingent. (*CJ*, 61–62)

Let's take this distribution as literally as possible. Kant implicitly invites us to draw a diagram of it, which might look like this:

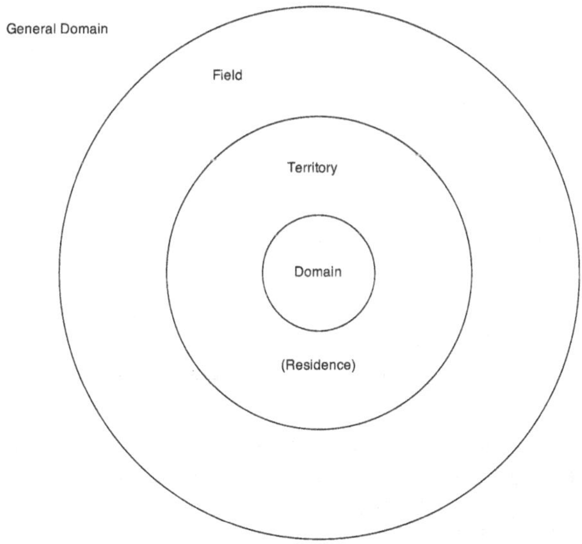

occupy that part of the general domain that falls outside the field. We would need to read this passage against the preface to the *Groundwork*, where the first great division of philosophy separates formal philosophy (logic), which does not deal with objects, from material philosophy, which then divides again into natural philosophy and moral philosophy, each of which contains a pure part and an empirical part. Note that the version given in the third *Critique* abandons an arborescent model (a common trunk divides into branches that divide again) in favor of a territorial model (frontiers have to be drawn in space). This territorial language is of course widespread in Kant, at least from the first *Critique* onward.

But we have immediately to complicate things, because Kant opens the following paragraph by saying that "our cognitive faculty as a whole has two domains, that of the concepts of nature and that of the concept of freedom; for it is *a priori* legislative through both" (*CJ*, 62). But the terrain or territory of these two domains is the same (the terrain of objects of possible experience), and so we must think that they can and even must share some objects, which would give the following diagram:

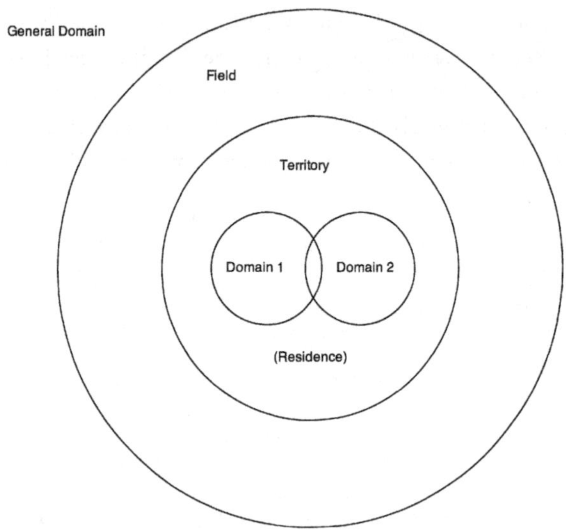

We shall see this still quite simple topography getting more and more complicated as Kant advances in his description. The fact that the two legislations bear on domains situated on the same terrain (domains that overlap at least somewhat, and perhaps completely) does not give rise to interferences at the level of legislation itself but to a mutual limitation (Kant uses the verb *einschranken*, which has become familiar to us) at the level of its effects. But the two domains remain separate to the extent that their objects are different in nature, or at least are considered in different lights or perspectives. Concepts of nature present their objects to intuition, as phenomena, whereas concepts of freedom present them as things in themselves, without that presentation taking place in intuition. Where there is theoretical knowledge, there is no thing in itself, and where there are things in themselves, there is no theoretical knowledge. Of such a "knowledge" (which if it claimed to be such would be, in us, finite beings, transcendental illusion), we must indeed have an Idea, which then takes its place in the field, but without giving rise to a terrain or, *a fortiori*, to a domain:

> There is thus an unlimited [unbegrenztes: so we were wrong to draw a frontier around the field within the general domain, but if we erase it we are at a bit of a loss as to how to represent the relations between the field and the general domain] but also inaccessible field for our faculty of cognition as a whole, namely the field of the supersensible, in which we find no territory for ourselves, and thus cannot have on it a domain for theoretical cognition either for the concepts of the understanding or for those of reason, a field that we must certainly occupy with ideas for the sake of the theoretical as well as the practical use of reason, but for which, in relation to the laws from the concept of freedom, we can provide nothing but a practical reality, through which, accordingly, our theoretical cognition is not in the least extended to the supersensible. (*CJ*, 63)

This already complicates the description given by Kant because, where we thought we were dealing with a concentric arrangement of field, terrain, and domain, we now see that things are more complex. Previously, it appeared that theoretical and practical cognition each had their domain within the terrain; now, the domain of the practical is, if not identified, at least placed in a strange relation with the (now unlimited) field that surrounds the terrain. To understand what is happening here, we clearly need to introduce a dynamic element into the picture, which would allow practical legislation to take place from out of the field while still aiming at the domain inside the terrain apparently occupied by theoretical legislation. This is why the famous gulf or abyss, the *unübersehbare Kluft*, the cleft over which one cannot see, is not simply a division or accentuated division between two sides of the same type and also why the attempt to throw a bridge over it (the bridge of judgment) is not as easy to conceive as is sometimes thought, unless we imagine a one-way bridge:[6]

> Now although there is an incalculable gulf fixed between the domain of the concept of nature, as the sensible, and the domain of the concept of freedom, as the supersensible, so that from the former to the latter (thus by means of the theoretical use of reason) no transition is possible, just as if there were so many different worlds, the first of which can have no influence on the second: yet the latter *should* [soll] have an influence on the former, namely the concept of freedom should [soll] make the end that is imposed by its laws real in the sensible world; and nature must [muß] consequently also be able to be conceived in such a way that the lawfulness of its form is at least in agreement with

6. At Dartford, near London, traffic crosses the Thames in one direction through a tunnel and in the other over a bridge. This might give a working representation of the relations in Kant between theory and practice.

> the possibility of the ends that are to be realized in it in accordance with the laws of freedom.—Thus there must [es muß] still be a ground of the *unity* of the supersensible that grounds nature with that which the concept of freedom contains practically, the concept of which, even if it does not suffice for cognition of it either theoretically or practically, and thus has no proper domain of its own, nevertheless makes possible the transition from the manner of thinking in accordance with the principles of the one to that in accordance with the principles of the other. (*CJ*, 63)

So if there is a possibility of transition from one domain to the other, this transition happens in one direction only (it is impossible to move from the theoretical to the practical, on pain of transcendental illusion), and this is done not by throwing a bridge over the abyss but by going under, through a tunnel; because the *Kluft* does have a bottom, it cuts into the common subsoil of the field, a sub-soil that is, however, super-sensible and that is shared by theoretical and practical cognition. This passage, or its possibility, is not itself of the order of theoretical knowledge. That it be possible to pass from the practical to the theoretical (that legislation according to freedom be compatible with legislation according to nature), that the moral law has effects that can be seen in the world, forms part of what makes that law the law that it is. It is duty's duty to realize itself in the phenomenal world. The moral law must, ought, or has to be able to actualize itself in the sensible world, according to a pre- or archi-moral duty we already signaled as the archi-prescription of prescription ("do it!"): Duty owes it to itself (*se doit*) to make itself real. But this primary *Sollen* (which must precede the distinction between nature and freedom, because it is the principle of their separation and their communication), according to which one has to have effects in the world, provokes in return another duty that this time owes it to itself to be a *Müssen*, according to which the legality of natural legality is such that it must, by its form, lend itself to this realization of moral ends. Only this consequence gives any substance to the archi-duty of duty, because if nature did not respond, duty could owe itself to itself *ad infinitum* without that duty ever becoming possible to carry out. It is necessary, then, for the duty of duty to be realizable as it ought to be, failing which it would not be duty and there would be no duty. There *ought to be* the *it is necessary that*, because *it is necessary* that duty *ought to be* done. This originary connivance between necessity and obligation, nature and freedom, *müssen* and *sollen*, mechanism and ends, will make judgment (which has not yet been named in the introduction) into an essentially teleological judgment.

The sensible world is thus the end of duty, or because duty is obligatory from the end, it is the end of the end. What Kant has not yet called "judgment" will be the faculty of this doubled-up end or of this movement that carries duty toward its end and ensures that the moral law will find in the natural world the formal condition of its possible realization. Consequently, and contrary to what one might think on reading the "typic" in the second *Critique*, the form of law, the *Gesetzmässigkeit* that the moral law supposedly borrows from nature, is, rather, given to nature by the form of law of the moral law. Nature has legal form in order to respond to the moral law; natural necessity is thus dictated by the moral law, which gives a (supersensible) ground to its necessity but, at the same stroke (by digging the tunnel), undermines this ground. Because natural necessity owes itself to duty, it is no longer quite necessary or quite natural. That the (legal) form of nature must accord with the possibility of ends is its end. The end of nature is that law find its end in it. And in this way, even the archi-determinative judgment of the first *Critique* is already teleological, because it must presuppose that nature is such that it will provide it with cases that fit the law that the understanding is in a position to prescribe to it. This is precisely what allows for the possibility of the transcendental position itself. The understanding is thus legislative with respect to nature in a very strong sense, which involves a prescriptive or pre-scriptive element—the understanding prescribes itself a nature such that the laws it pronounces will find cases in it. Nature is in this way made for the judgment that will make a case, and this *made for* already gives its end to nature as able to receive practico-moral realizations. Even the subsumptive determinative judgment, then, is determined in return by its apparent other, which returns through the tunnel to pop up in the middle, like a foreign legislator.

Kant says this much later, in §76 of the Critique of Teleological Judgment. Reason demands the unification of the diverse. But the understanding, insofar as it is tied to sensibility and therefore subject to a transcendental logic (for the transcendental is less what rises away from and more what comes back down to the singular and the empirical), can only proceed from the universal to the particular, in which it cannot fail to find something contingent. This contingent element must be brought back under the law, which is done by postulating a purposiveness of the contingent as such:

> But now since the particular, as such, contains something contingent with regard to the universal, but reason nevertheless still requires unity, hence lawfulness, in the connection of particular laws of nature (which lawfulness of the contingent is called purposiveness), and the a priori derivation of the particular laws from the universal, as far as what is contingent in the former is concerned,

> is impossible through the determination of the concept of the object, thus the concept of the purposiveness of nature in its products is a concept that is necessary for the human power of judgment in regard to nature. (*CJ*, 274)[7]

The apparently paradoxical consequence is that, for all its legality, nature must be fundamentally *contingent*. To be able to welcome the law, nature must not be necessary through and through. Natural necessity, seen from the point of view of its end (the law), is that it be contingent. The necessity of necessity is contingency. This chance of contingency (law's only chance) is not knowable as such but the object of a nonknowledge that calls for what is called judgment. For us to be able to judge from the end, there must be contingency, because only contingency calls for the end as the only chance of its legality. Necessity has no end, it is blind. For the end, this blindness must blind itself again in the contingency of blind chance.

Nature, then, has an end, a purpose: that of having a purposiveness, which it has only in contingency. That there be this end comes under neither theoretical cognition (for if we could demonstrate it, we would reduce contingency to natural necessity; this is why Kant constantly repeats that the principle of judgment—namely, that we must judge as if it were made to be judged—is only subjective, or at least is not objective, while functioning just as if it were objective, because otherwise there would be no "subject") nor practical cognition (there is no duty here) but underlies the possibility of both domains as the indispensable presupposition of their joining and separation. And yet, if this presupposition is what links the two domains beneath the abyss, it alone gives rise to the abyss. The theoretical and the practical are separated only because they are thus linked together by the purposive legality of the singular judgment. Kant's problem in the third *Critique* is thus not to bring together two domains that ran the risk of being too far separated but

7. See too the opening of §64: "In order to see that a thing is possible only as an end, i.e., that the causality of its origin must be sought not in the mechanism of nature, but in a cause whose productive capacity is determined by concepts, it is necessary that its form not be possible in accordance with mere natural laws, i.e., ones that can be cognized by us through the understanding, applied to objects of the senses, alone; rather even empirical cognition of their cause and effect presupposes concepts of reason. Since reason must be able to cognize the necessity in every form of natural product if it would understand the conditions connected with its generation, the *contingency* of their form with respect to all empirical laws of nature in relation to reason is itself a ground for regarding their causality as if it were possible only through reason; but this is then the capacity for acting in accordance with ends (a will); and the object which is represented as possible only on this basis is represented as possible only as an end." §67 will extend this logic to nature as a whole *qua* system, as we shall see in detail later.

precisely to think the frontier of these two domains, to think them together *as* separated. This is why, at the beginning of section 3 of the introduction, Kant repeats that we are not here dealing with a third domain but with what allows us to establish the legality of the other two domains, by tracing their frontiers:

> The critique of the faculties of cognition with regard to what they can accomplish *a priori* has, strictly speaking, no domain with regard to objects, because it is not a doctrine, but only has to investigate whether and how a doctrine is possible through it given the way it is situated with respect to our faculties. Its field [Feld] extends to all the presumptions of that doctrine, in order to set it within its rightful limits [um sie in die Grenzen ihrer Rechtmässigkeit zu setzen]. However, what cannot enter into the division of philosophy can nevertheless enter as a major part into the critique of the pure faculty of cognition in general if, namely, it contains principles that are for themselves fit neither for theoretical nor for practical use. (*CJ*, §64)

The critical chance of thought (of reason insofar as it is finally, in the end, devoted to morality) would then be the frontier as a separation that allows for a passage. This chance depends on contingency, which alone bears witness to the possibility in nature of a causality other than that of mechanism, and which, extended to the system of nature as such, will tell the truth of mechanism itself, as we shall see. But then, the whole Kantian topography is turned upside down when it comes to specifying the nature and place of judgment. Kant began by establishing the apparent mutual independence of the domains of nature and freedom; he then deduced a quasi-practical quasi-necessity of a one-directional transition between the two, which alone ensured their true separation. Now he is seeking a faculty to take charge of this uniquely critical activity.

Only here does analogy intervene, and as we have had several occasions to note, analogy analogizes endlessly (or bottomlessly). The analogy is not merely the bridge (or the tunnel) that crosses the abyss, it is simultaneously the abyss itself, which is starting to provoke cracks and fissures everywhere in the fields, terrains, and domains delimited so far. Kant takes another look at the frontier between understanding and reason and finds between the two the power of judgment (here named for the first time), "about which one has cause to presume, by analogy [nach der Analogie]" that it could also (by analogy, then, with the faculties of the understanding and of reason) have the means to legislate, or rather (because what is proper to the frontier is that it is not a domain) not to have its own legislation but "a proper principle of its own for seeking laws [ein ihr eigenes Prinzip nach Gesetzen zu suchen]."

Which would give judgment, *qua* bearer of its own principle, if not a domain ("even though it can claim no field of objects as its domain [wenn ihm gleich kein Feld der Gegenstände als sein Gebeit zuständе]" says Kant, insouciantly muddying any remaining terminological clarity of his own description), at least a terrain.[8]

To seek laws, for what is proper to judgment as such (i.e., when it is not simply pressed into the service of theoretical knowledge—which, while being already teleological, as we saw, does not need to judge in a strong sense to the extent that the law is already given to it and it only has to subsume the case)[9] is precisely to be seeking its own law. As we said, the whole Kantian system is teleological in that it is organized for the law. But we must not conclude from this, as is perhaps a common thing to do, that the law *qua* law is already given. To the contrary—and this is precisely why the general contingency of nature passes the understanding, which, for its part, believes in its necessity—purposiveness as legality of the contingent stretches out toward a law that has not yet come. Which is why judgment as such is essentially reflective (determinative judgment being the blind judgment of blind necessity) in search of its law. *Qua* reflective, judgment does not know how to judge but tries to judge. In judging, it calls for its law for which it can only wait. One can always draw a law from a judgment, but the law of judgment is that that law will never be certain. Judgment is made for a law it can never establish. Judgment itself thus has the structure of a purposiveness without purpose, a legality without law (*CJ*, §22), and, following the play of analogy,

8. Recall that in the initial description of the general domain of philosophy, there was some terrain with no domain, what Kant called the "residence," the *Aufenthalt*, the place for concepts that were lawful without being legislative, giving rise to rules that were empirical and thus contingent. This is the part of the general domain that judgment will occupy as its proper (non)domain.

9. This is no doubt why, in §74, Kant identifies determinative judgment with dogmatic procedure, reflective judgment with critical procedure: "We deal with a concept dogmatically (even if it is supposed to be empirically conditioned) if we consider it as contained under another concept of the object, which constitutes a principle of reason, and determine it in accordance with the latter. But we deal with it merely critically if we consider it only in relation to our cognitive faculties, hence in relation to the subjective conditions for thinking it, without undertaking to decide anything about its object. The dogmatic treatment of a concept is thus that which is lawful for the determining, the critical that which is lawful merely for the reflecting power of judgment" (*CJ*, 266). As Lyotard has most clearly brought out, critique is only really critical, only really itself, only comes to itself in reflective judgment. We might add that given the becoming-teleological even of the determinative judgment, critique entails a reflective judgment on the issue of the determinative judgment itself.

finds this structure in, or projects this structure into, some of the objects of its judgment. So the aesthetic judgment is "aesthetic," and so on without end.

But this structure is that of transcendentality as such. The transcendental is a movement beyond that comes back. Experience is empirical for the transcendental—in view of the transcendental, viewed from the transcendental—as nature is contingent for the law. The transcendental comes back to the empirical as law comes back to nature. But this means that the transcendental is (no more than) the empirical that comes back (to itself). And this analogy between the transcendental and the law is, rather, an identity. The transcendental names the being-law of law as such.[10] This (being-)law names a seeking after the law (still the *Seefahrer* or perhaps the astronaut), because we do not yet have the law and we will not have it, on pain of dogmatism: We only have the law of the law, which is its endless retreat. So the transcendental is not yet transcendental but what is nowadays called the quasi-transcendental. The transcendental can "be" transcendental only on condition of not *being* transcendental (for then it would be transcendent). What separates the transcendental from the transcendent is what dynamically separates the transcendental from the transcendent—namely, the frontier "itself." Saying that this separation is dynamic is also a way of saying that it is not done but that it is doing, as the becoming-transcendent of the transcendental and the becoming transcendental of the transcendent, which is the very tracing of the frontier. Every frontier transcendentalizes to the extent that it separates, and it prevents the achievement of that transcendentalization to the extent that it joins. The transcendental is the abyssal demultiplication of the frontier, along the frontier.

This is why Kant, under the name "cosmopolitanism," has to think at most an internationalism (the chance of cosmopolitanism lies this side of cosmopolitanism, it needs the frontier whose erasure it also projects) and why the end as (mortal) perpetual peace withdraws as a finality that must never reach its end. The chance of peace is not to be perpetual but perpetually in the process of putting off its perpetuity. Teleology thus understood puts an end to the end; it returns on itself. According to a logic that has been haunting us all along, the end of teleology is the end of teleology. "Zweckmässigkeit ohne Zweck" is no doubt naming nothing but that. "Purposiveness without

10. We must beware of this formulation, which is unduly ontological: law is not being and thus is not to be taken in terms of a "law-*being*," even if it can only be understood in relation to being. The reading of teleology we are attempting here tries to situate it between a being and an "oughting" of the law. The law of the law *is* not ought, and *ought* not to be.

purpose," "finality without end" still has too much end in its finality. So as not to be held hostage by the end, perhaps we could try other formulations: ((finality (without end) without end)), or "((finality (without finality)) without end)."[11]

This could easily bring us back to Epicurus. As we have seen, every time Kant states a crucial problem for his philosophy, the ghost of Epicurus comes to prowl around. And if Epicurus, before, was opposed to Plato for the antinomy in the first *Critique*, and to the Stoics for the relation between virtue and happiness in the second, here he will be opposed to Spinoza. As always for what we are interested in here, the context is one of antinomy, as expounded in the dialectic of teleological judgment.

The determinative judgment cannot have an antinomy, says Kant, because it is not autonomous, does not lay down a law. However, when we are dealing with the reflective judgment—in which, as we saw, the law is not given, but where judgment gives itself the law—judgment has to follow maxims for guidance, and these maxims can enter into conflict among themselves, giving rise to the possibility of an antinomy and, therefore, a dialectic, which calls for critique. Exploring empirical nature beyond what is legislated determinatively by the categories of the understanding, we are led to invoke the maxim that all natural products must be possible according to mechanical causality but also, sometimes, especially when we come across organisms, the maxim according to which at least this part of nature (but perhaps nature as a whole, understood according to the analogy between it and the organisms it contains) can be explained only by appealing to purposive causality, to final causes. Kant's presentation can give the impression that this antinomy is simply solved (by the end of §71, and even as early as §70, in the very statement of the antinomy, which on that reading would evaporate immediately) by insisting on the fact that these are merely maxims of investigation, regulative principles of our investigation and not constitutive principles of the objects of that investigation. There would be an obvious contradiction if one were to assert that an object were objectively caused both by natural mechanism and by final causality (a technic of nature) but no contradiction in appealing as a principle for judging nature (without claiming that this gives rise to objective knowledge), on the one hand to the maxim of mechanical causality (I have to judge according to that maxim as far as possible, for only this maxim puts me on the path to knowledge properly speaking, even if that

11. Perhaps we could exploit other semantic valences of the word *Zweckmässigkeit*, which also implies suitability, fitness, a being-opportune that conjures up a thought of chance and the event, the *kairos*, the right moment.

knowledge is not determinative) and, on the other, to the maxim of final causality (when the first maxim no longer serves, I have to judge some natural objects—most notably organisms, and even, following their example, nature as a whole—according to a quite different principle, that of final causality).

Kant's argument here is extremely delicate. If one were to maintain these two principles dogmatically (making them into determinative principles), there would indeed be an antinomy, because these two principles would be in contradiction. But as Kant points out, this contradiction would not be an antinomy of judgment, because by making these principles into principles determining objects, we would have provoked a contradiction in rational legislation itself with regard to nature, and that contradiction could not be resolved, because human reason cannot determine the objects of empirical nature. We do, of course, prescribe laws to nature, according to transcendental logic, but these laws cannot determine nature *qua* field of empirical investigation, in which, as we shall see in more detail, objects *qua* particular cases remain in part contingent with respect to the legislation of reason.

It cannot, therefore, suffice to insist that we are dealing only with maxims, regulative principles for the reflective judgment of empirical nature, in order to solve the antinomy of judgment, because it is only on the level of maxims that there is an antinomy of judgment (rather than of rational legislation itself). And yet Kant, at the end of a paragraph that presents itself as a mere preparation to the solution of the antinomy (§71: "Vorbereitung zur Auflösung obiger Antinomie"), can write the following:

> All appearance of an antinomy between the maxims of that kind of explanation which is genuinely physical (mechanical) and that which is teleological (technical) therefore rests on confusing a fundamental principle of the reflecting with that of the determining power of judgment, and on confusing the *autonomy* of the former (which is valid merely subjectively for the use of our reason in regard to the particular laws of experience) with the *heteronomy* of the latter, which has to conform to the laws given by the understanding (whether general or particular). (*CJ*, 261)

But Kant has already explained that an antinomy of judgment can arise only if the maxims of judgment are only maxims of judgment (and not principles determinative of objects). The antinomy of judgment does not result from a confusion of autonomy and heteronomy but from the fact that judgment is autonomous. The antinomy cannot be solved by simply recalling the same antinomy. Any appearance of a legislative antinomy (an insoluble contradiction) is removed by recalling the maxim-status of the mechanistic and finalist principles. It still remains to resolve the properly judgmental antinomy that results—the resolution of the antinomy of judgment is prepared by removing any appearance of an antinomy in the law.

So where exactly do we find the antinomy that remains to be resolved? In the very presentation of the antinomy in §70, Kant seems to suggest that the coexistence of the two maxims is fundamentally peaceful. But this peace of judgment about nature does not result from the equal status of the two maxims but a subordination of the one to the other, in the name of knowledge:

> For if I say that I must judge [beurteilen] the possibility of all events in material nature and hence all forms, as their products, in accordance with merely mechanical laws, I do not thereby say that they *are possible only in accordance with such laws* (to the exclusion of any other kind of causality); rather, that only indicates that *I should* [*soll*] always *reflect* on them *in accordance with the principle* of the mere mechanism of nature, and hence research the latter, so far as I can, because if it is not made the basis for research then there can be no proper cognition of nature [keine eigentliche Naturerkenntnis]. Now this is not an obstacle to the second maxim for searching after a principle and reflecting upon it which is quite different from explanation in accordance with the mechanisms of nature, namely the principle of final causes, on the proper occasion, namely in the case of some forms of nature (and, at their instance, even the whole of nature). (*CJ*, 259)

So the point is not to have both maxims available and choose one or other arbitrarily. In the perspective of knowledge, the principle of mechanical causality (in harmony with everything in the understanding that is legislative with respect to nature) comes first, and we stick with it as long as possible, moving to the other maxim only when the mechanistic explanation comes up short (for example, when faced with organisms). However—and this is where the antinomy will come into its own—the odd occasions on which one appeals to the purposive principle of judgment also serve as a pretext or a motive to judge similarly of nature as a whole (judging that nature is fundamentally teleological), which cannot fail to bring about a conflict between the two maxims, which henceforth are trying to apply to the same objects at the same time. The antinomy comes about as a result of abandoning any dogmatic claim to knowledge, which allows free competition between the two maxims of judgment.

We do not know if mechanical causality suffices to account for everything that is in nature, and we do not know this because natural particularities and their laws are, for us, empirical and therefore, at least in part, contingent. So we know that we cannot know nature through and through according to mechanical causality, despite the infinite field for judgment opened up by this principle in the scientific investigation of nature. We know that for us mechanical causality does not account for everything (for example, organisms). We could simply leave things at that (and there would be no antinomy). If our investigation of nature is driven by the search for scientific knowledge, we will follow the mechanistic maxim as far as possible, and the purposive maxim as regards organized beings, without further elaborating the "speculative" question of knowing whether (without making it a determinative principle) this latter maxim does not tend toward an inclusive understanding of nature as such, which would reverse the order of the hierarchy of maxims in favor of the maxim of purposive causality. That maxim tells us to judge as if nature involved a final causality, and for the purposes of the investigation of nature we can and even must remain with this subjective status of the maxim without making more of it. But we might also ask (while ruling out any theoretical knowledge in this respect) whether the invitation nature gives us to judge it according to the maxim of final causality does not take us further:

> Now one could leave this question or problem for speculation entirely untouched and unsolved, for if we are satisfied with speculation within the boundaries [Grenzen] of the mere cognition of nature, the above maxims are sufficient for studying nature as far as human powers reach and for probing its most hidden secrets. [But to the extent that we are not satisfied with this, and do try to go beyond those limits] It must therefore be a certain presentiment [Ahnung] of our reason, or a hint as it were given to us by nature, that we could by means of that concept of final causes step beyond nature and even connect it to the highest point in the series of causes if we were to abandon research into nature (even though we have not gotten very far in that), or at least set it aside for a while, and attempt to discover first where that stranger [Fremdling] in natural science, namely the concept of natural ends, leads. (*CJ*, 261–62)

Suspending scientific research in this way, in the name of speculative reason, does not mean one is falling back into the dogmatism that consisted in taking a subjective principle for a determinative principle but rather opening a question, a problem, as Kant says, "a wide array of controversial problems." And these controversies have indeed taken place in the tradition: Either it has been asserted that the technic of nature (its at least apparent operation according to final causality) is not intentional (and thus is not really a final causality but rather "identical with the mechanism of nature or dependent on one and the same ground, where, however, since in many products of nature this ground is often too deeply hidden for our research, we attempt to ascribe it to nature by analogy with a subjective principle, namely that of art, i.e., causality in accordance with ideas" [*CJ*, 181]) or that it is intentional and that there really is a final causality. Kant, running the risk of confusing the reader, calls the claim that the technic of nature is not really one the system of idealism (in the sense that the final causality operates only at the level of the idea) and realism the system according to which there really is such a final causality.

As is often the case in Kant, there is some degree of convergence between the history of philosophy and the *a priori* deductions of reason: Reason alone suggests a matrix of four possible ways of approaching the problem of the objective purposiveness of nature—and it turns out that these four possibilities have indeed been realized in the texts of the tradition. Kant, very satisfied with this convergence, which means that the dogmatic resources of reason have all been exploited, henceforth leaving room only for critique (according to the schema laid out in the first preface to the first *Critique*), adds a footnote:

> One sees from this that in most speculative matters of pure reason the philosophical schools have usually tried all of the solutions that are possible for a certain question concerning dogmatic assertions. Thus for the sake of the purposiveness of nature either *lifeless matter* or a *lifeless God* as well as *living matter* or a *living God* have been tried. Nothing is left for us except, if need be, to give up all these objective *assertions* and to weigh our judgment critically, merely in relation to our cognitive faculty, in order to provide its principle with the non-dogmatic but adequate validity of a maxim for the reliable use of reason. (*CJ*, 263n)

If we clearly must not conclude too rapidly that, in order to orient himself in thinking, Kant begins by appealing to the tradition, we must also beware of accepting too readily that critique has been able to overcome that tradition. As we shall see, Kant has the greatest difficulty establishing the status of his "maxims" here (the whole drama of this antinomy) and, by the same token, separating the properly critical moment of his thinking from what the tradition presents dogmatically. As we shall not cease verifying, it is contingency that plays a crucial role here, and we shall see that, in spite of appearances, it is again from Epicurus that Kant will have the greatest difficulty taking his distance.

Each of Kant's two ways of approaching the problem in turn divides into two. On the side of idealism, we have on the one hand, as we saw earlier, Epicurus (and Democritus), and on the other Spinoza:

> The *idealism* of purposiveness (I always mean objective purposiveness here) is now either that of the *accidentality* or of the *fatality* of the determination of

> nature in the purposive form of its products. The first principle concerns the relation of matter to the physical ground of its form, namely the laws of motion; the second concerns the *hyperphysical* ground of matter and the whole of nature. The system of *accidentality*, which is ascribed to Epicurus or Democritus, is, if taken literally, so obviously absurd that it need not detain us; by contrast, the system of fatality (of which Spinoza is made the author, although it is to all appearance much older), which appeals to something supersensible, to which our insight therefore does not reach, is not so easy to refute, since its concept of the original being is not intelligible at all [nicht zu verstehen ist]. (*CJ*, 263)

This "absurdity" of the Epicurean system (Democritus never reappears in the rest of the text and the question of any differences there may be between Democritus and Epicurus, which was to occupy a young German philosopher a few decades later, is not even raised), which is here dismissed in the same way as in the "Universal History" text, is the object a little later of a fuller explanation as to its absurdity:

> The systems that contend for the idealism of final causes in nature [i.e., those who argue that there are no such causes objectively speaking] concede to its principle a causality according to laws of motion (through which natural things purposively exist [i.e., there is an appearance of purposive causality, which is really only a mechanical causality]), but they deny *intentionality* to it, i.e., they deny that nature is intentionally determined to its purposive production, or, in other words, that an end is the cause. This is *Epicurus's* kind of explanation, on which the difference between a technique of nature and mere mechanism is completely denied [according to Epicurus there is only mechanical causality that, in some cases, produces effects which misleadingly seem to have been produced by final causality], and blind chance is assumed to be the explanation not only of the correspondence of generated products with our concepts of ends, hence of technique, but even of the determination of the causes of this generation in accordance with laws of motion, hence of their mechanism, and thus nothing is explained, not even the illusion in our teleological judgments, and hence the putative idealism in them is not demonstrated at all. (*CJ*, 264)

As always, the rejection of Epicurus turns out to be more complicated than Kant's initial gesture would suggest. For what is the basis of the refutation here? Not, as one might have expected, the fact that Epicurus simply denies all final causality in the name of mere mechanism (which would be enough to motivate rejection on the grounds of dogmatism, as in the first *Critique*, where, it will be remembered, the ambiguity in the presentation of Epicurus depended on the possibility of making his [anti-]theses into mere *hypo*theses leading to an enlargement of knowledge) but indeed the way he understands mechanical causality itself when he writes it off to chance. According to Epicurus as read by Kant, the only causality is causality by chance, which immediately removes all possibility of understanding anything at all. The appearance of final causality is then "explained" by the reality of a mechanical causality, which is not even a causality because it rests entirely on chance. Epicurus, called in to show that the appearance of finality in nature is not the result of an intention, shows too much from Kant's point of view by refusing even the principle of nonintentional mechanical causality, which makes the question of causality in general fall even below the opposition between intentionality and nonintentionality into pure chance, which explains nothing and is absurd by virtue of invoking absurdity (chance) as the principle for explaining anything at all.

So chance remains in an excessive and eccentric position with respect to the needs of Kant's demonstration. To fill this square in his matrix (the nonintentional/idealist square), Kant did not need a doctrine as radical as that of Epicurus, which, as he presents it, is not even a mechanistic dogmatism. Unless—and this is the suspicion that will henceforth guide our reading of the antinomy—in Kant's logic, mechanism without final causality will always be doomed to the abysses of chance, in which case, as always, Epicurus, excessive with respect to the position Kant assigns to him in the demonstration he is attempting here, will not really have been dismissed and will continue to prowl around the antinomy as what we might call its negative resource.

Recall Kant's procedure thus far. The antinomy of judgment results from the possibility for reason to appeal, in its consideration of nature, to two incompatible maxims: This antinomy is an antinomy of judgment—rather than a contradiction in the legislation of reason itself—only to the extent that we are in fact dealing with two maxims (regulative principles). In the perspective of the investigation of nature (in the optic of natural science), the coexistence of these two maxims is not a problem so long as we give priority to the maxim of mechanical explanation and follow it as far as possible, appealing to the finalist maxim only when the former no longer works (i.e., as we shall see, at the moment of contingency). But, following the (natural) movement of speculation, one can suspend this priority of the mechanical maxim and give priority to the finalist maxim, on the grounds that natural contingencies (as seen from the point of view of mechanism) may give us a clue as to a more inclusive natural purposiveness to which our reason cannot be indifferent and which would indeed be the question of transcendental philosophy. In the tradition, there are four main ways of dealing with this problem of at least apparent natural purposiveness, but the Epicurean way is absurd, for not only does it attempt to reduce purposiveness to mechanism (which in itself is not so different from what the naturalist must do to attain a true knowledge of nature), it also reduces mechanism to chance. It remains to be shown that that is the fate of all mechanistic explanation as such (and thus of any knowledge of nature in the theoretical sense and, in the end, of any determinative judgment) if it is not subordinated to the finalist maxim, which by the same token becomes much more than a simple "subjective" maxim. And this disturbs all the oppositions on the basis of which Kant is trying to think here, beginning with the oppositions between the constitutive and the regulative,[12] the determinative and the reflective, the contingent and the necessary, among others. In this perspective, the excessive position of Epicurus will give us something like a negative truth of Kant's thinking.

Kant thus disposes of the four traditional ways of dealing with the question of natural purposiveness: Epicureanism is "absurd," as we have just seen; Spinozism is unintelligible, in that it ends up positing a "blind necessity" (*CJ*, 265) that is the counterpart of the "blind chance" (*CJ*, 264) of Epicureanism; hylozoism is unsatisfactory because not only is the attribution of life to matter a simple category error but it also relies on a vicious circle (we suspect on the basis of organisms that nature as a whole is perhaps also organized in terms of final causality; hylozoism explains the purposiveness of the parts by simply presupposing the purposiveness of the whole, which is what we were supposed to be explaining); and theism is dogmatic in that we would first have to prove the impossibility of an exhaustive explanation according to mechanical causality before having grounds to posit in determinative fashion the existence of a superior intelligence outside nature. Having thus disposed of the four traditional ways of dealing with the problem, Kant needs to motivate the properly critical explanation of the antinomy (and even the bare presentation of the antinomy, because we are still waiting to find out exactly how this antinomy really is an antinomy), and this he attempts in §74. To have grounds for a dogmatic use (for a determinative judgment, then) of the concept of a thing as a natural end (namely the concept of a thing as part of a nature subject to final causality), we would have to be able to establish the objective reality ("objective," as always in Kant, according to the conditions of possibility of an experience for us) of this concept. One might be tempted to think that this concept *must* be objective, because it is undeniable that it comes to us in a context of empirical conditions, which must be subject to the laws of the understanding in general, which would then provide the

12. See *Opus Postumum*, 57, on the "transition" to Physics: "Regulative principles that are at the same time constitutive."

necessary principle of subsumption. But we cannot abstract this concept from experience (i.e., produce it *qua* concept by a process of abstraction from the singular conditions in which it shows up in given empirical situations), because it is a concept possible only as a rational principle of the judgment we bring to bear on the object. Which amounts to saying that we can never see a natural end as such (in a moment we shall see that all we ever see is a contingency), but we can judge a given object as being the result of a causality other than a mechanistic causality. But judging in this way, according to a rational principle indeed, but one the objective validity of which remains undemonstrable, we cannot be proceeding by subsumption according to a determinative judgment. So the principle remains regulative for a reflective judgment and thus susceptible to a treatment that is merely (but radically) critical (i.e., one that, given the position of judgment as we saw it in the introduction, cannot ever advance beyond critique to doctrine).

Because the judgment brought to bear according to this principle is necessarily brought to bear on the basis of a natural datum (what we judge to be a natural end—an organized being—is indeed found in nature), it seems to involve a contradiction, which will be the formal marker of the impossibility in which we find ourselves of making it into an objectively established concept giving rise to determinative judgments (and therefore objective knowledge). For to the very extent that the object in question is found in nature, it must necessarily involve necessity entailed by laws, whereas *qua* natural end it involves contingency with respect to those same laws. So the antinomy properly speaking is here: The point is not that we can invoke one or other of two maxims of investigation of which the one relays the other when the first fails, because the concept that guides one of those maxims (at least) (i.e., the one that guides the purposive maxim) is apparently split by two contradictory suppositions, of necessity and of contingency. This antinomy (in the very concept of natural end) can be resolved, says Kant, only by placing "end" and "nature" on radically different planes, which has as a consequence that the concept of natural end can never be objectively established:

> As a concept of a *natural product* it includes natural necessity and yet at the same time a contingency of the form of the object (in relation to mere laws of nature) in one and the same thing as an end; consequently, if there is not to be a contradiction here, it must contain a basis for the possibility of this thing in nature and yet at the same time a basis of the possibility of this nature itself and its relation to something that is not empirically cognizable nature (supersensible) and thus is not cognizable at all for us, in order to be judged in accordance with another kind of causality than that of the mechanism of nature, if its possibility is to be determined. (*CJ*, 267)

The contingency with respect to mechanical causality revealed by the form of organized beings, then, refers us not only to a different maxim to guide our research but refers us beyond nature as such, or at least toward a thinking of the whole of nature as grounded in something nonnatural and unknowable. The impossibility of getting to the end of our determinative-subsumptive judgments according to mechanical causality, the fact that we stumble over contingencies (namely, objects the organization of which is indubitable and yet escapes our mechanistic explanations), does not allow us to posit a purposive causality as objective (because we understand it not at all) but obliges us to think of the possibility of nature in general, the sphere of mechanical causality, as not itself falling, *qua* totality, under the law of that same mechanical causality that, in general, holds sway within it.

So the antinomy resides in the fact that, faced with organized beings, we find ourselves unable not to appeal simultaneously to both causalities, and its resolution consists in referring purposive causality (which had appeared in nature in the form of organized beings, which are contingent with respect to mechanical causality) to the unknowable (and hence super-natural) realm of the supersensible. The concept of natural end will, then, remain forever problematic and will never be able to motivate dogmatic responses, be they positive or negative. The concept of purposive causality does indeed exist objectively (as in human art and technology), as does that of a mechanical natural causality; what cannot attain to such objectivity is the concept of a *natural* purposive causality, for such a concept cannot be drawn from experience (by abstraction, as we were just saying) or posited as necessary for an experience to be possible. Such a concept will remain forever problematic because even if, *per impossibile*, I managed to show that some natural objects really were the intentional productions of a divine artistic understanding, I would in so doing simply withdraw them from the domain of nature, whereas the problem was that of knowing now to understand them as natural products. We can preserve the naturality of nature only by invoking in a merely problematic way a concept the (positive or negative) objectivity of which will never be established. Nature needs this strange concept of a nature other than simply natural nature, this phantom nature of which all we know is that we need it. I will attempt to show that once again this structure is that of transcendentality itself.

The fact that this concept is fundamentally problematic, then, does not above all mean that we could do without it. The problematic concept of natural end is in a certain sense necessary. How? In that it is necessary for necessity. We saw earlier that the study of nature in view of knowledge must lean toward the maxim of judgment according to mechanical causality, a judgment that is perfectly in accord with the necessary, determining, character of the law of nature (even if that law be, in the event, an empirical one). But the movement of Kant's thought, which consisted initially in "suspending" this investigation to answer the speculative, transcendental call of the other maxim, leads to the point where, at least when faced with organized beings, it is impossible for us not to invoke the two causalities simultaneously and to refer the second to the unknowable supersensible. But this ("subjective," regulative, problematic) reference of purposive causality beyond nature as such turns out, after the suspension of scientific investigation, to be indispensable to the progress of that investigation and even to its possibility as such.

Because, as Kant says in §75, the fact of making the concept of natural purposiveness merely a principle of my judgment (the result of the particular, limited, constitution of human rationality) merely confirms the necessity of this concept that escapes natural necessity: "It is in fact indispensable for us to subject nature to the concept of an intention if we would even merely conduct research among its organized products by means of continued observation; and this concept is thus already *an absolutely necessary maxim for the use of our reason in experience*" (*CJ*, 269; emphasis added). This necessity as regards organized beings taken piecemeal, as it were, cannot fail, as we have seen, to lead us to thinking about nature as a whole. Now Kant, having established—contrary to the apparent movement of the beginning of the antinomy, which seemed to concede priority when it came to knowledge to the maxim of mechanical causality—that we must necessarily invoke the purposive maxim for all knowledge of organized beings, wants to move on to the totality without giving up on the question of knowledge (the necessity of the purposive maxim for knowledge of some beings must lead us to try it out on nature as a whole) but does not want to suggest that the problem is still essentially situated on the same level. Whence a paragraph that has to start out on the terrain of knowledge in order to jump beyond it:

> It is obvious that once we have adopted such a guideline [ein solcher Leitfaden] for studying nature and found it to be reliable we must [müßen] also at least attempt to apply this maxim of the power of judgment to the whole of nature, since by means of it we have been able to discover many laws of nature which, given the limitation of our insights into the inner mechanisms of nature, would otherwise remain hidden from us. [Do not, however, imagine that that is the principal reason for performing that extension:] But with regard to the latter use this maxim of the power of judgment is certainly useful, but not indispensable, because nature as a whole is not given to us as organized (in the strictest sense of the term adduced above). By contrast, this maxim of the reflecting power of judgment is essential [essentially necessary, wesentlich notwendig] for

> those products of nature which must be judged only as intentionally formed thus and not otherwise, in order to obtain even an experiential cognition of their internal constitution; because even the thought of them as organized things is impossible without associating the thought of a generation with an intention [mit Absicht]. (*CJ*, 269)

So the finalist maxim leads us, on the basis of its grounding at the level of knowledge, to ask the question of the totality of nature. This question cannot, strictly speaking, be situated at the level of empirical knowledge (the maxim can always serve as a maxim for knowledge but does not essentially enter into the thought of nature as totality). But at least this much follows: The purposive maxim has turned out to be necessary as regards a part of nature (namely, organized beings). And this necessity of the purposive maxim also makes necessary the thought of a certain contingency of nature (thought of as mechanism). But if nature is therefore not thinkable (by us) as entirely necessary, then nature *qua* totality must itself be considered to be contingent and must therefore, still for us, be thought of as the work of a super-natural intelligence:

> Hence natural things which we find possible only as ends constitute the best proof of the contingency of the world-whole [der vornehmsten Beweis für die Zufälligkeit des Weltganzen], and are the only basis for proof valid for both common understanding as well as for philosophers of the dependence of these things on and their origin in a being that exists outside of the world and is (on account of that purposive form) intelligent [verständigen]; thus teleology cannot find a complete answer for its inquiries except in a theology. (*CJ*, 269)

So by dint of explicating what is merely a maxim of the faculty of reflective judgment, Kant has sent us off beyond nature as such, toward God. But, according to a movement that is none other than the becoming-transcendent of the transcendental, this movement runs the risk of carrying us much too far. The thought of a purposive causality in nature can only refer us beyond nature to God, but it will never demonstrate the existence of God, which remains, then, here at least, a purely subjective necessity of our limited faculty of judgment. We can never establish the existence of God in this way because, as Kant recalls, we can never see natural ends as such, but only certain objects the thought of which we cannot even formulate without judging according to final causality.

The whole teleology, which thus finds its end in a theology, is radically subjective. What does this mean here? That human reason, which is, *ex hypothesi*, limited compared to the reason of other possible rational beings, cannot do without the purposive maxim (or, therefore, its theological consequence) and that the limit of reason that makes the maxim necessary for us simultaneously makes impossible for us any objective proof in this regard. Such an objective proof (which would establish that final causality is constitutive of the object and not merely regulative for the judgment we are in a position to bring to bear on the object) would be equivalent to showing that the maxim in question was valid not only for us but also for superior intelligences. And one senses the impossibility of such a demonstration: To the very extent that human reason is limited, any conception of a reason that could go beyond those limits is itself limited by the very limits it would be claiming to go beyond, according to the very structure of transcendentality, the structure of the *Grenze*—we transgress the frontiers of human reason only to the extent that we are transgressing *frontiers*, which thus by definition hold us short of what such a transgression wanted to achieve. One can cross the frontiers of human reason only the better to draw them. Any "objective" proof is thereby circumscribed, and everything that is not susceptible of objective proof (including the very objectivity of that objectivity, as we shall see in a moment) never will be. So it is not simply that we are condemned to appeal to the purposive maxim because of a negative limit from which superior intelligences would not suffer, because the very idea of such intelligences is positively produced only by the structure of that same limit (and so the infinite is finite). The limit produces both what is limited and what is beyond it, but what is beyond it *is beyond it* by the very fact of this limit. Reason thus produces itself both as understanding (at home inside the limit, grounding an "objectivity" entirely subordinate to the limit) and as reason (the limit itself as a bilateral frontier folding its outside back toward its inside, whence it cannot fail to externalize itself, to turn itself back out). This is literally what Kant says in the "Remark" that is §76:

> Reason is a faculty of principles, and in its most extreme demand it reaches to the unconditioned, while understanding, in contrast, is always at its service only under a certain condition, which must be given. Without concepts of the understanding, however, which must be given objective reality, reason cannot judge at all objectively (synthetically), and by itself it contains, as theoretical reason, absolutely no constitutive principles, but only regulative ones. One soon learns that where the understanding cannot follow, reason becomes excessive, displaying itself in well-grounded ideas (as regulative principles) but not in objectively valid concepts; the understanding, however, which cannot keep up with it, but which would yet be necessary for validity for objects, restricts the validity of those ideas of reason solely to the subject, although still universally

> for all members of this species, i.e., understanding restricts the validity of those ideas to the condition which, given the nature of our (human) cognitive faculty or even the concept that we can form of the capacity of a finite rational being in general, we cannot and must not conceive otherwise, but without asserting that the basis for such a judgment lies in the object. (*CJ*, 271–72)

One senses that all of Kant's frontiers are beginning to tremble here. On the basis of the apparently anodyne antinomy of the faculty of judgment (judge according to mechanism or purposiveness), Kant, having apparently defused the antinomy by appealing to the merely subjective character of the maxims in question, has, by exploring further the very subjectivity of the purposive maxim, exceeded nature as a whole to ground it in a principle of subjectivity that is so radical that it removes any "objective" definition of objectivity. The objectivity of the objective is overtaken by a principle that can never achieve objectivity (while dealing it a radical blow) and whose supposed "subjectivity" *de jure* precedes the very opposition of subjective and objective. The understanding (and thereby any use of the faculty of determinative judgment) is in the service of a reason that is merely the exposure of that understanding to its own frontier, where its finitude is, as it were, denounced before a principle of excess that is none other than the supposed regulative principle of reflective judgment itself. *Qua* rational (excessive), the reflective judgment (always, it will be remembered, in search of its law) "grounds" the understanding in an "objectivity" that is strangled by the subjective finitude of a reason that is only its own turning back toward an absolute exteriority. It will follow that henceforth Kant will have the greatest difficulty maintaining clear frontiers between the subjective and the objective, the constitutive and the regulative, the dogmatic and the problematic, the understanding and reason, the critical and the doctrinal.

This consequence can, clearly enough, give rise to two apparently opposite movements. On the one hand, Kant can register a certain satisfaction of human reason, grounded on the resemblance between what is objective and what is subjective but necessary to the subject insofar as it can have objects. He says in §75:

> Now if this proposition, grounded on an indispensably necessary maxim of our power of judgment, is completely sufficient for every speculative as well as practical use of our reason in every human respect, I would like to know [so möchte ich wohl wissen] what we lose by being unable to prove it valid for higher beings, on purely objective grounds (which unfortunately exceed our capacity). (*CJ*, 270; Paul Guyer adds a question mark here not found in the German text)

But this implied rhetorical question ("I would like to know") and the satisfaction it might indicate if we take it to be a rhetorical question also invite a more literal reading:[13] I would like to know, I would *really* like to know, but everything I have said shows that unhappily I can never know, only judge. Human reason, just now self-satisfied, is here somewhat needy and miserable. What we lack will never be the object of theoretical knowledge for us, just because we lack it. But just this indeterminate lack is the principle of judgment as reflective judgment—that is, as characterized by lack (of the law for the case). The self-sufficiency and self-satisfaction of human reason are thus grounded in its radical insufficiency as understanding, its deficit of objectivity that thus becomes the reason of (human) reason itself.

Human reason is in this way characterized by a certain necessity of contingency. The nonobjectivity of the principle of purposive causality, the absence of the law for some cases at least, the contingency in and of nature are necessary for our understanding. This curious necessity drives Kant to give "examples" in this remark to §76, "examples, which are certainly too important as well as too difficult for them to be immediately pressed upon the reader as proven propositions, but which will still provide material to think over and can serve to elucidate what is our proper concern here."[14]

And indeed, two examples will prepare the way for what we have just called the necessity of contingency. First "example": It is necessary for human understanding to make a distinction between possibility and actuality (*Wirklichkeit*). We can represent a thing to ourselves (by its concept) without that thing's being actually given to us. The actuality of things comes to us solely via our sensibility, according to the first *Critique's intuitus derivativus* (B72). But we can imagine (in the modality of the possible, then) an understanding that would give itself objects directly by thinking them, without it being necessary for it to go via sensibility. For such an understanding, the distinction

13. According to a procedure brilliantly exploited by Paul de Man in *Allegories of Reading* (New Haven, CT: Yale University Press, 1979), 9–12.

14. These examples will, then, function like regulative principles for a reflective judgment in order to demonstrate the necessity of regulative principles and reflective judgments. *Qua* examples, these examples are contingent, and they are examples *of* the contingent—which is nonetheless necessary. Clearly, this use of "examples" goes beyond the description of the exemplarity of the example given in the first *Critique*, where examples are called the *Gängelwagen*, what Kemp Smith memorably translated as the "go-cart" (Guyer and Wood have "leading-strings," Pluhar "walker") of judgment (A134/B173), a kind of provisional prosthetic to help with a lack of natural aptitude. Here, however, these "examples" could never become "proven propositions," and so the prosthesis is originary and irreducible.

between possibility and actuality would be irrelevant, whereas for us (who need such a distinction), such an understanding is thinkable only according to one of the terms of that same opposition. An understanding (impossible for us) that would not recognize the meaning of possible can be represented (possible for us). One of terms of this opposition (necessary for us) allows us to think its nonpertinence. But this radicalization of the possible is only possible. The possible (as opposed to the actual) remains necessary for us so we can represent to ourselves, in the mode of the possible, its disappearance into an identity with the actual. The possibility of representing the end of the possible thus confirms the necessity of the possible. The very fact of the separation of sensibility and understanding allows us to think their nonseparation.

This separation of the possible and the actual for us is none other than the separation between the necessary and the contingent. The absolutely necessary (where the separation of the possible and the actual would lose all relevance) is only possible and thus contingent. The contingent is necessary for us to be able to represent its disappearance in the absolutely necessary.

Second "example." Just as we must (necessarily) admit necessity (in the mode of the contingent), we are conscious of the moral law, and we must thus presuppose causality through freedom:

> Now since here, however, the objective necessity of the action, as duty, is opposed to that which it, as an occurrence, would have if its ground lay in nature and not in freedom (i.e., in the causality of reason), and the action which is morally absolutely necessary [die moralisch-schlechtin-notwendige Handlung] can be regarded physically as entirely contingent (i.e., what necessarily should [sollte] happen often does not), it is clear that it depends only on the subjective constitution of our practical faculty that the moral laws must [müßen] be represented as commands (and the actions which are in accord with them as duties), and that reason expresses this necessity not through a be [Sein] (happening [Geschehen]) but through a should-be [Sein-Sollen]. (*CJ*, 273)

So there is necessity and necessity. The morally necessary is physically contingent (what ought necessarily to happen must not necessarily happen, and even most often does not happen, might even never happen, is totally contingent, necessarily contingent). Why is this? Because reason is not mankind's only faculty, it is related to sensibility and thereby to nature (to a possible nature). The thing that gives nature as an object of possible experience, and as object of such an experience, as phenomenon, what gives rise to theoretical knowledge and to the necessity of *Sein* or *Geschehen*—namely, sensibility—by the same token withdraws *Sein* from the intelligible world and gives it the *Sollen*. And this is another version of the paradox of the possible and the actual that we were just reading. The fact of sensibility here gives the separation of possible and actual as the separation between *Sein* and *Sollen*:

> Which would not be the case if reason without sensibility (as the subjective condition of its application to objects of nature) were considered, as far as its causality is concerned, as a cause in an intelligible world, corresponding completely with the moral law, where there would be no distinction between what should be done and what is done, between a practical law concerning that which is possible through us and the theoretical law concerning that which is actual through us. (*CJ*, 273)

Just as it is possible for us to represent to ourselves a world in which the modality of the possible would not have a place, it is equally possible—and in fact we ought, this is duty itself—to represent to ourselves a world from which duty would be absent, in which *Sollen* would merge with *Sein*, in which the law would not take the form of a command that constrains us. It is possible for us to do so, and in fact we ought to do so; this means also that we are free to do so. That is what freedom is. If freedom *qua* "formal condition" of this intelligible world, in which *Sollen* and *Sein* merge, remains for us an excessive concept (*überschwenglicher Begriff*) that can determine nothing as to objective reality, this is because "freedom" has meaning for us (doubly for us: once as our freedom itself, a second time as our concept or Idea of that freedom) only to the extent that it does not dissolve in a purely intelligible world (that would by this very fact be unintelligible for us) in which causality by freedom would merge with causality by necessity and would find its end in that merging. Which is, of course, the meaning of what Kant is trying to think under the name of regulative principle, which brings with it the whole issue of the Ideas of Reason.

So, for us, freedom will consist exemplarily (recall that we are dealing with "examples" in §76) in thinking nonobjectively the end of freedom in the (un)intelligible world. To give any meaning to freedom, we must, then, be in part constrained by a mechanical necessity (in sensible nature) and thus equally constrained by the moral law that presents itself to us as imperative and command. And this free thought of freedom—which is free only by dint of constituting nothing objectively, by dint of its ought-to-be-realized in a world in which, if in fact it were realized, it would not be free—which, says Kant, by making of freedom a mere regulative principle "does not determine the constitution of freedom, as a form of causality, objectively," this thought in no way devalues freedom by refusing it any objective status but "indeed does so with no less validity than if it did determine freedom objectively [mit nicht minderer Gültigkeit, als ob diese geschähe]." Being able to represent to ourselves a world in which freedom and necessity would merge like actuality and possibility, then, we can only represent such a world to ourselves, and the only chance we have of representing it is by hanging on tight to the very distinction the disappearance of which that representation seems to promise. Our freedom depends on our possibility of representing its end and so depends on our having of freedom a final idea. According to a schema that Kant is about to refine and aggravate, but which we shall see to be the schema of the Ideas as such, the Idea of freedom is an Idea only to the extent that it projects its own end (i.e., the moment at which it would become concept rather than Idea, constitutive rather than regulative principle, or at least the moment at which these distinctions would disappear in what they made possible). Kant says that it has no less value than if it were the case; but if it were the case it would have no value at all, because "being the case" here is precisely *geschähe*, and as we have seen, *geschehen* is on the side of *Sein*, not of *Sein-Sollen*. The case as such cannot be free.

Freedom considered as the formal condition of an intelligible world is, then, inaccessible to us as an objective concept and must remain forever problematic. But the freedom of freedom consists in precisely this problematic status. And it is precisely this structure (which is, I repeat, the same as that of transcendentality as such) that Kant will formalize under the name of purposiveness. For the two "examples" he has just given serve to elucidate a thinking of purposiveness that thinks together lawfulness and contingency even before the distinctions between concept and Idea, theory and practice, etc.

Recall the abyssally analogical structure of §76, which condenses the very structure of Kant's thought, at least as it is expounded in the introduction to the third *Critique*. The examples given by Kant are linked by operators of analogy that have a cumulative effect:

> *Just as* [So wie] in the theoretical consideration of nature reason must assume the idea of an unconditioned necessity of its primordial ground, *so*, in the case of the practical, *it also* presupposes [so setzt sie auf] its own unconditioned (in regard to nature) causality, i.e., freedom, because it is aware of its moral command [. . .] *Likewise* [Ebenso] [. . .] (*CJ*, 273–74; emphasis added)

The first two examples have opened the way to what will bring the series to an end. They have allowed us to think what one might call a certain free possibility that can only be thought in the evanescent perspective of its own disappearance, a perspective called "Idea." This thought will now find a formulation that, in the context of a judgment supposed to give a certain mediation between theory and practice, will in fact enfold and transgress them at one and the same time. *Ebenso*, then:

> Likewise, as far as the case before us is concerned [was unsern vorhabende Fall befrifft: that is, the case of judgment (which is always judgment of a case) insofar as it is divided in its antinomy between mechanism and purposiveness], it may be conceded that we would find no distinction between a natural mechanism and a technique of nature, i.e., a connection to ends [Zweckverknüpfung] in it, if our understanding were not of the sort that must go from the universal to the particular, and the power of judgment can thus cognize no purposiveness in the particular, and hence make no determining judgments, without having a universal law under which it can subsume the particular. But now since the particular, as such, contains something contingent [etwas Zufälliges] with regard to the universal, but reason nevertheless still requires unity, hence lawfulness, in the connection of particular laws of nature (*which lawfulness of the contingent is called purposiveness* [emphasis added]), and the *a priori* derivation of the particular laws from the universal, as far as what is contingent in the former is concerned, is impossible through the determination of the concept of the object, thus the concept of the purposiveness of nature in its products is a concept that is necessary for the human power of judgment in regard to nature but does not pertain to the determination of the objects themselves, thus a subjective principle of reason for the power of judgment which, as regulative (not constitutive), is just as necessarily valid for *our human power of judgment* as if it were an objective principle. (*CJ*, 274)

Everything trembles here. This regulative (and therefore "subjective") concept, which alone can provide for a lawfulness of the contingent (but without such lawfulness the contingent would remain contingent, natural necessity would be partial and incomplete, depressing for reason), which cannot by definition achieve necessity, is "just as necessarily valid [. . .] as if it were an objective principle." And even more necessary than necessity, because without this regulative principle, judgments of objective necessity would have no meaning, would not converge toward the unity demanded by reason, which is given only in teleology. Judgment would thus be the place from which proceed necessity and contingency, mechanism and freedom, archi-contingent necessity of contingency, archi-necessary contingency of necessity. This preobjective condition of objectivity, this place where all the key terms of Kantian thought can be exchanged and analogized, is clearly enough the blind origin of critique itself, but thereby also its essential resource, without which there would be no critique, properly speaking, but merely preparation or propaedeutic for doctrine. This point, reached via a thinking of teleology, must also precede all teleology and, therefore, all theology too.

Can we satisfactorily call this point, which precedes Kant's distinction between speculative and practical, "finitude"? Logically no, because we have seen it to precede the distinction between finite and infinite. "Finitude," especially when thought in the limiting form or privileged example of human mortality, can give the condition described by Kant a certain "existential" pathos that has had its day but that remains dependent on a thinking of God (of a God who is essentially, always already, dead), which falls short of Kant's thinking in this regard. It would not be difficult to show that Kant's thinking about God is merely thinking the same blind spot as fundamentally analogical, according to the ana-logics we follow in the Appendix around the distinction between *Grenze* and *Schranke*, because it is precisely around God that Kant pushes furthest with his analogism, and this thinking again passes through the problem of cosmopolitanism.

In the "Methodology of Teleological Judgment," which Kant places as an appendix to the third *Critique*, and having reinforced the subordination of mechanism to teleology that we saw happening little by little in the antinomy, Kant, via the question of what the ultimate end of nature considered as a teleological system can be, comes to pose again the question of war and peace. Man is indeed the ultimate end of nature but only insofar as "he is the only being on earth who forms a concept of ends for himself" (*CJ*, 295). The ultimate end would be, then, that there be ends, postultimate ends, the end that there be always more ends. Since our reading of Aristotle in Chapter 1, we immediately suspect that this structure of the postultimate will bring us back to the archi-originary. What comes at the end is the possibility of seeing that there must be an end and that that end is the possibility of setting oneself still further ends. Clearly, it is not enough to say in this context simply that the ultimate end is man himself, because man is, at least in part, part of nature considered as mechanism. So the ultimate end cannot be man as such but something in man, and this ultimate end can be either an end that nature can bring about through its beneficence (i.e., happiness) or else something that man can realize by exploiting nature (i.e., culture). Obviously the first of these cannot be the one, because man comes up with such a diversity of ideas as to what constitutes happiness (a constant refrain in Kant's moral philosophy) and also, on the one hand, it is not in man's nature to be satisfied with what nature gives him and, on the other, nature spares him none of the trials and tribulations suffered equally by all other animals. And this is not all. Man also has natural dispositions that are "absurd." What are these dispositions? Exactly those that earlier Kant wrote off to natural providence—namely, the oppressive and warlike tendency that makes man (considered as a natural being) work toward the destruction of his species. So here is a paradox: as ultimate end of nature, man, being of nature, is not the ultimate end (because if he were, he would be remaining in nature viewed as mechanism). If so-called natural man were the end of nature, nature would not even be a teleological system but pure mechanism, and thus would have no ultimate end. For man to be the ultimate end of nature considered as a teleological system of ends (and he must be, otherwise nature would be merely a mechanism without end or meaning, even for scientific exploration), it must be that what in man constitutes this end is a capacity to go beyond nature as such. What man must do to be the final end of nature is to project another end beyond nature, and that end is no longer in nature as its ultimate end but outside nature as its final end (no longer as *letzter Zweck*, then, but as *Endzweck*, according to Kant's distinction). Man is the final end only because he can give himself ends after the ultimate end, and that can only be done by culture, because culture is precisely the development of the capacity for ends in a rational being. Properly speaking, then, the ultimate end of nature is not man but culture: "Only culture can be the ultimate end that one has cause to ascribe to nature in regard to the human species" (*CJ*, 299). The ultimate end of nature is thus the end of nature in culture, its apparent other, or else the becoming-culture of nature on its human frontier.

Culture is not a simple thing, and Kant distinguishes between the culture of skill (*Geschicklichkeit*) and the culture of discipline (*Zucht [Disziplin]*). These two determinations of culture are situated, we might say, on two sides of a frontier. Although skill is part of culture rather than nature, it is nonetheless on the side of nature, as a condition of possibility of the realization of ends of all sorts ("the foremost subjective condition of aptitude for the promotion of ends in general," as Kant puts it [*CJ*, 299]), but it cannot of itself guide the will in the choice of ends to be realized; the culture of discipline will take care of that by behaving in a negative way toward what in man is natural—namely, passions and desires:

> [It] consists in the liberation of the will from the despotism of desires [Begierden], by which we are made, attached as we are to certain things of nature, incapable of choosing for ourselves, while we turn into fetters the drives [Triebe] that nature has given us merely for guidance [die uns die Natur nur statt Leitfäden beigegeben hat] in order not to neglect or even injure the determination of the animality in us, while yet we are free enough to tighten or loosen them, to lengthen or shorten them, as the ends of reason require. (*CJ*, 299)

Everything we followed in Kant's political writings belongs to the culture of skill, which, while remaining on the side of nature, never stops leaving nature behind (for, as we saw, politics is nothing but the leaving-behind of nature, never accomplished by mankind). All the negativity we saw at work in natural providence is summed up here in a striking formula: The culture of skill gives rise to what Kant calls a "splendid misery [glänzende Elend, brilliant distress]," because not only must there be inequality, and therefore oppression, among men for the culture of skill to develop, says Kant clearly with Rousseau in mind, but the development made possible gives rise to an increase of misery (*Plagen*: torments) on both sides (the oppressors as much as the oppressed) either through external violence or internal insatiability. This brilliant distress is nonetheless linked to the end of nature that is reached here, even if this end is not ours—which is where we come back to cosmopolitanism and its inner inhibition:

> The formal condition under which alone nature can attain this its final aim [Endabsicht] is that constitution in the relations of human beings with one another in which the abuse of reciprocally conflicting freedom is opposed by lawful power in a whole, which is called *civil society*; for only in this can the greatest development of the natural predispositions occur. For this, however, even if humans were clever [klug] enough to discover it and wise enough to subject themselves willingly to its coercion, a *cosmopolitan* whole, i.e., a system of all states that are at risk of detrimentally affecting each other, is required. (*CJ*, 299–300)

This is, then, the argument that we followed in the "Universal History" text. But just as we were able to see in *Perpetual Peace*, this cosmopolitan perspective must not be realized, and this nonrealization, in its very violence, forms part of the realization of the end of nature (soon not to be ours)—namely, the development of culture as aptitude for ends. Culture (of skill, still) is no other than that brilliant distress that would be overcome by the cosmopolitanism that must not come about:

> In its absence, and given the obstacles that ambition, love of power, and greed, especially on the part of those who are in power, oppose to even the possibility of such a design, war (partly of the kind in which states split apart and divide themselves into smaller ones, partly of the kind in which smaller ones unite with each other and strive to form a larger whole) is inevitable, which, even though it is an unintentional effort of humans (aroused by unbridled passions), is a deeply hidden but perhaps intentional effort of supreme wisdom *if not to establish then at least to prepare the way* for the lawfulness together with the freedom of the states and by means of that the unity of a morally grounded system of them, and which, in spite of the most horrible tribulations which it inflicts upon the human race, is nevertheless one more incentive (while the hope for a peaceful state of happiness among nations recedes ever further) for developing to their highest degree all the talents that serve for culture. (*CJ*, 300; emphasis added)

This culture of skill, which is on the side of nature, then, develops while remaining in nature (animality, warfare). Kant must now distinguish it from the other culture, the culture of discipline, which we said was on the other side of the natural frontier. But he will have the greatest difficulty in operating this distinction, and for good reason. On the one hand, as we saw, our natural drives (purposive for us *qua* animal species) encourage the development of culture while making more difficult (*erschweren*) the development of man as a rational being; on the other hand, then, there is the other culture, the culture of discipline, which must take us beyond nature. This culture, *qua* culture, must still take off from nature as its ultimate end (*letzter Zweck*). Where the culture of skill is answerable to an *Endabsicht* of nature, a final intention or aim, the culture of discipline will answer to a "purposive effort [ein zweckmässiges Streben]," of nature still, in view of an *Endzweck* yet to come. This culture of discipline must oppose all the penchants that, as we just saw, contribute to the culture of skill, because the "end of nature [der Zweck der Natur]" remains that of getting mankind over the natural frontier.

So there must be a cut. Remaining in nature (or, as we would say, on the frontier of nature), we will never arrive at the end (i.e., the end of all the other ends, the end even of the final end [culture], which remains fundamentally natural). All these ends must have their end, but for it to be their final end, their *Endzweck*, it must be cut from them. If this final end of ends were merely the end of nature, it would never make it out. So all previous ends (including the ultimate end, the *letzter Zweck*) must be finalized by a further end, which is their true end only by not exactly being their end, only by not belonging to them. Which is what Kant says, literally, at the beginning of §84: "A *final end* is that end which needs no other as the condition of its possibility [Endzweck ist derjenige Zweck, der keines andern als Bedingung seiner Möglichkeit bedarf]" (*CJ*, 301). The *Endzweck* does not need that of which it is the end to be its end. And reciprocally, that of which this end is the end (nature) cannot bring it about, because in that case the end would be dependent on and conditioned by the very thing (nature) that knows nothing unconditioned. Everything in nature is conditioned, so the end of ends cannot be found in it.

Kant considers this end to be human, still, in the sense that man is supposedly the only natural being to act by final causality all the while representing to himself the final finality of this finality as being necessary, unconditioned, and thus outside nature. But the humanity thus identified is again divided according to the fractal frontier demultiplication of nature that is our privileged "object." For if, on the one hand, one can always say that man is the final goal of nature, to the extent that natural affairs must have some such end if they are not to fall back into the blind necessity or contingency of the natural mechanism, on the other hand, one must say that, *qua* final end, precisely, man becomes cut from all teleology and all nature:

> The being of this sort is the human being, though considered as noumenon: the only natural being in which we can nevertheless cognize, on the basis of its own constitution, a supersensible faculty (*freedom*) and even the law of the causality together with the object that it can set for itself as the highest end (the highest good in the world).
>
> Now of the human being (and thus of every rational being in the world), as a moral being, it cannot be further asked why (*quem in finem*) it exists. His existence contains the highest end itself, to which, as far as he is capable, he can subject the whole of nature, or against which at least he need not hold himself to be subjected by any influence from nature. (*CJ*, 302)

Nature in its totality, then, is teleologically subordinate to a natural ultimate end (mankind) and again to a nonnatural final end (mankind again). But *qua* end cut from that of which it is the end, *qua* end without finality (*Zweck ohne Zweckmässigkeit*, we might say), man (noumenal man, certainly) is no longer human. Just as the end of nature (in nature) is not quite natural, so the end of man (in man) is not quite human. Teleology arrives at its end only by cutting itself from its end to which it is, however, endlessly tending.

Of course Kant appeals to God to solve the problem that is persisting here and that is none other than the insistence of the frontier, now pushed inside as the frontier between phenomenal man and noumenal man. But as we shall see, God, called in to put an end to the end without end of interrupted and interminable teleology, will turn out to be just another name for the frontier, *Deus terminus*.

Having dismissed physical theology (because we can conclude nothing as to the supreme cause of nature while remaining within nature), Kant turns to ethical theology. He is trying to explain how we get across the frontier between moral teleology (for which we are still beings in the world, and for which the point is to understand the relation between our ends and the end of those ends in the world—i.e., reply to the question of knowing, given that we are beings in the world among other beings, how we can bring about that end in that context) and a moral theology. Moral theology necessarily appears, because moral teleology cannot help but ask whether we need to go looking beyond the world for a principle that can explain the relation in the world between the moral and the natural.

As always when in comes to morality, Kant systematically invokes here what is obvious, in the sense of what anyone at all can understand, "even the most common understanding" (*CJ*, 308) "the commonest judgment of healthy human reason" (*CJ*, 309), "even the most common human reason" (*CJ*, 314). What even this common understanding can understand is that nature would have no end were it not for mankind and that it is *qua* moral being that mankind can lay claim to that place. What is man *qua* moral being? A rational being "*under* moral laws" (i.e., rational in the sense of a type of reason capable of giving itself unconditional laws):

> The moral laws, however, have the unique property that they prescribe something to reason as an end without a condition, thus do exactly what the concept of a final end requires; and the existence of such a reason, which in the relation to ends can be the supreme law for itself, in other words, the existence of rational beings under moral laws, can alone be conceived of as the final end of the existence of a world. If, on the contrary, this is not the case, then there is either no end at all for the existence of a world in its cause, or it is grounded in an end without a final end. (*CJ*, 315)

For there to be an *Endzweck*, there must be a reason able to give itself an end according to the structure of an *Endzweck* (i.e., an unconditioned end). The unconditioned end is that there be an unconditioned end. The point is not to have such ends realized (impossible, and this impossibility is a positive condition of possibility for moral laws and, as we shall see, for God) but to be able to give them to oneself as ends to-be-realized. Reason giving itself its unconditional law, reason being unto itself its own supreme law, this end cut from all ends, or rather reason able to think itself as its own supreme law, is the only possible *Endzweck* for any world at all. To sum up a little brutally: The end is that one can think the end. The end is the end to the extent that it manages to think itself as the (unconditioned) end and is thus the end of everything. And the end, in this thinking the end, gives itself an end that is unrealizable (according to natural causality), an end that must not be realized but that nonetheless remains to be realized. To safeguard the tendentiality of this *to-be-realized* we are obliged to postulate a moral author of the world—namely, God.

God occupies in this reasoning a place that is extremely difficult to pin down and that Kant will further complicate in the paragraphs to come. The final end can only be mankind able to set himself moral (unconditioned) ends. But as these ends, if they are to be moral, must be capable of realization in the natural world in which there reigns only mechanical causality—that is, as the practical necessity in which we find ourselves to realize in the world what is prescribed by moral laws "is not congruent with [stimmt . . . nicht . . . zusammen] the theoretical concept of the *physical possibility* of producing it if we do not connect our freedom with any other causality (as a means) than that of nature" (*CJ*, 316)—we must admit, subjectively, the existence of God as moral author of the world, for this accord to be possible.

This "moral proof" of the existence of God is valid only for the finite beings we are (i.e., beings who cannot find the agreement between their freedom and natural causality). It "proves" the existence of God without demonstrating it, but it must (müßen) be admitted in order to maintain the *to-be-realized* of the moral law. If we were content to stay on the nature side of the frontier, the moral law could never apply to any case; but if we passed too rapidly to the other side, there would be no cases (contingencies) at all. For the moral law to be prescriptive, what is prescribes must be perpetually to be realized, and this, as we saw, is what gives rise to the teleological structure. And for this teleological structure to maintain itself in its purposiveness before its end, without being realized, then we must admit the moral proof of God.

Just like the principle of natural purposiveness itself, which, recall, was as necessary as necessity, necessary with a necessity before all necessity, so God is necessary for the moral law, which is the only truly final end of all the structures of purposiveness we have gone through. On the level of practical necessity, strictly speaking, God is, indeed, less necessary than the moral law as such, but, just as the prenecessary necessity of natural purposiveness was, in the end, necessary for natural necessity itself, the necessity of God, less necessary than strict moral necessity, is necessary (for us) for this practical necessity to have a chance—like peace—in the perpetually relaunched structure of its *to-be-realized*.[15] The whole problem of Kant's thinking of God will consist in keeping him in this exiguous but capital place. And in fact, by giving a "proof" in this way, even a "subjective" proof, Kant has no doubt already proved too much, which is why he devotes the next paragraph to a limitation (*Beschränkung*) of this moral proof, which always runs the risk of going too far in the direction of theoreticist objectivity, in the very crossing of the frontier between teleology and theology.

Kant repeatedly takes up this argument in these paragraphs. Here in §86: in following the principle of theoretical reflective judgment, we can sufficiently

15. Again, this structure seems to be misrecognized by Hegel in his critique of Kant. In putting the maxim of the action of giving money to the poor through the test of the categorical imperative, the point is not at all, as Hegel pretends to believe in the *Natural Law* essay, to project the end of poverty, thus eliminating the very thing that gave rise to the possibility of moral action, but to inscribe this singular act in the perspective of a *to-be-realized* that must precisely never arrive at its realization (its end).

establish that the possibility of a world containing purposive products of nature entails the thought of a final end. But the concept of a final end is a concept of our practical reason alone:

> No use of this concept is possible except solely for practical reason in accordance with moral laws; and the final end of creation is that constitution of the world which corresponds only to that which we can give as determined in accordance with laws, namely the final end of our pure practical reason, insofar as it is to be practical [so fern sie praktisch sein soll].—Now in virtue of the moral law, which imposes this final end upon us, we have a basis for assuming, from a practical point of view, that is, in order to apply our powers to realize it, its possibility, its realizability [Ausführbarkeit], hence also a nature of things corresponding to that end (since without the accession of nature to a condition that does not stand within our own power its realization would be impossible). Thus we have a moral ground for also conceiving of a final end of creation for a world. (*CJ*, 320)

So this reasoning gives us reasons to believe in a final end of creation. But to go from that to the conclusion that there must be a God, two more inferences are needed: first, that the author of the world must be intelligent (which we have already assumed for the purposive products of nature) and secondly that he must be moral (otherwise this is not God but a demon or a demiurge). These inferences can in no way give rise to an objective proof but operate merely for our finite reason: We cannot claim to say that such a being exists but only that we have no way of understanding, without supposing such an author, how to refer the moral law, and thus its final end, to its objects. For us, the abyss to be crossed between moral causality and natural causality can be bridged only on condition that we suppose, purely for the use of our practical reason, the actuality or effectivity, the *Wirklichkeit*, but not the objective existence, of such a moral author-legislator.

God, then, is an idea that is necessary for us on the level of practical reason and in the mode of reflective judgment. If we attribute qualities to him (and we have seen in §86 that we must indeed attribute to him the qualities of omniscience, omnipotence, absolute goodness, etc.), we must above all not do so in a theoretical manner. What is proper to God is precisely to put an end to nature while remaining radically cut from it; so he must above all not be the object of a theoretical knowledge of the type we can have of nature. The fact remains that we must attribute qualities to him if the idea of God is not to remain completely indeterminate and thus useless. How are we to do so? Precisely by analogy. We think the qualities of the Supreme Being only by analogy, and we *think* these qualities by analogy: We do not *know* (*erkennen*) these qualities, but we *think* (*denken*) them. So we think them by analogy with a knowledge we do not have; thought is the analogy of knowledge.

Kant's difficulty here is patent and comes from the fact that he is trying to think together the frontier between speculative and practical reason, between knowledge and thought, and between constitutive and regulative principle. The difficulty, which the appeal to analogy is supposed to solve but which it complicates infinitely, consists in the fact that under the name of God, Kant is advancing a thought of relation as such, whereas he has at his disposal only a language of possible objects.

> Thus just as we name a cause after the concept that we have of its effect (though only with regard to its relation [ihrer Relation] to the latter), without thereby meaning to determine its internal constitution intrinsically by means of the properties that are all that we know about such causes and which must be given to us by experience [. . .] so we must assume something that contains the ground of the possibility and the practical reality, i.e., the realizability, of a necessary moral final end; but given the constitution of the effect that is expected from it, we can conceive of it as a wise being ruling the world according to moral laws, and in accordance with the constitution of our cognitive faculties we must conceive of it as a cause that is distinct from nature, only in order to express the *relation* [Verhältnis] of this being transcending all of our cognitive faculties to the object of *our* practical reason, without on that account theoretically attributing to it the only kind of causality of this sort that is known to us, namely an intelligence and a will, indeed without meaning to make an objective distinction between the causality that we conceive in this being itself with respect to what is a final cause for us and its causality with respect to nature (and its purposive determinations in general); rather, we can assume this distinction only as subjectively necessary, for the constitution of our cognitive faculty, and as valid for the reflecting but not the objectively determining power of judgment. (*CJ*, 321–22)

All of this, then, on the side of possible knowledge. From the theoretical point of view, we know nothing of God objectively, but from the practical point of view, the same principle, here regulative for a reflective judgment, indeed becomes constitutive for a determinative judgment, but solely on the practical level:

> But when it comes to the practical sphere, such a *regulative* principle (for prudence or wisdom)—namely, to act in conformity with something, as

> an end, which given the constitution of our cognitive faculties can only be conceived by us as possible in a certain way—is at the same time *constitutive*, i.e.,practically determining. (*CJ*, 322)

Kant's problem is obvious. Up until now there was, not an identity, of course, but something like a proportionality that managed the relations between the couples theoretical-practical, concept-Idea, constitutive-regulative, determinative-reflective. Thus, for example, the whole slow drift of the antinomy of judgment toward the primacy of the teleological, and in the end the practical was doubtless programmed since the first *Critique* by the very distinction between concept and Idea of Reason. It was indeed the radically reflective nature of some judgments that led us to theology, with all the consequences that result for teleology and its internal cut. Here, however, as we arrive apparently toward the end, we discover (this is exactly the sense of what earlier we said was necessary for necessity) that this regulative side turns constitutive. This is again and always the problem of the applicability of the moral law and the *to-be-realized* of the final end. As the moral law is (for us) only moral and the law insofar as it is applicable (i.e., determinative with regard to its cases, as in morality we are dealing with constitutive principles), the figure of God has the job of making possible this conversion of the regulative into the constitutive while preventing any attempt to cross back over the frontier and to enter the domain of theoretical knowledge on such a basis.

This is why, having spent a paragraph congratulating himself as to the advantages of this way of conceiving of God as cut from all objectivity, Kant has to confront the question of exactly what has been proved by the moral proof thus constructed and duly limited. In other words, in what way are we to hold for true what is proved in the proof? Literally, what is the kind of holding-for-true ("der Art des Führwahrhaltens") of this proof?[16]

Every proof, says Kant, following his usual analytic method, must not only persuade (*überreden*) but convince (*überzeugen*). Or rather, he adds immediately, already complicating the description in a way that is like the formalization of the structure of the *to-be-realized*, convince or tend to convince, to work on conviction, "auf Überzeugung wirke." This means that proof must be based on objective grounds, because otherwise the understanding is simply seduced and not truly convinced. But a proof that tries to convince can in turn be of two sorts: either it seeks for what the object is *in itself* or else what

16. Guyer translates "Art des Führwahrhaltens" as "kind of affirmation" and relates it to the analytic philosophy notion of "propositional attitude."

it is *for us*; the first corresponds to the determinative judgment, the second to the reflective judgment. In this second case, the proof absolutely does not work on conviction if it is based on theoretical principles. If, however, it is based on a practical rational principle, it can still lay claim to a true moral conviction. But between conviction properly speaking and mere persuasion, we find proofs that *work on* conviction, that *tend to* convince, in the sense that they are on the way to conviction: "A proof, however, *tends to conviction* without actually convincing if it is merely led onto the path to conviction, i.e., if it contains only objective grounds for that, which, although they are not sufficient for certainty, are nevertheless of the sort that do not serve merely as subjective grounds of the judgment for conviction" (*CJ*, 327).

Kant will now show how the four degrees of holding-for-true that can be identified (namely: rigorous proof by syllogisms; proof by analogy; plausible opinion; hypothesis) cannot be attained by what claims to be a proof of the existence of God. But among the four possibilities thus dismissed, one poses some problems. And, as if by chance, this is proof by analogy.

As for a rigorous proof of the existence of God, Kant refers us to the first *Critique*, where he demonstrates that, given that by definition we cannot have an intuition of a being beyond nature, the concept of God remains forever problematic. But the question of analogy merits a longer treatment and is further complicated by a long note that will detain us in a moment.

> One can, of course, *think* of one of two heterogeneous things, even on the very point of their heterogeneity [eben in dem Punkte ihrer Ungleichartigkeit], by means of an *analogy** with the other; but from that respect in which they are heterogeneous we cannot draw an inference [Schliessen, conclude] by means of the analogy, i.e., transfer this characteristic of the specific difference from the one to the other. (*CJ*, 328–29)[17]

Analogy serves to *think* but not to *conclude*. The note called for by the word *Analogie* undertakes to clarify this assertion. In it, we read that analogy is the identity of a cause-and-effect relation despite a difference of objects. And before following the main text that will discuss the possibility of analogy between man and God as to technical activity, the note takes as a first example an analogy between man and beast with respect to this same technical activity:

17. Translation modified. Given the rather dramatic nature of Kant's claims, here and in the following quotations I prefer "heterogeneous" to "dissimilar" for *ungleichartig* and "conclude" to "infer" or "make an inference" for *Schliessen* and make cognate changes as appropriate.

> Thus, in comparing the artistic actions of animals with those of human beings, we conceive of the ground of the former, which we do not know, through the ground of similar effects in humans (reason), which we do know, and thus as an analogue of reason, and by that we also mean to indicate that the ground of the artistic capacity in animals, designated as instinct, is in fact specifically different from reason, but yet has a similar relation to the effect (comparing, say, construction by beavers with that by humans). (*CJ*, 328n)

We are thinking these two (supposedly) heterogeneous things (human reason and animal instinct) according to the analogy of their effects and thus placing the analogy precisely at the point of heterogeneity between man and animal. This allows me to *think* animal instinct (which I do not know), but Kant will show that it does not allow me to *conclude*, by transferring the specific mark of mankind (reason) onto the beaver, that animals act rationally.

But, as the analogy must be good for something, I can nonetheless, in spite of the impossibility of concluding by analogy that animals are rational, conclude something by analogy:

> Yet from the comparison of the similar mode of operation in the animals (the ground for which we cannot immediately perceive) to that of humans (of which we are immediately aware) we can quite properly conclude *in accordance with the analogy* that the animals also act in accordance with *representations* (and are not, as Descartes would have it, machines), and that in spite of their specific difference, they are still of the same genus as human beings (as living beings). The principle that authorizes such a conclusion lies in the fact that we have the same ground for counting animals, with respect to the determination in question, as members of the same genus with human beings, as humans, insofar as we compare them with one another externally, on the basis of their actions. There is *par ratio*. (*CJ*, 328n; tr. mod.)

That was the first exemplary analogy, then: An analogy to show what an analogy is, or rather what it is to conclude by analogy. In analogy, one can permit oneself to draw certain conclusions to the extent that there is *paritas rationis*—and we ought to be able to draw some conclusions about analogy as such from this example. The second analogy that follows will allow us to draw the right conclusions about analogy. This second analogy, in which the beast is replaced by God, has an analogical relation with the first. *Ebenso*, says Kant:

> Likewise, in the comparison of the purposive products of the causality of the supreme world-cause in the world with the artworks of human beings, I can conceive of the former in an analogy to an understanding, but I cannot conclude to this property in the world-cause by means of the analogy; because

> here the principle of the possibility of such a conclusion is precisely what is missing, namely the *paritas rationis*, for counting the highest being as part of one and the same species along with human beings (with regard to their respective causalities). The causality of the being in the world, which is always sensibly conditioned (even its causality through understanding) cannot be transferred to a being that has no generic concept in common with the former except that of a thing in general. (*CJ*, 328; tr. mod.)

In the analogy between man and beast, then, we think these two heterogeneous things at the point of their heterogeneity, without for all that being able to cross the frontier of that heterogeneity to a conclusion that would posit that beasts are rational. But we can conclude that animals and man both act according to representations (instinctually for the former, rationally for the latter) for we have equal reason to think so in both cases. But the analogy between man and God, which also allows us to think two heterogeneous beings at the point of their heterogeneity (the nature of their causality), does not have an intermediate concept that would allow for a conclusion of the same type. The man-God analogy is thus only partially analogous with the man-beast analogy: It allows us to think that there is an analogy between man and God but not that there must be the possibility of concluding by analogy any objective characterization of the nature of God. Which is as much as to say that the man-God analogy is only analogically analogical, because here we are lacking precisely the *paritas rationis* that gives rise to the analogy in the first place. Or rather we might say that the man-God analogy, being only analogically analogical, capitalizes the being-analogy of the analogy.[18]

18. In the various versions of his lectures on Logic, Kant gives much less rich explanations of analogy, always in the context of induction and always saying that induction and analogy are merely "crutches" for the understanding, but crutches we cannot do without. In the so-called Dohna-Wundlacken version of the Logic, however (a transcript of the 1792 course, here a session from August 20), we find the following (the text includes several conjectural readings by its editor, Kowalewski): "According to the inference by analogy, if 2 things agree under as many determinations as I have become acquainted with, then I infer that they agree also in the other determinations. I infer, then, from some determinations, which I cognize, that the others belong to the thing too. This is an inference of a provisional judgment. One reserves the right to change it. No logician has yet developed analogy and induction properly. This field still lies open." In the margin, Kant writes, "An inference according to analogy, that animals have souls—But . . . why? If wasps have drunk from the forbidden honey and now wish to sting, then they fall, but they have [. . .] Faculty of desire. This holds for plants, too, the fly-trap. They seek air and sun and water" (in *Lectures on Logic*, tr. J. Michael Young [Cambridge: Cambridge University Press, 2004], 503–4).

This much in the note. In the main text, there are also two analogies, and the second is the analogy between man and God. But this time the first, exemplary, analogy, the analogy of analogy itself, directly following from the definition of analogy we read a moment ago, is directly political:

> But from that respect in which they are heterogeneous we cannot *conclude* by means of the analogy, i.e., transfer this characteristic of the specific difference from the one to the other. Thus, in analogy with the law of the equality of effect and countereffect in the mutual attraction and repulsion of bodies, I can also conceive of the community of the members of a commonwealth in accordance with rules of justice, but I cannot transfer the specific determinations of the former (the material attraction and repulsion) to the latter and attribute them to the citizens in order to conceive of a system which is called a state. (*CJ*, 329; tr. mod.)

As we saw earlier, State organization is thinkable only analogically: The right that holds together the members of the community must not be force but can be thought only by analogy with force. It is striking in Kant's definition of analogy that the thing we want to think and the place where we must not conclude coincide. "That respect in which they are heterogeneous" is exactly what we are interested in, the very reason why we are resorting to the analogy at all: I can get a sense of right only by appealing to the force that it precisely is not, that it *above all* is not. Analogy is thus fundamentally inhibited and frustrating: It allows what it by the same token makes impossible (i.e., a thinking of heterogeneity as such). This is what will come to the fore in the second analogy given in the main text, in which, as in the note, we are dealing with God. Here too there is an analogy between the two analogies:

> Likewise, we can very well conceive of the causality of the original being with regard to the things in the world, in analogy with an intelligence as the ground of the forms of certain products that we call artworks, as natural ends (for this occurs only for the sake of the theoretical or the practical use we have to make of this concept by our cognitive faculty, with regard to the natural things in the world, in accordance with a certain principle); but from the fact that among beings in the world the cause of an effect that is judged as artistic has to be attributed to intelligence we can by no means infer by an analogy that the very same causality that we perceive in humans must also pertain to the being who is entirely distinct from nature in regard to nature itself; because this touches the very dissimilarity in their effects that must be conceived between a sensibly conditioned cause and the supersensible original being, and thus cannot be transferred from the former to the latter.—In the very fact that I am to con-

> ceive of the divine causality only in analogy with an intelligence (a faculty with which we are not acquainted in any being other than the sensibly conditioned human being) lies the prohibition against attributing this intelligence in a strict sense to the supersensible original being. (*CJ*, 329)

It is precisely because it is analogical that it cannot be proper: The best proof that we do not know what we are talking about when we talk about God is that we are talking about him analogically. To say that we can only think of God as if he were an understanding is to say that God is precisely not an understanding. We home in on the point of heterogeneity between God and us, what makes God God, by making use of analogy, which teaches us that at this point of heterogeneity we understand nothing. The road of analogy is, therefore, constitutively blocked, it leaves us stuck at the very point where we thought we ought to be able to touch the goal. Faced with the possibility that the reader might feel a little disappointed here, Kant adds a note:

> One does not thereby lose anything in the representation of the relation of this being to the world as far as either theoretical or practical consequences are concerned. To wish to investigate what it is in itself is a pretension that is as purposeless as it is futile. (*CJ*, 329n)

Knowing nothing of God as such, then, is of no importance and even of no interest. The analogical approach, which cuts us from God just where it seemed to promise to reveal Him, is by that very fact perfectly adequate, leaves no regrets, because "God" here is precisely the name only for the pure relation to the world of an agency the logic of which is dictated by a teleology constitutively cut from its end. The *Endzweck*, recall, is an *Endzweck* only if it depends not at all on that whose end it is, only if it is cut from it. Analogy answers perfectly to this structure of the cut, espouses the cut by inscribing it right on the point of heterogeneity. Nothing is lacking here, for the cut has nothing negative about it but is the positive condition of Kant's thinking of God as pure relation. By precisely not allowing us to conclude the objective existence of God, the analogy turns out to be perfectly adequate to the mode of being of God, which cannot by definition be that of a knowable object.

So, among the four possibilities of the *Fürwahrhalten* discussed in §90 (logical proof, analogy, opinion, and hypothesis), none of which allows one to conclude that God exists, analogy is set apart from the rest, because where the other attempts are simply inappropriate (no logical proof in the absence of any intuition of God; no plausible opinion because there is no possible continuity between this-worldly reasons and other-worldly aims; no hypothesis, because it would presuppose that what it puts forward is at least possible, whereas we have no reason at all to admit the possibility of God as object), analogy gives the exact measure of the thinking of God of which we are capable: God is perfectly analogical.

Teleology, then, which cannot not end up in a theology, does so according to its own proper structure (i.e., being cut from its end), which alone makes it a teleology. Cut from its end, teleology does not lose its guiding thread (which, as we have seen as we venture on this interminable reading, has no end, precisely, and just that is its finality) but prolongs it indefinitely in analogy, which describes exactly this relation to an end from which one is radically cut. As always in Kant, we must not see in analogy an ersatz theoretical knowledge—this is what §90 has just shown: Nothing is lacking in our representation of the relation of God to the world so long as this representation remains merely analogical, and if nothing is lacking, that is because this analogical representation is, precisely, not a substitute or surrogate for some missing theoretical knowledge. Analogy is not a substitute for theoretical knowledge but always has a practical import. Which is why, in the following paragraph, Kant comes to the problem of the relation between this mode of *Fürwahrhalten* and practical belief.

If we take up again the question of knowable objects, no longer on the side of the object ("What can we know *of God*?") but on our side ("What can *we know* of God?"), we discover three sorts of knowable things: things of opinion (*Sachen der Meinung [opinabile]*), facts (*Tatsachen [scibile]*), and things of belief (*Glaubensachen [mere credibile]*). I can have an opinion only with respect to an empirical possibility that I might one day verify (so I can be of the opinion that there is intelligent life on other planets, because it is in itself possible that one day I could go and check this out) but never with respect to an Idea of Reason (because that would make it into mere fiction). Facts are where I can prove an objective reality (where there is a corresponding intuition). But there is one exception among facts and among the Ideas of Reason, and this is the Idea of freedom, which makes sense only to the extent that it can be made manifest by real actions in the world of experience. The factuality of freedom (none other than the *to-be-realized* of the moral law) is part of its Idea, which, as we saw for the law, must comprise its own realizability as a determining feature. Freedom is a fact and can therefore be known, even if it remains an Idea (because, *qua* concept, it is *überschwenglich* for theoretical reason, for the understanding). But the idea of freedom, when it is thought according to the moral law, entails other Ideas that go beyond the domain of theoretical concepts, and these Ideas will be the object of belief but a belief that must be practical. This means that freedom can be bought under the moral law only if we admit the Idea of the supreme Good to be realized in the world:

> Of this sort is the *highest good* to be achieved in the world through freedom, the objective reality of the concept of which cannot be proved adequately in any experience possible for us, and hence for the theoretical use of reason, but the use of which is nevertheless commanded by practical pure reason for the best possible realization of that end, and which must thus be assumed to be possible. (*CJ*, 333)

And, says Kant, if we admit the supreme Good as an object of belief, we must also admit, for the same reasons, the conditions of its realizability (namely, the immortality of the soul and the existence of God). And these are really the only true objects of belief (because everything we believe on the basis of another's testimony, for example, really implies a probative experience somewhere and can thus in principle become a known object),[19] and belief becomes essentially a matter for practical reason, which, in order to be practical, has to give itself the structure of its own *to-be-realized*, according to the interrupted teleology we are following here.

It remains, however, to clarify the exact relation between the moral law and the final end it commands us to bring about, for which we have to admit God as merely an object of practical belief. For the cut that alone gives meaning to the Idea of the final end (which, recall again, is final only to the extent that it is cut from everything of which it is the end) intervenes again between the moral law strictly conceived and what that same law commands; or, better, the cut intervenes within the moral law itself as its very structure, that in a moment Kant is going to describe as the structure of a promise. But—and this is Kant's problem—as such, the moral law is precisely not a matter of ends, on pain of falling into what the *Groundwork* and the second *Critique* call the hypothetical or technical imperative. The moral law is expressed as categorical imperative and is thus unconditioned and unconditional. So how are we to articulate it with what Kant has just demonstrated? We must try to articulate it with God and the final end, because otherwise the whole teleology would again fall back into mechanism and theoreticism: The teleology depends entirely on the positing of the final end, and the coherence of this final end depends on its relation with freedom thought under the aegis of the moral law. If the moral law did not

19. This distinction is placed into question in recent work by Derrida. See, for example, *Demeure: Maurice Blanchot* (Paris: Galilée, 1998).

command us to realize the supreme Good as final end, there would be no freedom other than contingency (i.e., we would be subject to blind chance or blind necessity). Kant attempts this articulation first of all by situating the cut between the necessity of the law as such, on the one hand, and the partial contingency of the final end, on the other:

> Consequently, the concept of God acquires the distinction of counting as a matter of faith in our holding-for-true only through its relation to the object of our duty, as the condition of the possibility of attaining the final end of that duty; by contrast, the very same concept can still not make its object valid as a fact, because although the necessity of duty for the practical reason is quite clear, still the attainment of its final end, insofar as it is not entirely in our own power, is assumed only for the sake of the practical use of reason, and is thus not practically necessary like duty itself. (*CJ*, 334–35)

Duty is necessary (i.e., known *a priori* by reason) and is thus entirely within our power. The final end, however, escapes us at least in part and cannot therefore attain necessity. However, there must be this final end in its very nonnecessity, and, following a structure that is becoming familiar to us, this is necessary for necessity. Just as natural necessity needed teleology to safeguard its necessity (the necessity of necessity), so practical necessity, to the extent that it entails a necessity of realization (which is why the Idea of freedom can lay claim to its status as a fact and save the teleology) needs this nonnecessary final end if its necessity is to be properly practical. As is often the case, it is in a note that Kant tries to untangle these very complex relations:

> The final end, the promotion of which is imposed upon us by the moral law, is not the ground of duty; for this lies in the moral law, which, as a formal practical principle, guides us categorically, regardless of the object of the faculty of desire (the matter of the will), hence regardless of any end. This formal property of my actions, in which alone their inner moral worth consists, is entirely in our power; and I can perfectly well abstract from the possibility or unrealizability of the ends that I am obliged to promote in accordance with that law (because only the external value of my actions consists in them) as something that is never completely in my power, in order to see only that which is my own doing. Yet the aim [die Absicht] of promoting the final end of all rational beings (happiness, insofar as it is consistent with duty) is still imposed precisely by the law of duty. (*CJ*, 335n)

So here is the crux of the problem: The "formal" character of the moral law, which alone guarantees its necessity, allows for the possibility of abstracting from ends and their realization or realizability in general. But I ought not follow this possibility opened by the law, because that same law imposes on me the duty not to ignore ends. Which means that the morality of the moral law (what is too rapidly called its "formalism") is immediately counteracted by a movement toward the end, and this movement also forms part of the morality of the moral law. The categorical imperative orders me to act according to its purely formal law, but it also orders me to *act* (i.e., to pursue an end and make something happen). The maxim of my action must survive the formal test of the law, but my action is moral only if I do it, if, then, I realize some end; and this end, whatever it be, must also contribute to the pursuit of the final end. As to this incursion of moral action into the world of nature, we have known since the Antinomies of Pure Reason that theoretical reason does not understand it at all:

> But speculative reason cannot understand the realizability of this final end at all (either on the part of our own physical capacity or on the part of the cooperation of nature); rather, on the basis of such causes, as far as we can rationally judge, it must hold the assumption of such a success of our good conduct in mere nature (inside and outside of us), without the assumption of God and immortality, to be unfounded and empty even if well-intended, and, if it could be completely certain of this judgment, it would regard the moral law itself as a mere deception of our reason in a practical respect. But since speculative reason is fully convinced that the latter can never happen, but by contrast those ideas the object of which lies beyond nature can be conceived without contradiction, it must acknowledge those ideas as real for its own practical law and the task that is thereby imposed, thus as real in a moral respect, in order not to contradict itself. (*CJ*, 335n)

While not understanding this at all, theoretical reason is nonetheless necessitated to believe it, on pain of contradiction. Practical reason ought not be, must not be, has not to be a mystification of theoretical reason, and theoretical reason has to believe it, had better believe it, to the extent that the whole teleological structure of reason—the rationality of reason itself—depends on it. And this is indeed the structure of the *Endzweck*, itself a rigorous consequence of teleology: All teleology must finalize its ends, however complex and numerous they be, by appeal to a final end, which must logically be cut from that of which it is the end. It is obvious that this end, which alone gives meaning to that of which it is the end, structurally speaking, escapes the comprehension of everything it finalizes. The "practical belief" that results as the only rational possibility of still orienting oneself in this structure takes the form of the kind of belief one can have in a promise. Better believe that the promise will be kept and fulfilled, but the promise as such excludes all certainty as to its realization (which is why it is hard to make a clear distinction between promise and threat)[20] and thus represents the constitutive frustration, the productive inhibition of theoretical reason, which thus finds itself grounded in a slightly vacant confidence. Kant again resorts to a note to clarify his position:

> Faith (as *habitus*, not as *actus*) is reason's moral way of thinking in the affirmation of that which is inaccessible for theoretical cognition. It is thus the constant fundamental principle of the mind to assume as true that which it is necessary to presuppose as a condition for the possibility of the highest moral final end, on account of the obligation to that, although we can have no insight into its possibility or into its impossibility.*
>
> * [Kant's note:] It is a matter of trusting the promise of the moral law: not a promise that is contained in the moral law, but one that I put into it, and indeed on a morally adequate basis. For a final end cannot be commanded by any law of reason without reason simultaneously promising its attainability, even if uncertainly, and hereby also justifying the affirmation of the only conditions under which our reason can conceive this. (*CJ*, 335–36 and n)

Teleology comes to an end here. Which means that it interrupts itself rather than fulfills itself—or perhaps that it fulfills its interruption. Just as it was necessary for peace that peace not be realized, it is necessary for practical reason that the moral law—the *telos* of the whole Kantian system, which gives meaning to all rational activity as such (even in the theoretical domain)—be merely promised. Or rather, for the moral law itself makes no promises, does not contain this promise, as Kant says, it is necessary that I promise myself the law, that I promise myself the realization of what the law commands—namely, to make the law. I promise myself that the law, which is inaccessible as such, forever, forever unrealizable, remains nonetheless practicable as something always to come; or rather, for the law cannot really be some thing, that what I call the law is only the practice of the path that I am tracing with the end of the thread in my hand, a *Seefahrer* in spite of everything, and that is thus not even a path but just the minimal movement that carries me forward just enough for me to believe in this forward movement, not only in uncertainty as to the end to be reached but in the certainty, not only that I will never reach the end, but that I will never know what the end is, because there is no end beyond what I am doing here and now in promising myself to go on, or

20. As Derrida has conclusively shown, any promise, in order to be a promise, must bring with it the necessary possibility of its nonrealization and thus the constitutive threat that it not be kept.

at least (because in the belief the promise gives me I do not know which way is onward, merely that I must go on) to take a step in nature, that uncrossable frontier, toward the singular, violent encounter on the occasion of which, the chance or opportunity, the *Zweckmässigkeit* of which I will again promise (as I am already promising without promising), promise myself the law that I will no more know then than now, as I take another step, holding in my hand the end of the thread I have always been dragging behind me, this point of free heterogeneity that therefore I am.

Brought this far by teleology, encouraged by those natural contingencies that call for teleological judgment, that encourage me to judge nature as a whole to be the work of an intelligent and moral God, I find myself now abandoned by teleology, abandoned to the pure teleology without *telos* of the promise I make myself as to the moral law, while the world around me can break up into scattered raw matter:

> The moral proof (which of course proves the existence of God only in a practical respect although one that is also indispensable for reason) would thus always remain in force even if we found in the world no material for physical teleology at all or only ambiguous material for it. We can conceive of rational beings who see themselves surrounded by a nature that gives no clear trace of organization but reveals only effects of a mere mechanism of raw matter, and who on that account, and given the alterability of some merely contingently purposive forms and relations, seem to have no ground to infer an intelligent author, in which case there would also be no suggestion of a physical teleology; nevertheless, reason, which in this case gets no guidance from concepts of nature, would still find in the concept of freedom and the moral ideas that are grounded upon that a practically sufficient ground for postulating the concept of an original being in accordance with these, i.e., as the concept of a divinity, and for postulating nature (even our own existence) as a final end in accordance with that concept and its laws, and of course with respect to the indispensable command of practical reason. (*CJ*, 341–42)

If, then, we have no need of natural teleology in order to think the being-teleological of teleology as such, if freedom alone would suffice, one might imagine that one would think that teleology better, more purely, without the encouragement or "confirmation" given by natural teleology, which in the end has nothing to do with the final end, cut from the world of which it is the end. Reason as such has no use for the physico-teleological proof of the existence of God. It only serves to make a finite and failing reason more receptive to the real proof, the moral proof, which as such can very well do without it.[21]

Seen from the vantage of reason itself, the natural contingencies that demand to be judged teleologically really are contingent. Which is as much as to say that Epicurus could have been right about natural mechanism without that changing anything for reason. But which is also as much as to say that one cannot see from the point of view of reason, that we are not there yet, that teleology in general makes no sense unless one has not reached its *telos*, a *telos* that one never could reach. The whole teleological structure, including the projected *telos* that determines it while remaining cut from it, depends on our being always somewhere in the middle, depends on the *telos* remaining for us a promise, thus uncertain, and that therefore we have no certainty at all as to the teleological nature of teleology. Which is also what is called freedom. Here, now, *point de téléologie, point de liberté.*

Can we identify this point with Kant's thinking of the transcendental imagination and ultimately with time itself? No more than with finitude, to the extent that such a reading, despite its obvious power, remains within a reading of Kant that misrecognizes the radicality of judgment, even within the first *Critique*, by having undue faith in what phenomenology can put up against a "scholastic" logic.

Rather, we must try to think this "point" (which is clearly not *a* point) according to the fractal logic of the frontier and the radical exteriority it allows us to think. As spectral residue of a nature that never was before this residue, the frontier, unsublatable trace of exteriority and therefore of any identity at all (even that of time, of which Heidegger's conception would be the most powerful attempt to hold together identity and difference—but the frontier is also the trace of a spacing unsublatable by time itself), can only relaunch the scattering play of ana-logy or ananalogy without ever promising to gather it into a *logos* speakable as such. Ana-*logos* precedes *logos*. Whence the violence inscribed in the frontier as thought by Kant in the failing perspective of perpetual peace, and whence too a certain stupid literality of

21. Kant's argument is supposed to provide a proof of the existence of God. This proof draws its strength and its rationality from its very theoretical insufficiency. This is a practical proof in the sense that in the end it proves nothing and is entirely held in the open structure of the promise. In this sense, God depends on the absence of any proof of his existence, which comes down to the thought that believing in God (in this Kantian way) and not believing in God come to the same thing. Given Kant's proof, we cannot (not) believe in God. The frontier, on which we are still putting in time, persists as this very (im)possibility. In this sense, God is just a name for the quasi-transcendental as general condition of everything, pure *Deus terminus.*

everything we have suggested here. The stupid resistance of the frontier to thinking is clearly enough the chance of thinking, which survives and even thrives only by not quite being able to think what it thinks. In this way the essence of peace, be it in the literal sense or, analogically, peace in philosophy, excludes its perpetuity. Nothing is thought in the peace of the graveyard; true peace is agitated and threatened, perpetually, here too, on this final frontier.

Finis

The violence, the inderacinatable radical evil of the quasi-natural and perpetual frontier that Kant cannot absorb, is precisely what Hegel criticizes in the *Elements of the Philosophy of Right*, under the unsurprising name of *contingency*. According to the remark to §333:

> there is no praetor to adjudicate between states, but at most arbitrators and mediators, and even the presence of these will be contingent, i.e. determined by particular wills. Kant's idea [Vorstellung] of a *perpetual peace* guaranteed by a federation of states which would settle all disputes and which, as a power recognized by each individual state, would resolve all disagreements so as to make it impossible for these to be settled by war presupposes an *agreement* between states. But this agreement, whether based on moral, religious, or other grounds and considerations, would always be dependent on particular sovereign wills, and would therefore continue to be tainted with contingency.[1]

Hegel's whole philosophy is of course an attempt to sublate contingency into necessity, without simply erasing the place of the contingency thus sublated.[2] If we wished to put some pressure on this *Aufhebung* of contingency

1. G.W. F. Hegel, *Elements of the Philosophy of Right*, ed. Allen Wood, tr. B. H. Nisbet (Cambridge: Cambridge University Press, 1991), remark to §333. See already the youthful piece entitled "The German Constitution," in *Hegel's Political Writings*, tr. T. M. Knox (Oxford: Clarendon Press, 1964), 208.

2. There are countless reflections on the contingent and the necessary throughout Hegel. For example, in the preface to the *Philosophy of Right*, Hegel protests against a current tendency to suppose that "the spiritual universe is [. . .] at the mercy of contingency and arbitrariness" (14); the very first paragraph of the *Encyclopedia Logic* asserts that "thought will be satisfied with nothing short of showing the *necessity* of its facts" (tr. William Wallace [Cambridge: Cambridge University Press, 1975], §1), and parallel assertions are to be found in the introduction to the *Aesthetics* (tr. Knox [Oxford:

into necessity (i.e., *Aufhebung* itself) to the test, at least in Hegel's political philosophy, we would need to look not so much toward the individual, as has recently been suggested in an improbable attempt to recover Hegel for liberalism,[3] but indeed toward the frontier. For Hegel, the frontier of the State is thought with a rigor found nowhere else in the tradition, first in that the State for Hegel is possible only within a plurality of States ("Without relations with other states, the state can no more be an actual individual than an individual can be an actual person without a relationship with other persons" [remark to *Philosophy of Right*, §331]) and that this plurality necessarily and explicitly involves violence along the frontier. From early to late, from the youthful text on the German Constitution (153)[4] through the essay on Natural Law[5] to the *Philosophy of Right* itself, Hegel constantly insists that a State is a State only if it really, *Wirklich*, defends itself on its frontier, and in so doing, obliges Civil Society, everything within the frontier, to recognize its vanity and nullity, as it exposes itself with all its values of property, security, and even life to exteriority and destruction in the name of the State, and therefore of Spirit, thus revealing its ethical truth in warfare. It follows that for Hegel the State is never truly established, because its reality consists only in what he calls "involvement with contingent occurrences [der Verwicklung

---

Clarendon Press, 1975], 1:11, 22, 24); the *Natural Law* essay reproaches empiricism with "lack[ing] in the first place all criteria for drawing the boundary between the contingent and the necessary" (64). In the remark on Free Will appended to §145 of the *Encyclopedia Logic*, again, "The problem of science, and especially of philosophy, undoubtedly consists in eliciting the necessity concealed under the semblance of contingency." But contingency is not simply to be denied. On the contrary: the passage continues, "That, however, is far from meaning that the contingent belongs to our subjective conception alone, and must therefore be simply set aside, if we wish to get at the truth." See also Bernard Mabille, *Hegel: l'épreuve de la contingence* (Paris: Aubier, 1999).

3. Jean-Claude Pinson, *Hegel, le droit et le libéralisme* (Paris: Presses Universitaires de France, 1989).

4. "A multitude of human beings can only call itself a state if it is united for the common defence of the entirety of its property. What is self-explanatory in this proposition must none the less be stated, namely that this union has not merely the intention of defending itself; the point is that it defends itself by actual arms, be its power and success what they may" ("The German Constitution," in *Hegel's Political Writings*, tr. T. M. Knox, 143–242 [Oxford: Clarendon Press, 1964], 153).

5. "War preserves the ethical health of peoples in their indifference to specific institutions, preserves it from habituation to such institutions and their hardening. Just as the blowing of the winds preserves the sea from the foulness which would result for peoples from a continual calm, so also corruption would result for peoples under continual or indeed 'perpetual' peace" (*Natural Law*, 93).

mit zufälligen Begebenheiten]" (*Philosophy of Right*, §323) at the moment of risk that is the confrontation on the frontier in time of war, which is the essential moment of the State. The State is itself only in thus exposing itself to a destruction that is always really, effectively, possible. This contingency, which is essential to the definition of the State, a contingency that takes the form of war as the truth of the frontier, must of course be sublated, which is what Hegel attempts in the remark to the following paragraph:

> The ethical *moment of war* is implicit in what was stated above. For war should not be regarded as an absolute evil [Übel] and as a purely external contingency whose cause is therefore itself contingent, whether this cause lies in the passions of rulers or nations [Völker], in injustices, etc., or in anything else which is not as it should be. Whatever is by nature contingent is subject to contingencies, and this fate is therefore itself a necessity. (remark to §324)

And yet, this contingency that is apparently only apparent, and which ensures the transition between "External Sovereignty" and "International Right" properly speaking, is not sublated for all that. It is perhaps necessary that the contingent encounter another contingent, but that necessity of contingency is not yet proper Hegelian necessity. Which explains why in §340, the last paragraph of "International Right," we should still be talking about this contingency, and even in an extreme form:

> Since states function as *particular* entities in their mutual relations, these relations will encompass the most supremely animated play of the inner particularity of passions, interests, ends, talents and virtues, violence [Gewalt], wrongdoing, and vice, as of external contingency in the greatest dimensions of appearance [der äusseren Zufälligkeit, in der grössten Dimensionen der Erscheinung], a play in which the ethical whole itself—the autonomy of the state—is exposed to contingency. (§340; tr. mod.)[6]

As is well known, this contingency—that Hegel, sure of himself, expounds here almost complacently, and to which he can allow much greater scope than almost any other philosopher, certain as he is of his dialectic—will be sublated in Universal History, thus at a level that is inaccessible to the State *qua* State. Because the State as such must remain in its particularity, within its limits, finite and *beschränkte*, limited, closed in, enclosed in its frontier, where

6. I have modified Nisbet's translation considerably here, based on the French translation by André Kahn (Paris: Gallimard, 1940) and advice on how to construe Hegel's difficult German here from Rodrigo Bueno Therezo and Julia Ireland, to both of whom I am extremely grateful.

it acts only in its own interests and is entirely ignorant of the *Weltgeist*, even if the *Weltgeist* is residing with it at the moment in question. In that case, the State would be merely the unconscious bearer of reason according to reason's famous "cunning" (and in Hegel reason *just is* that cunning, by which it advances only by virtue at every step forward of an enormous retreat, to draw from the ahistorical reserve of nature and passion the means to progress, all the while claiming to be moving beyond nature and passion) (§345).

This sublation, crucial to the whole structure of the *Philosophy of Right*, and thereby the whole of Hegel's philosophy, is quite problematic. To avoid universal history's being reduced to the mere judgment of power (i.e., "the abstract and irrational necessity of a blind fate" [§342]), to avoid remaining basically on the same level as Kant, "infected with contingency," Hegel must transform the situation we have just sketched out, which is essentially a situation of spatial dispersion (whence the importance of the frontier) into a temporal sequence, according to a sublation that is also essential to the speculative dialectic as such. This he does in §346 by distributing a fragmentary "principle" of Spirit to each people, "a plurality of separate entities," in what he calls "*geographical* and *anthropological* existence," and then by insisting in a perfectly dogmatic way that "*only once in history can [each nation] have this epoch-making role*" (§347). By insisting, *contra* Hegel, on an unsublatable spatiality of the frontier, a resistance of the frontier (as spectral return of nature) to this historicizing sublation, and thus insisting on a persistence of contingency, we are apparently going to situate ourselves at the very beginning of World History, or rather (but this is the whole of Hegel) at a beginning that is not even a beginning, a prehistorical beginning of history:

> It is the childhood of History. Substantial forms constitute the gorgeous edifices of Oriental Empires in which we find all rational ordinances and arrangements, but in such a way, that individuals remain as mere accidents. [. . .] All the elements of a complete State—even subjectivity—may be found there, but not yet harmonized with the grand substantial being. For outside the One Power—before which nothing can maintain an independent existence—there is only revolting caprice, which, beyond the limits of the central power, roves at will without purpose or result. Accordingly we find the wild hordes breaking out from the Upland—falling upon the countries in question, and laying them waste, or settling down in them, and giving up their wild life; but in all cases resultlessly lost in the central substance. [. . .] On the one side we see duration, stability—Empires belonging to mere space, as it were (as distinguished from Time)—unhistorical History;—as for example, in China. [. . .] On the other side, the Form of Time stands contrasted with this spatial stability. The States

> in question, without undergoing any change in themselves, or in the principle of their existence, are constantly changing their position towards each other. They are in ceaseless conflict, which brings on rapid destruction. [. . .] This History, too (i.e., of the struggles before-mentioned) is, for the most part, really unhistorical, for it is only the repetition of the same majestic ruin.[7]

If we are justified in finding that Hegel is being dogmatic in sublating our violent dispersion of States haunted by the nature (the contingency, radical evil, the perpetual nonperpetuity of peace) that returns to prowl along their frontiers, then we would have here, before history, a figure of something Hegel cannot historicize or can only repress by historicizing. The "ceaseless conflict," what we are here calling the frontier, would then be the nonhistorical ground of history that survives history (just as China and India, nonhistorical empires, have, according to Hegel, outlived history, whereas Persia, the first historical empire, is historical by virtue of having passed away in history, an ephemeral rose superior to the enduring mountains, closer to spirit). This nonhistorical ground of history would be a pernicious nomadic and barbarous errancy, far from the essence. War on the frontier, or—less tautologically—simply the frontier, is thus both what is essentially historical in Hegel, what makes history advance, and something nonspiritual, contingent, and thus nonhistorical, the nonhistorical historicity of a history that will not, clearly enough, have reached its end in the German empire.

Hegel will not have sublated that frontier, because it is what gives rise to a nonspiritualizable difference, to what alone provokes thought. It means we will never reach the end, that the end is a certain in-terminability that is the very structure of the term. The certainty we henceforth have of not knowing the end should not push us to return to the beginning or, indeed, to any given point in the middle (this is not at all about any "return to Kant"). But what our halt around Kant will have taught us is that there are *only* halts and in them a certain spirit of critique that begins to be lost as soon as it becomes critique (i.e., once it is carried out in anticipation of a doctrine to come). This critical position of critique, this crisis of critique, obliges it to have quite different relations to the tradition than those entertained by Kant himself.

So we have not tried to read Kant in a Kantian way (as will have been noticed), while nonetheless claiming to *read* Kant. Reading him, we clearly take a step outside what philosophers call "philosophy," because philosophy in that sense is the refusal, in principle, of reading. And if, as we have just too

7. G.W. F. Hegel, *The Philosophy of History*, tr. J. Sibree [1899] (Mineola, NY: Dover, 1956), 105–6.

rapidly claimed, the Hegelian reading of Kant is the most consistent of all refusals of reading, then we cannot follow Hegel (while reserving for another occasion the pleasure of *reading* him), it follows that we do not know where we have arrived, here at the term of our book, and more especially do not know what might come next.

Appendix: On Transcendental Fiction (*Grenze* and *Schranke*)

Let me suggest provisionally that fiction (or at least literary fiction), in its traditional (philosophical) determination, always has to do with a certain beyond.[1] That it puts us in adventurous touch with something over the frontier, with other worlds, with ghosts (perhaps, as we shall see, with ghost ships). And that, reciprocally, any beyond always runs the risk of falling prey to fiction, so that as soon as philosophy ventures into it, it runs the risk of finding itself somewhere it never should be.

Jacques Derrida claims that it is on the frontier of philosophy and literature—or rather, where this frontier trembles—that philosophy is most called to thought.[2] One imagines that such a frontier (especially if it were to turn out to be essentially unstable) has a complex structure that is difficult to pin down. My working hypothesis here, in what will be both rather elementary and rather dry (for which I apologize), is that this structure must have an at least analogical relation (but we shall see that analogy is part of our problem and cannot solve it) with the structure of the frontier as Kant presents it, and especially in the famous and obscure discussion in the *Prolegomena* of the distinction between limit and bound, bound and limit, border and boundary, perimeter and periphery, barrier and gate, *Grenze* and *Schranke*.[3]

I shall be trying to show not that philosophy and literature are two domains with a frontier (even a vague or uncertain frontier) that separates them

1. This is an adapted translation of a text originally written in French for the conference Passions de la littérature at Université de Louvain-la-Neuve, Belgium, July 1995, and subsequently published in the volume of the same name edited by Michel Lisse (Paris: Galilée, 1996), 141–60.

2. Jacques Derrida, *Parages* (Paris: Galilée, 1986), 10.

3. These two terms have been variously and inconsistently translated into English (and other languages). I shall most often leave them in German in what follows.

more or less successfully, but that where there is a frontier (even a sharp or distinct frontier), or perhaps where there is an effort to *think* the frontier, there is something like literature. This "literature" (as tends to be the case in Kant) can be something from which one suffers, of which one bears the passion (as one says the passion of Christ), while enjoying it more or less secretly. "Something like literature" would then be (as Jean-Luc Nancy has brilliantly shown from a quite different point of view)[4] Kant's passion, or at least the passion of a Kant reread after Derrida—reread, then, with a view to subjecting the Kantian transcendental (or finding it already subjected) to the strange kind of twist we have gotten used to calling the quasi-transcendental.

And so, by way of an exergue, as an example of this double passion, this famous paragraph that I cite without commentary, in which the whole *Critique of Pure Reason* is at stake:

> We have now not only traveled through the land of pure understanding, and carefully inspected each part of it, but we have also surveyed it, and determined the place for each thing in it. This land, however, is an island, and enclosed in unalterable boundaries by nature itself. [Dieses Land aber ist eine Insel, und durch die Natur selbst in unverändliche Grenzen eingeschlossen.] It is the land of truth (a charming name), surrounded by a broad and stormy ocean, the true seat of illusion, where many a fog bank and rapidly melting iceberg pretend to be new lands and, ceaselessly deceiving with empty hopes the voyager looking around for new discoveries [den auf Entdeckungen herunschwärmenden Seefahrer], entwine him in adventures from which he can never escape and yet also never bring to an end. But before we venture out on this sea, to search through all its breadth and become certain of whether there is anything to hope for in it, it will be useful first to cast yet another glance at the map of the land that we would now leave, and to ask, first, whether we could not be satisfied with what it contains, or even must be satisfied with it out of necessity, if there is no other ground on which we could build; and, second, by what title we occupy even this land, and can hold it securely against all hostile claims. (*CPR*, A235–36/ B294–95)

Kant not only makes a difference between these two terms *Grenze* and *Schranke* (an operative difference, as they used to say) but he makes that difference the object of an explicit reflection in the first edition of the *Critique*

4. Jean-Luc Nancy, *Le Discours de la syncope: 1. Logodaedalus* (Paris: Aubier-Flammarion, 1976).

(1781) and then, in the *Prolegomena* (1783), pushes this reflection to the point of making this distinction a key to the understanding of his entire thought, at least as far as pure speculative reason is concerned—and this leaves more than a trace in the second edition of the *Critique* (1787).

In Kant's discussions of the limits and boundaries of the understanding, which are of course legion, the dominant German term in general is *Grenze*. Thus, at the outset of the preface to the first edition of the first *Critique*, explaining how on the basis of the principles reason cannot fail to employ in the sphere of experience it finds itself impelled to go beyond experience and to invoke principles that are of no use in that sphere:

> By doing this, however, human reason plunges into darkness and contradictions; and although it can indeed gather from these that they must be based on errors lying hidden somewhere, it is unable to discover these errors. For the principles that it employs go beyond the boundary of all experience [da sie über die Grenze aller Ehrfahrung hinausgehen], and hence no longer acknowledge any touchstone of experience. The combat arena of these endless conflicts is what we call *metaphysics*. (*CPR*, Aviii)

There would be dozens of examples of this usage that one could quote, as much in passages that remain unchanged from one edition to the next as in some additions that are found only in the second edition.[5]

It is true that one also finds uses of the word *Schranke*, notably in a passage from the "Discipline of Pure Reason," in which Kant proposes an extended analogy between our knowledge in general and our knowledge of the terrestrial globe. Kant wants to make a distinction between two forms or mo-

5. For example, in a note to the preface to the second edition: "This method, imitated from the method of those who study nature, thus consists in this: to seek the elements of pure reason in that *which admits of being confirmed or refuted through an experiment*. Now the propositions of pure reason, especially when they venture beyond all boundaries of possible experience [wenn sie über alle Grenze möglicher Erfahrung hinaus gewagt werden], admit of no test by experiment with their *objects* (as in natural science): thus to experiment will be feasible only with *concepts* and *principles* that we assume a priori by arranging the latter so that the same objects can be considered from two different sides, *on the one side* as objects of the senses and the understanding for experience, and *on the other side* as objects that are merely thought at most for isolated reason striving beyond the bounds of experience [Erfahrungsgrenze]. If we now find that there is agreement with the principles of pure reason when things are considered from this twofold standpoint, but that an unavoidable conflict of reason with itself arises with a single standpoint, then the experiment decides for the correctness of that distinction" (*CPR*, Bxviii–xixn).

dalities of ignorance (an ignorance that, he recalls, should incite me to pursue my inquiry rather than abandon it) or rather two forms *and* two modalities of ignorance. I can first be ignorant either of things or of the determination and the limits (*Grenzen*) of my knowledge. Each of these two forms of ignorance can have two modalities. The ignorance in question can be contingent: A contingent ignorance of things calls for a dogmatic inquiry into the things in question; a contingent ignorance of the limits of my knowledge calls for a critical inquiry into the limits (*Grenzen*, still) of my possible knowledge. But that my ignorance be necessary (second modality, then, and apparently of both forms at once, for Kant no longer talks of things, is already on the limit) cannot be established empirically by observation (*Beobachtung*) but solely by critical means, by the deepening (*Ergründung*) of the primary sources of knowledge.

We must therefore distinguish the determination of the limits (*Grenzbestimmung*) of our knowledge, which can only be done on the basis of *a priori* grounds, from a mere limitation (*Einschränkung*) because of what Kant calls "a merely indeterminate cognition of an ignorance that is never completely to be lifted" (*CPR*, A758/B787). The first ignorance, which is necessary, determined by a *Grenze*, gives rise to science, whereas the second, contingent and limited, only gives rise to a perception.

If I represent the earth as flat ("as a plate," says Kant, in a passage we already had occasion to quote earlier [68–69]), I can learn from my experience that however far I go there is always ahead of me more space into which I could still advance. In this way I know the *Schranken* of my own knowledge of the earth at a given moment (the circle closed by the horizon that represents the limit of my current perception and even the sum of all I have seen in all the circles I have thus known as I went around the earth), but I do not know the *Grenzen* of all possible geography (*Erdbeschreibung*). But if I learn that the earth is a sphere, then, on the basis of a tiny part of the surface of that sphere, I can know it (without experience of what its surface may contain) in its scope (*Umfange*), its size, and its *Schranken*.

My knowledge, so long as I restrict myself to the data of immediate experience, is thus limited; it has *Schranken* that do not correspond to the *Grenzen* of what I could know if I set off from the knowledge (Kant does not say how I get that knowledge) of the sphericity of the globe. But having progressed to such knowledge and what it makes possible, I now know these *Grenzen* (of the writing of the earth) as *Schranken* (of the earth itself, in the analogy here being used). If one does not know that the earth is spherical, then one will rather imagine the sum of knowledge (acquired in the circle of an apparently flat space surrounded by a horizon) as analogous to our current little circle:

a big circle, then, on a flat surface, limited by a horizon that one can never embrace with a single glance and that one imagines to be the horizon of an unconditioned totality (for the circle must contain the whole of possible experience). But, says Kant, all the questions of our pure reason concern what might be found beyond this horizon, or else, *allenfals*, at best, for that matter, also on its frontier (*Grenzlinie*, its boundary line).

Hume's error[6] was to imagine that one can simply put such questions in their place beyond the horizon as mere fictions, but however useful that may be, this second, skeptical, step (*zweite Schritt*) of reason (the first being the dogmatic step), which would be the step of rest or temporary dwelling, for skepticism is also here presented as a *Ruheplatz* (a resting place, a step that is not a step, a halting step) where reason can reflect on its dogmatic wandering (for dogmatism is here a wandering, whereas in the celebrated preface to the second edition of the *Critique* it is rather skepticism that is presented as a nomadism and dogmatism would rather be sedentary), where it can make a sketch of the region in which it finds itself, better choose the path it is to take, but where it cannot establish a fixed abode (this is not "ein Wohnplatz zum beständigen Aufenthalte [a dwelling place for constant residence]"). Only critique, the third step, can render such residence possible, precisely by fixing the boundaries, the *Grenzen* here explicitly opposed to the limits, the *Schranken*, of knowledge. Where skepticism can merely conjecture that reason is limited (and that the questions it raises fall in part beyond those limits), critique establishes *a priori* the boundaries of reason.

Which is precisely why we have to change analogies and compare our reason to a sphere rather than an indefinite flat surface, as we saw earlier. For the problem in representing reason as a flat surface is that such a surface is in principle unlimited, and so any limit in it can only be empirical and uncertain, put in place *a posteriori*, whereas what makes a sphere a good representation of reason is that its limits are rigorously determinable *a priori*. The object of the analogy (the sphere) therefore has *Schranken* that mean it can represent reason that has *Grenzen*, whereas the flat surface, having

6. Recall that according to the *Prolegomena*, Hume, already a geographer of human reason in the *Critique* (A761/B788), now become a *Seefahrer* himself, may have awakened Kant from his dogmatic slumber, "but deposited his ship on the beach (of skepticism) for safekeeping, where it could then lie and rot, whereas it is important to me to give it a pilot, who, provided with complete sea-charts and a compass, might safely navigate the ship wherever seems good to him, following sound principles of the helmsman's art drawn from a knowledge of the globe" (*Prolegomena*, 11–12).

as such neither *Schranken* nor *Grenzen*, can only give rise to the tracing of indeterminate or at best merely empirical limits.

Let us leave aside for now this minimal sign of a complication in the distribution of *Grenzen* and *Schranken* (a complication that consists in the fact that the one can figure the other in an analogy), because the general distribution of the two terms still seems clear and coherent. *Grenzen* are on the side of necessity, the *a priori*, and critique; *Schranken* on the side of contingency, the *a posteriori*, the empirical, and skepticism.

And, it would seem, it is exactly in this sense that Kant picks up this distinction again in the *Prolegomena*, the very subtitle of whose conclusion names the *Grenzbestimmung* of pure reason.[7] Kant repeats that we can claim knowledge only in the context of a possible experience but that this does not mean that we have to give up on things in themselves, which of course we cannot know but with which we can have a relation other than a theoretical knowledge-relation. The frontier between phenomena and things in themselves is complex and difficult to describe. Kant says this:

> Our principles, which limit [einschranken] the use of reason to possible experience alone, could accordingly [i.e., if they closed off the frontier of possible experience to such an extent that nothing was supposed to subsist beyond] become *transcendent* and could pass off the limits [Schranken] of our reason for limits [Schranken again] on the possibility of things themselves (for which *Hume's* Dialogues can serve as an example), if a painstaking critique did not guard the boundaries [Grenzen] of our reason even with respect to its empirical use, and set a limit [here *Ziel*, a term, an aim, a final point] to its pretensions. (§57, 102)

Our reason, then, does indeed have *Schranken*, which, one must believe, are contingent but which always might present themselves as the *Grenzen* of all reality. And these contingent limits might present themselves as such precisely on critical grounds, if those grounds were to be no longer immanent but, according to the celebrated but obscure distinction from the first *Critique*, transcendent. And what is a transcendent principle? Precisely, a principle that not only transgresses the limits of the field of experience through error or lack of caution but incites one to cross those limits and even to overthrow them. In the *Critique*, the frontier between *Grenze* and *Schranke* begins to be a little less distinct here:

7. This conclusion comprises §§57–60, with the overall title "Von der Grenzbestimmung der reinen Vernunft" ("On Determining the Boundary of Pure Reason").

> We will call the principles whose application stays wholly and completely within the limits [Schranken] of possible experience *immanent*, those that would fly beyond these boundaries [Grenzen: so here, *Schranken* and *Grenzen* are not distinguished, they are the same thing, in this passage that remains the same from one edition to the next] *transcendent* principles. But by the latter I do not understand the *transcendental* use or misuse of categories, which is a mere mistake of the faculty of judgment when it is not properly checked by criticism, and thus does not attend enough to the boundaries of the territory [die Grenze des Bodens] in which alone the pure understanding is allowed its play; rather, I mean principles that actually incite us to tear down all those boundary posts [Grenzpfähle] and to lay claim to a wholly new territory that recognizes no demarcations anywhere. Hence *transcendental* and *transcendent* are not the same. The principles of pure understanding we presented above should be only of empirical and not of transcendental use, i.e., of a use that reaches out beyond the boundaries of experience [Erfahrungsgrenze]. But a principle that takes away these limits, which indeed bids us to overstep them, is called *transcendent.* (A295–96/B352)

In the *Critique*, then (in the second edition, which dates from after the *Prolegomena*, as much as in the first), a transcendent principle does not respect a frontier that can just as well be called *Grenze* as *Schranke*. In the *Prolegomena*, however, what runs the risk of being transcendent is a principle that tries to pass off simple *Schranken* as *Grenzen*. It is no longer so much the case that this principle incites one to cross the frontier but that it posits this frontier as being uncrossable, whereas one *ought* to cross it but only in a certain way, which remains to be specified. In the *Critique*, the transcendent tries to erase the frontier, whether it be boundary or limit (the distinction matters little, because the principle in question wants, precisely, to sweep away anything to do with it, move into a domain with no demarcations, and can therefore happily erase the frontier between these two ways of thinking the frontier), whereas in the *Prolegomena*, the transcendent is transcendent (or rather, our good immanent principle, or our transcendental principle that prescribes immanence, also runs the risk of becoming transcendent) by wanting to close off this perspective that before it was transcendent to want to open.

Let me suggest that it is precisely this confusion—or this indetermination in the determination of the frontier, the vagueness here affecting the frontier supposed to pass within the concept "frontier," between *Grenze* and *Schranke*—that the *Prolegomena* want to clear up, and let us accept an empirical explanation (namely, that Kant did not have the time or the energy to change everything) for the maintenance of the confusion in the second edition of the *Critique*. Let us return, then, to the way things are presented in the *Prolegomena*. We cannot accept that the frontiers of reason be *Schranken* (because then we should have not only to give up knowing what is beyond them but relegate that beyond to the status of mere fiction, as does Hume);[8] they must, then, be *Grenzen*. Only the latter can be traced securely and rigorously, and only the latter also allow a certain crossing of the frontier (a crossing that would be blocked by its determination—an indeterminate determination, moreover, because it would be empirical and contingent—as *Schranke*) toward what lies beyond. Critique, which will establish once and for all the *Grenzen* of reason, will also allow, in so doing, a certain crossing of these *Grenzen*.[9]

Kant attempts to make his distinction clearer by pulling the whole spatial or topographical analogy toward *Grenzen* (whereas in the *Critique*, at least in the passage we have just been quoting, *Grenzen* and *Schranken* both work in a spatial register) by giving a different version of the *Schranken*, which will do

8. "From which he concluded that reason has no power at all to think such [causal] connections, not even merely in general, because its concepts would then be bare fictions [Erdichtungen] and all of its cognitions allegedly established *a priori* would be nothing but falsely marked ordinary experiences" (*Prolegomena*, 7–8).

9. This would perhaps be the place to look for a properly Kantian riposte to Hegel's complaints in the *Science of Logic* about *Die Schranke und das Sollen* (trans. A.V. Miller as *Limitation and the Ought* [Atlantic Highlands: Humanities Press, 1990], 131). Hegel famously complains, with Kant clearly in mind: "Great stress is laid on the limitations of thought, of reason, and so on, and it is asserted that the limitation *cannot* be transcended. To make such an assertion is to be unaware that the very fact that something is determined as a limitation implies that the limitation is already transcended. For a determinateness, a limit, is determined as a limitation only in opposition to its other in general, that is, in opposition to that which is *free from the limitation*; the other of a limitation is precisely the *being beyond it*. [Es pflegt zuerst viel auf die Schranken des Denkens, der Vernunft usf. gehalten zu werden, und es wird behauptet, es könne über die Schranke nicht hinausgegangen werden. In dieser Behauptung liegt die Bewußtlosigkeit, daß darin selbst, daß etwas als Schranke bestimmt ist, darüber bereits hinausgegangen ist. Denn eine Bestimmtheit, Grenze ist als Schranke nur bestimmt im Gegensatz gegen sein Anderes überhaupt als gegen sein Unbeschränktes; das Andere einer Schranke ist eben das Hinaus über dieselbe.]" (ibid., 134). As is clearer in the German, Hegel makes no real effort to respect the complex distinction Kant is at least attempting to make between *Schranke* and *Grenze* (and, if anything, inverts the terminology). It might be argued that what Kant says about the *Grenze* in the *Prolegomena* is precisely an attempt to think through the "self-transcending" logic of the limit in general. The deconstructive demonstration of his failure does not, of course, commit one to accepting the Hegelian solution to the problem.

all it can to exclude them not only from the sphere of knowledge but from any spatial intuition, even of a plane. Kant first offers a definition to clarify this evanescent distinction:

> Boundaries [Grenzen] (in extended things) always presuppose a space that is found outside a certain fixed location, and that encloses that location; limits [Schranken] require nothing of the kind, but are mere negations that affect a magnitude insofar as it does not possess absolute completeness. Our reason, however, sees around itself as it were a space for the cognition of things in themselves, although it can never have determinate concepts of those things and is limited [eingeschränkt] to appearances alone. (*Prolegomena*, 103–4)

In the determination of reason, then, we are indeed dealing with *Grenzen* and not with *Schranken* (which are a simple negation, a contingent measure of the incomplete nature of our current knowledge, for example), with limits and not with boundaries, even if Kant still says that reason is limited by its boundaries. The space reserved for things in themselves (which for its part can have neither *Grenzen* nor *Schranken*, being none other than the unlimited field into which we were being invited by the transcendent principle) remains a space of knowledge or cognition without concept, the space of the Ideas of reason, and it alone gives dignity to metaphysics (for were it not for this space, if reason were simply limited to the domain of the understanding, it would be content with mere positive science). How are we to represent the crossing of this frontier, demanded by reason and permitted in such a complicated way by critique? Kant will appeal to a more and more complex topography to figure it.

In mathematics and the natural sciences, there are indeed *Schranken* but no *Grenzen*. One might expect that Kant would explain this by saying that these two sciences do not posit any space beyond themselves and that they know only the contingent bounds of their knowledge at a given moment of their development. The *Schranken* would thus be pushed back regularly toward an ideal completeness that would never be reached in fact. But this is not exactly how Kant presents things. He does recognize that progress within mathematics or natural sciences is *de jure* infinite, but instead of making *Schranken* the contingent limits constituted by the current horizon of these sciences he makes of them something quite different—namely, the apparently necessary and essential frontier of these disciplines, insofar as they are limited, indeed, but insofar as they do not approach these limits:

> As long as reason's cognition is homogeneous, no determinate boundaries [bestimmte Grenzen] can be thought for it. In mathematics and natural science

> [examples, then, of such homogeneous rational cognition] human reason recognizes *Schranken* but not *Grenzen*; that is, it indeed recognizes that something lies beyond it to which it can never reach, but not that it would itself at any point ever complete its inner progression. (*Prolegomena*, 104)

Note how much has changed: *Grenzen* are now the term of a progress, basically a *telos*, whereas *Schranken* are no longer the contingent limits of a specific cognition but something like the boundaries of a discipline. Kant continues:

> The expansion of insight in mathematics, and the possibility of ever new inventions, goes to infinity; so too does the discovery of new properties in nature (new forces and laws) through continued experience and the unification of that experience by reason. But *Schranken* here are nonetheless unmistakable, for mathematics refers only to *appearances*, and that which cannot be the object of sensory intuition, like the concepts of metaphysics and morals, lies entirely outside its sphere, and it can never lead there; but it also has no need whatsoever for such concepts. (*Prolegomena*, 104)

And now Kant continues: "Es ist also kein kontinuierlicher Fortgang und Annäherung zu diesen Wissenschaften, und gleichsam ein Punkt oder Linie der Berührung." This sentence, which carries a good part of the weight of the demonstration, remains desperately obscure. "There is therefore no continuous progress and advancement toward those sciences, or any point or line of contact, as it were" (*Prolegomena*, 104).[10] What seems clear is that these sciences do not push us to approach what does indeed constitute their frontier, the *Schranke* that separates them from metaphysics, because they are absorbed in their proper internal (and infinite) task, and this task can be pursued *ad infinitum* without metaphysical questions ever arising. Pursuing mathematics or the natural sciences as such, one never finds oneself confronted with the frontier of these disciplines (or if one does, one can imagine this would be only contingently so, and then one should turn aside to continue doing math or science). Whereas the science of *Grenzen* (namely, metaphysics itself) is distinguished from mathematics and the natural

10. The earlier English translation by Paul Carus ("extensively revised by James W. Ellington" [Indianapolis: Hackett, 1977]) is clearly erroneous: "There is therefore a continuous progress and approach to these sciences; and there is, as it were, a point or line of contact," translating as though the German had *ein* rather than *kein*. Although this is clearly an error, the reading is not completely implausible, to the extent that one might think that these sciences of *Schranken* are what they are insofar as they continually push back their limits without ever reaching complete knowledge.

sciences, insofar as its frontier is concerned, by needing to approach its frontier by its very nature and even inducing the permanent temptation of the transgression of the frontier; or rather—for this is the complication that has dictated from afar all these attempts to make distinctions—the transgression of the *Schranken* that metaphysics also involves and that are precisely not the *Grenzen*—mathematics and the natural sciences remain sagely (or can remain sagely) within the frontiers drawn by their respective *Schranken* in a way that metaphysics cannot.

This is as much as to say that the frontier, so far as metaphysics is concerned, is dynamic.[11] *Grenzen* are a bit like *Schranken* but as dynamically crossed and forbidden at one and the same time. And this is exactly the end or purpose of the natural dialectic of reason, a dialectic that is both the very rationality of reason and its radical contestation. One might say that Kant's thought here is very tense, caught in the risk of pure reason's coming apart by its very inner tension:

> But metaphysics, in the dialectical endeavors of pure reason (which are not initiated arbitrarily or wantonly, but toward which the nature of reason itself drives), does lead us to the *Grenzen*; and the transcendental ideas, just because they cannot be avoided and yet will never be realized, serve not only actually to show us the *Grenzen* of reason's pure use, but also the way to determine such *Grenzen*; and that too is the end of this natural predisposition of our reason. (*Prolegomena*, 104)

For this natural tendency must above all not be a movement of deregulation or dispersion but, *qua* natural, while escaping *ex hypothesi* from the explanations of natural science, must be susceptible to a teleological description from which Hume, but also the ghost of Epicurus, always wandering around this central and frontier zone of Kant's thought, must be banished. Thus it is this very tendency of our reason, to go to the limit and even to go beyond the limit, that gives rise to metaphysics as such, which at bottom is concerned only with this very movement according to which reason recognizes itself at its limit:

> The end of this natural predisposition of our reason, which bore metaphysics as its favorite child, whose procreation (as with any other in the world) is to be ascribed not to chance accident but to an original seed that is wisely organized toward great ends. (*Prolegomena*, 104–5)

11. I use this term less in the Kantian sense than in that of the nonlinear dynamics of so-called chaos theory.

For metaphysics is more natural in us than any other science and to that extent can even less than others be considered the product of a mere arbitrary choice.

What does it mean to say that nature, via metaphysics, pushes us to recognize or determine *Grenzen*? First, that having recognized *Schranken*, reason cannot be satisfied with them. And this nonsatisfaction translates as a certain transmutation of *Schranken* into *Grenzen* (for we are getting to the point of contact, they are the same thing, just as—and this is no doubt still the same thing—phenomena and things in themselves are the same thing), operated by a change of sign, from negative to positive, and of quality, from rupture to contact, from nonrelation to relation, from cut to continuity:

> Above (§§33, 34)[12] we noted *Schranken* of reason with respect to all cognition of mere beings of thought; now, since the transcendental ideas nevertheless make the progression up to these limits necessary for us, and have therefore led us, as it were, up to the contiguity of the filled space (of experience) with empty space (of which we know nothing—the *noumena*), we can also determine the *Grenzen* of pure reason; for in all *Grenzen* there is something positive (e.g., a surface is the *Grenze* of corporeal space, yet is nonetheless itself a space; a line is a space, which is the *Grenze* of a surface; a point is the *Grenze* of a line, yet is nonetheless a locus in space), whereas *Schranken* contain mere negations. (*Prolegomena*, 105)

So, there are *Schranken*, not to be crossed, but as one approaches them, one cannot fail to try to cross them. This temptation (according to §33, there is in the pure concepts of the understanding something *Verfänglich*, insidious, leading one astray, a principle of seduction that is a result of their very purity), produced by the negative, forbidding character of the *Schranken*, operates a remarkable conversion whereby they become *Grenzen* (i.e., a point, line, or surface of contact with the beyond insofar as it is empty). The negativity of *Schranken* tended paradoxically to positivize the beyond, to make of it a domain that was forbidden but by that very fact a domain of the same nature as the domain of experience, desirable, like a better world or a fictional world, whereas the positivization of the frontier itself, as *Grenze*, will confirm the void beyond as void for knowledge but thereby allow a certain accessibility for reason as nonknowing. The minimal but infinite difference between *Schranke* and *Grenze* consists then in the fact that reason, as understanding,

12. These are the paragraphs that resume the schematism and the phenomenon/noumenon distinction: The pure concepts of the understanding are not *in* experience, whence the tendency to think that they could lead us beyond all possible experience.

can approach the former without ever comprehending it, whereas the *Grenze* is part of the space of reason, which understands that it cannot understand the beyond of the understanding precisely by comprehending the *Grenze* itself. The *Grenze* thus becomes two-faced (whereas the *Schranke*—this was its very negativity—had one face only, on the inside), and reason finds a certain contentment by integrating its outer surface, by which it touches on the void.

The *Grenze*, then, comprises the *Schranke* and the minimal transgression of the *Schranke* that consists in recognizing that it has another side. This makes of it the place of a certain contradiction or conflict that infiltrates Kant's very syntax:

> If we combine the injunction to avoid [Verbot . . . zu vermeiden] all transcendent judgments of pure reason with the apparently conflicting command to proceed to concepts that lie beyond the field of immanent (empirical) use, we become aware that both can subsist together, but only directly on the *Grenze* [aber nur gerade auf der Grenze] of all permitted use of reason—for this *Grenze* belongs just as much to the field of experience as to that of beings of thought—and we are thereby at the same time taught how those remarkable ideas serve solely for determining the *Grenze* of human reason; that is, we are taught, on the one hand, not to extend cognition from experience without bound [unbegrenzt], so that nothing at all remains for us to cognize except merely the world, and, on the other, nevertheless not to go beyond the *Grenze* of experience and to want to judge of things outside that *Grenze* as things in themselves. (*Prolegomena*, 108)

So where is the duplicity of the *Grenze*, its double positivity? Clearly in a double interdiction: 1) Do not transgress the *Grenze* in order to judge what lies beyond it as still forming part of what lies on this side (i.e., the objects of experience); and 2) do not transgress the *Grenze* in order to judge what lies beyond as *not* forming part of experience (i.e., as things in themselves). What is the frontier here, on the frontier, between these two negative injunctions? There are things beyond the frontier, and the frontier belongs to the field of those things (as well as to the field of the objects of possible experience). The frontier signals that one must not judge them as though they belonged in the field of experience but also that one must not judge them as though they did not belong there (as though they were things in themselves). What lies beyond the *Grenze* of experience is indeed the field of things in themselves, but one must not judge them as such, for no (determinative) judgment is permissible as to things in themselves, on pain of not respecting their radically unknowable character and making them objects of an experience, be it an empirically impossible experience. The objects of the transcendental Ideas, then, are to be taken not as objects of experience or as objects beyond experience (that would be fiction) but as the frontier itself, in the crossing that does not cross, in its nontransgressive transgression. Caught in the double bind of these apparently conflicting interdictions, reason stands and gathers itself, picks itself up, on its own frontier, in the fleeting no-man's-land—its only proper homeland where it will never manage to orient itself—the vanishing space between its inner edge (experience) and its outer edge (noumena).

So one judges the domain beyond the frontier neither according to the domain this side of the frontier nor according to its beyond but according to the join between the two. This pure judgment, which must then be neither one side of the frontier nor the other, will bear solely on the relation between the two sides, on what crosses the frontier insofar as it is crossing and not insofar as it will cross or has crossed. The *Grenze* is thus determined as the pure suspense of a frontier in the pure event of its never-accomplished tracing. Reason as such (insofar as it is not limited to the understanding but insofar as it does not just let itself go either) is to be found precisely here, busy only tracing this double line, or tightrope-walking always on the point of falling into the empirical or else into the transcendent void.

One might wonder if it is by chance that the example that Kant takes here is that of God. Among the three Ideas of reason that Kant enumerates (immaterial being, world of the understanding taken as a whole, supreme Being), why choose the third to illustrate the problem posed by the *Grenze*? Can God be an example? "Wir wollen ein Beispiel vom Begriffe des höchsten Wesens hernehmen," says Kant. He is happy to concede to Hume all Hume's arguments against theism, and even against the supposed proofs of deism, but intends to hang onto what he calls "der Satz der deistichen Behauptung selbst," the proposition of the deistic affirmation itself. For one cannot literally attribute to God an understanding and a will, on pain of reducing Him to the dimensions of strictly human reason, but if one is content merely to attribute to God ontological predicates (eternity, omnipresence, omnipotence), one has thereby thought nothing determinate at all. Kant's response, supposed to allow the maintenance of the deistic affirmation, is that one *behaves as if* . . . or rather that one *speaks as if*, without really extending to the field of Ideas concepts belonging to the field of the understanding:

> But we hold ourselves to this *Grenze* if we limit [einschränken: no *Grenze* without *Schranke*] our judgment merely to the relation that the world may have to a being whose concept itself lies outside all cognition that we can attain within the world. For we then do not attribute to the supreme being any of the properties *in themselves* by which we think the objects of experience, and we

> thereby avoid *dogmatic* anthropomorphism; but we attribute those properties, nonetheless, to the relation of this being to the world, and allow ourselves a *symbolic* anthropomorphism, *which in fact concerns only language* [emphasis added] and not the object itself. (*Prolegomena*, 108)

The *Grenze*, then, the *point of (no) reason* where reason hangs on the event of its own possibility as pure relation between two domains where it is not entirely itself (for on the one side of the *Grenze* it is merely understanding and on the other it is *Schwärmerei* and fiction)—this *Grenze*, at least as to what concerns the transcendental Idea of a Supreme Being, avoids falling under the two interdictions we have seen by resorting to the *as if*, to the symbol, or, as we shall see in a moment, to analogy. In its ownmost point, reason posits the pure relation that gives it its reality by giving it its limit, and it is all about language. The object itself escapes us on both sides of the frontier. It is not subject to the categories of the understanding and is inaccessible to us as a thing in itself, but we can posit the relation between these two domains by what we can call either mere language or pure language, *nur die Sprache*, language as the pure affirmation of the relation as analogical.

Here then is the last paragraph of §57:

> If I say that we are compelled [genötigt: this is a necessity rather than an obligation] to look upon the world *as if* it were the work of a supreme understanding and will, I actually say nothing more than: in the way that a watch, a ship, and a regiment are related to an artisan, a builder, and a commander,[13] the sensible world (or everything that makes up the basis of this sum total of appearances) is related to the unknown—which I do not thereby cognize according to what it is in itself, but only according to what it is for me, that is, with respect to the world of which I am a part. (*Prolegomena*, 108)

Reason recognizes its *Grenze*, then, in speaking only by analogy of the relation between that *Grenze*'s two sides. The *as if*, the determining role of which in Kant's moral thought is well known, here plays in (as) the definition of pure reason (by) itself as a play of language that avoids all objective transgression of the limit while allowing reason to find itself to be other than the understanding. Reason recognizes itself at the limit in analogy. Faced with

13. We immediately wonder as to the compatibility of these examples, in which analogy already appears to be playing a complex role, for everything we know about Kant would encourage us to be wary of thinking there was any identity between the watchmaker-watch relation and the commanding officer-regiment relation; if this were already an analogy, this would be an analogy of analogy, a kind of multiplication of analogy that we shall see in a moment to be part of what makes analogy analogy.

the extreme precariousness of the situation of reason here, Kant quickly ends his section and opens a new one, which will take on the task of explaining and justifying this recourse:

> §58. This type of cognition is cognition *according to analogy*, which surely does not signify, as the word is usually taken, an imperfect similarity between two things, but rather a perfect similarity between two relations in wholly dissimilar things.*
>
> * [Kant's note:] Such is an analogy between the legal relation of human actions and the mechanical relation of moving forces: I can never do anything to another without giving him a right to do the same to me under the same conditions; just as a body cannot act on another body with its motive force without thereby causing the other body to react just as much on it. Right and motive force are here completely dissimilar things, but in their relation there is nonetheless complete similarity. By means of such an analogy, I can therefore provide a concept of a relation to things that are absolutely unknown to me. E.g. the promotion of the happiness of the children =a is to the love of the parents =b as the welfare of humankind =c is to the unknown in God =x. which we call love: not as if this unknown had the least similarity with any human inclination, but because we can posit the relation between God's love and the world to be similar to that which things in the world have to one another. But here the concept of the relation is a mere category, namely the concept of cause, which has nothing to do with sensibility. (*Prolegomena*, 108–9n)[14]

So what is placed in relation in Kantian analogy is already relations: The analogy posits a relation of relations, not of objects. If, as is the case here, the relational concept in play in the relation related by the analogy is a category (here, causality), and therefore already pure with respect to the sensibility (even if saying, as does Kant, that it therefore has nothing to do with the sensibility seems a little strong in the context in which the categories are elaborated), one can see the advantage for reason that is seeking to maintain itself on its frontier as the place that identifies it most securely: pure analogy of pure reason as pure relation of pure relations.

The *Grenze*, then, is essentially a limit-place (surface, line, or point) where

14. This argument around analogy, with some of the same examples and internal analogies, will return in §90 of the *Critique of Judgment*, where much of the work is again done in a difficult footnote that pushes the thought of analogy, at least in the case of God, far toward a thought of heterogeneity, which can be shown to disrupt or interrupt the whole structure of teleology with what I believe to be grave consequences that go well beyond Kant. I comment at length on these passages in Chapter 5. In our immediate context, it might be worth recalling that this description of proportional analogy (a : b :: c : x) mirrors Aristotle's famous analysis of the structure of metaphor in the *Poetics*.

reason speaks itself analogically—and so always differently—but where it thereby speaks itself as such. Reason according to Kant would thus be the faculty of the pure relation that can speak itself only by analogy. The domain of the understanding serves to provide pure reason with material for analogies with which it can think itself at and as its limit. And this limit, the *Grenze* "itself," the place of analogy, is already an analogy, at least to the extent that reason does not literally have a frontier. An analogy, then, to speak the proper (i.e., analogical) place of analogy, an analogy of analogy following a fractal multiplication that also gives us a precious analogy for thinking the frontier more generally. And to the extent that the *Grenze* is thus fundamentally analogical, and can only be analogical (as the pure relation as such is, properly speaking, nothing), it can give rise to different substitutions, including *Schranke*, from which Kant's initial effort was to separate it as clearly as possible. And so, when Kant comes to resume what seems less and less like a demonstration and more and more like an analogical drift, *Schranke* can reappear as the proper term for a *Grenze* become in turn a mere analogy; here is the very beginning of §59:

> At the beginning of this note [Kant means the whole conclusion of this part of the *Prolegomena*, which began with §57] I made use of the metaphor [Sinnbild] of a *boundary* [Grenze] in order to fix [festzusetzen: set down firmly] the limits [Schranken] of reason with respect to its own appropriate use. (*Prolegomena*, 111)

Grenzen, which, you will remember, must above all not be confused with *Schranken*, were therefore from the start in a position we might call metaphorical—analogical—with respect to *Schranken*, that they were content to present in a fashion that is imaged but nonetheless firm and solid. The abyss of analogy opens up here never to close again, for from the moment that one of the terms of what one had to believe was a distinction and even an opposition can take the place of the other to present it more vividly, then it follows that the whole conceptual scaffolding that we have had such trouble deciphering begins to wobble and could fall at any moment. We would then have to start out again from this sentence and reread this whole conclusion from its beginning, saying to ourselves that each time the word *Grenze* appears it might always be merely the analogical or metaphorical figure of its apparent opposite. This is no doubt why Kant, having tried to clarify things by calling *Grenze* an image or a metaphor (*Sinnbild*, an allegory, even), sees himself obliged to go back on everything that was argued in §§57 and 58, but this does no good, to the extent that he cannot get rid of the analogical language of frontiers, which is now contaminated by a radical uncertainty as to its conceptual status. Whence a paragraph entirely made up of concessions and corrections, struggling to keep its balance (I will simply emphasize some of the [ana-]logical articulations without further commentary):

> The sensible world contains only appearances, which are still not things in themselves, which latter things (noumena) the understanding must **therefore** assume for the very reason that it cognizes the objects of experience as mere appearances. Both are considered together [befasst] in our reason, and the question arises: how does reason proceed in setting boundaries [begrenzen] for the understanding with respect to both fields? Experience, which contains everything that belongs to the sensible world, does not set a boundary for itself [begrenzt sich nicht selbst]: from every conditioned it always arrives merely at another conditioned. That which is to set its boundary [Das, was sie begrenzen soll: that which must (obligation) bound it] must [muß] lie completely outside it, and this is the field of pure intelligible beings. For us, **however**, as far as concerns the *determination* of the nature of these intelligible beings, this is an empty space, and to that extent, if dogmatically determined concepts are intended, we cannot go beyond the field of possible experience. **But** since a *Grenze* is itself something positive, which belongs as much to what is within it as to the space lying outside a given totality, reason **therefore**, merely by expanding up to this *Grenze*, partakes of a real, positive cognition, provided that it does not try to go out beyond the boundary, since there it finds an empty space before it, in which it can indeed think the forms for things, but no things themselves. **But** *setting the boundary* [B e g r e n z u n g] to the field of experience through something that is otherwise unknown to it is indeed a cognition that is **still** left to reason from this standpoint, whereby reason is **neither** locked inside the sensible world **nor** adrift outside it, **but**, as befits knowledge of a *Grenze*, restricts itself [sich einschränkt] solely to the relation of what lies outside the *Grenze* to what is contained within. (*Prolegomena*, 111–12)

The knowledge proper to reason limits itself to its bounds, is bound to its limit. At the limit, reason is bounded by exposing itself to the void that gives the pure relation of pure reason as pure endless analogy. Reason as such shrinks until it subsists only as the surface, line, or point of the frontier itself, minimally positive.

The attempt to trace a secure and definitive frontier between *Schranke* and *Grenze* is thus doomed to fail. Any determination in general is affected by this, because this failure is the end of the end of pure reason, which finds itself only by losing itself in the zero thickness of the pure frontier as place of analogy without term.

Does this mean that "analogy" is the proper name of what we are trying to articulate here? Certainly not, because there can be no propriety of analogy. The *ana-logos* always remains to one side of the *logos*, bordering or lining it without letting itself be comprehended by it, or letting itself be comprehended solely as its *Grenze*, which immediately relaunches the whole machinery. Reason, exposed by Kant according to a certain ana-logics of logic, speaks itself and loses itself not in the empty space beyond the frontier but at the frontier itself as pure analogy. But one senses that analogy can never be pure, as it is purely a placing in relation. Like the frontier as such, analogy as such is nothing, and so there is analogy only in a dispersion of uncontrollable, in(de)terminable singularities, always in the now of the event of the frontier. Analogy is only ever analogical, relaunches itself indefinitely as the unlimited limit of thought or as the pure relation of thought and language. The frontier, as Aristotle knew, is infinite, interminable, a term without term. Kant never finishes tracing it, putting a term to it, limiting himself to bounds, bound to limits. This is his cross, his passion, that gives rise to a reading that I cannot say is either literary or philosophical, that really starts I know not where, and finds its end I know not how.

Index

Sara Guyer and Brian McGrath, series editors

Sara Guyer, *Reading with John Clare: Biopoetics, Sovereignty, Romanticism.*

Philippe Lacoue-Labarthe, *Ending and Unending Agony: On Maurice Blanchot.* Translated by Hannes Opelz.

Emily Rohrbach, *Modernity's Mist: British Romanticism and the Poetics of Anticipation.*

Marc Redfield, *Theory at Yale: The Strange Case of Deconstruction in America.*

Jacques Khalip and Forest Pyle (eds.), *Constellations of a Contemporary Romanticism.*

Geoffrey Bennington, *Kant on the Frontier: Philosophy, Politics, and the Ends of the Earth.*